SYMBOL AND NEUROSIS

SELECTED PAPERS OF
LAWRENCE S. KUBIE

Edited by
HERBERT J. SCHLESINGER

With an introduction by
EUGENE B. BRODY

Psychological Issues
Monograph 44

INTERNATIONAL UNIVERSITIES PRESS, INC.
New York

Library of Congress Cataloging in Publication Data

Kubie, Lawrence Schlesinger, 1896-1973.
  Symbol and neurosis.

  (Psychological issues ; v. 11, no. 4 : Monograph ; 44)
  Bibliography: p.
  Includes index.
  CONTENTS: Brody, E. B. Lawrence S. Kubie's psychoanalysis. — The fallacious use of quantitative concepts in dynamic psychology. — Instincts and homeostasis. [etc.]
  1. Neuroses — Addresses, essays, lectures.
2. Psychoses — Addresses, essays, lectures. 3. Symbolism (Psychology) — Addresses, essays, lectures.
4. Psychoanalysis — Addresses, essays, lectures.
I. Schlesinger, Herbert J. II. Title. III. Series.
[DNLM: 1. Neuroses. 2. Symbolism. 3. Psychoanalytic theory. WI PS572 v. 11 no. 4 / WM460 K95s]
RC454.4.K8 1978   616.8'9   77-92177
ISBN 0-8236-6291-8
ISBN 0-8236-6290-X pbk.

CONTENTS

Foreword — by HERBERT J. SCHLESINGER   vii

LAWRENCE S. KUBIE'S PSYCHOANALYSIS, by EUGENE B.
    BRODY   1

1 THE FALLACIOUS USE OF QUANTITATIVE CONCEPTS IN
    DYNAMIC PSYCHOLOGY   41

2 INSTINCTS AND HOMEOSTASIS   52

3 THE DISTORTION OF THE SYMBOLIC PROCESS IN NEUROSIS
    AND PSYCHOSIS   87

4 THE CENTRAL REPRESENTATION OF THE SYMBOLIC
    PROCESS IN PSYCHOSOMATIC DISORDERS   115

5 THE FUNDAMENTAL NATURE OF THE DISTINCTION
    BETWEEN NORMALITY AND NEUROSIS   127

6 A RECONSIDERATION OF THINKING, THE DREAM
    PROCESS, AND "THE DREAM"   162

7 THE RELATION OF PSYCHOTIC DISORGANIZATION TO
    THE NEUROTIC PROCESS   170

8 IMPAIRMENT OF THE FREEDOM TO CHANGE WITH
    THE ACQUISITION OF THE SYMBOLIC PROCESS   185

9 THE DRIVE TO BECOME BOTH SEXES   191

References   264

Index   271

About the Authors   279

FOREWORD

Lawrence S. Kubie

(1896-1973)

The death of Larry Kubie took from the world a man of great stature—a teacher and researcher, a keen critic of professional and social affairs, a gadfly whose life and thoughts influenced several generations of students. The members of the Editoral Board of *Psychological Issues* mourn the passing of their teacher, colleague, and friend. By publishing a selection of his papers we both memorialize the man and facilitate access to some of his major ideas.

The problem of selecting a group of papers to represent a man of such wide-ranging interests is formidable. He wrote more than 300 articles, reviews, and books, on neurophysiology, psychoanalytic theory and practice, education, the delivery of mental health services, and the arts and literature, to mention but a sample. In the end, the constraints of space and a certain ruthlessness that is one of the few prerogatives of editorship yielded the present collection.

In making the final selection I was guided by a wish for thematic unity among the papers. The papers selected represent a central theme of Kubie's enduring contribution. As the title, *Symbol and Neurosis,* suggests, they mainly have to do with the relationship of what Kubie called the neurotic and psychotic processes and freedom, which are linked in his conception by the symbolic process that characterizes preconscious functioning. Throughout his career these issues appeared and reappeared in Kubie's writings, and we believe this selection of papers represents his best statements of them.

Since considerations of space and unity prevented inclusion of all of our favorite papers, I take the opportunity on behalf of myself and my editorial advisors (chiefly Robert S. Wallerstein, Robert R. Holt, and Philip S. Holzman) to commend to the reader the several additional papers listed below.

The Repetitive Core of Neurosis. *Psychoanalytic Quarterly,* 10:23-43, 1941.

The Nature of Psychotherapy. *Bulletin of the New York Academy of Medicine,* Second Series, 19:183-194, 1943.

Some Unsolved Problems of the Scientific Career. *American Scientist,* 41:596-613, 1953, and 42:104-112, 1954.

The Pros & Cons of a New Profession: A Doctorate in Medical Psychology. *Texas Reports on Biology and Medicine,* 12:692-737, 1954; reprinted in *Medical & Psychological Teamwork in the Care of the Chronically Ill,* ed. M. Harrower. Springfield, Ill.: Thomas, pp. 125-170, 1955.

(with Hyman A. Israel) "Say You're Sorry." *The Psychoanalytic Study of the Child,* 10:289-299. New York: International Universities Press, 1955.

I would like to express particular thanks to Mrs. Bernard Rabinowitz, Lawrence Kubie's daughter, editor, and literary executor. Ann Rabinowitz graciously consented to this project to honor her father and facilitated its completion at every step.

Herbert J. Schlesinger

LAWRENCE S. KUBIE'S PSYCHOANALYSIS

EUGENE B. BRODY

Introduction: An Appreciation

SOME PERSONAL HISTORY

I first knew Lawrence Kubie—Larry, as he soon asked to be called—in January of 1948 in the role of a psychotherapy supervisor. This famous and uncompromising man was a warm, tolerant, and utterly supportive mentor. Our interchange in those days was chiefly about patients, his and mine, as I was the house physician for a number of his private cases hospitalized in the Yale Psychiatric Institute. But we also talked at length about research, literature, and the arts. He numbered many creative and well-known people among his friends and patients and was intensely interested in the portrayal of human nature in drama and story.

Another common interest was in the relation of brain function to psychoanalytic concepts. Many of us at Yale in that era were simultaneously working with patients in the hospital and doing research with monkeys and chimpanzees in John Fulton's laboratories, housed in the same building. Larry was a significant bridging personality, and for some neuroscientists the only person whose psychoanalytic ideas could be taken seriously. His capacity to communicate across disciplinary barriers was immense.

He also had the capacity to make people feel his intense and authentic interest in them as unique individuals. His impact on others was to an important degree personal and immediate. He was a superb clinical supervisor and critical

1

discussant of research papers. His influence lives in hundreds of former students, colleagues, and friends, as well as in patients—many of whom were influential leaders in their own fields. All felt that they had been personally touched by an exceptional human being.

Larry and I remained in close touch although I moved from New Haven to Baltimore in 1957. In 1961, leaving his Manhattan practice, he too came to Baltimore, where he had been a medical student and house officer at Johns Hopkins. He accepted the post of Director of Training at Sheppard Pratt Hospital, then directed by Harry Murdock. At the same time it was my privilege to appoint him a clinical professor in the Department of Psychiatry at the University of Maryland School of Medicine, where he remained an active teacher and consultant until his death in 1973. We also collaborated closely on the *Journal of Nervous and Mental Disease*—he was Editor-in-Chief and I was Consulting Editor from 1961 until we switched posts in 1968. His influence on the *Journal* and on our department was significant and lasting.

A MAN FOR OUR TIME

With the need for replicable and reviewable data in mind, Kubie was among the first to call for audio and later video records of psychoanalytic sessions and samples of free association under controlled conditions. He was also among the first to advocate systematic interdisciplinary studies of behavior including the participation of seasoned psycho-analysts, housed in special schools or institutes, and using a central computerized data registry. A proposal, evolving since its first appearance in 1954, for a degree combining elements of psychoanalytic education with aspects of medicine, psychology, and the social sciences, still exerts a significant influence on psychiatric teaching centers throughout the country (Kubie, 1954b). This idea, its elaborations and beginning applications, has been reviewed by Holt (1971), and in modified form has been actualized in a joint program at the University of California and the Mt. Zion Hospital in San Francisco.

His books and papers touched almost every aspect of human

behavior. René Spitz remarked that his works are "so numerous that only the term 'polyhistor' could be applied to their author" (1969, p. 81). Although he often provoked disagreement, he invariably struck intellectual sparks capable of igniting the thoughts and creative impulses of others. Creativity itself was one of the human phenomena which occupied his attention. Characteristically, he did not limit his interest to the intrapsychic mechanisms involved in the emergence of original ideas, but was concerned, as well, with the development of child-rearing methods and schools that might foster the talents of gifted children and young adults. These concerns reflected an abiding sensitivity to man as a social being with the capacity to transcend some of the apparent constraints of biological evolution; deliberate social change in particular, Kubie thought, might facilitate the emergence of neurosis-free persons able to use their mental capacities in wholly new ways. His article, "A Research Project in Community Mental Hygiene: A Fantasy" (1952c), was a pioneering effort. It bespoke an optimism not yet dimmed when, in one of his last papers (1968), he underlined the fallacies and pitfalls in what had come to be known as "the community mental-health movement" in the United States.

PSYCHOANALYSIS AS SCIENCE

Kubie was a gifted theoretician, but the wide-ranging nature of his ideas makes it difficult to tie them together. Nor do they all fit easily into the established structure of psychoanalysis. This may account for the fact that they seem to be less frequently referred to in the psychoanalytic literature than in that of related humanistic and scientific disciplines. Nevertheless, his diverse contributions stemmed from a personally integrated conception of a psychoanalytic theory, broadly conceived with its biological base, and including the full range of conscious and unconscious events that take place in the human mind.

He very much wanted to make psychoanalysis an exact science and believed that definitive formulations would some day be achieved. At least one critic, though, felt that his optimism about the potential yield of interdisciplinary research was "reaching for the stars." He was fond of saying, "The tree of psychoanalytic theory needs drastic pruning!" (Some analysts felt his pruning was so drastic that his theoretical tree was no longer recognizable as psychoanalysis.) In his earliest writings he referred conventionally to the energetic and structural concepts, but these fell away, leaving a dynamic and developmental psychology with major emphasis on unconscious conflict and defense as they involve symbolic processes. He soon expressed his belief that psychic energy was an inadequate and nonheuristic explanatory concept (1952b). Later he referred to "a gain in simplicity and clarity for psychoanalysis, if the descriptive 'structural' metaphors can be dropped from our vocabulary, both because of their static implications and because of their vulnerability to anthropomorphic misuse as pseudoexplanatory principles" (1967, p. 172).

From time to time, in addition to "pruning," he used other expressions that suggested sharpness and decisiveness. I remember being impressed, for example, when in the course of supervising one of my early psychotherapy cases he spoke of making interpretations "with surgical precision." He valued the "stricter" use of concepts and terms. The need to cast the clinical observations of psychoanalysis into the experimental mold continued to be evident in his later years when he wrote of a life history as illustrating the elements of the neurotic process "with the clarity of a laboratory demonstration" (1967, p. 177).

His concern with interdisciplinary research, unyielding devotion to scientific method, and persisting attention to the biological substrata of behavior—particularly in neurophysiology—had visible roots in his earliest work. Like Freud, he began his career with research in neurohistology, and was regarded as a highly promising clinical neurologist.

Two important years, 1928 to 1930, were spent in London. There, in addition to working at the National Hospital in Queens Square, he was analyzed by Edward Glover. I sometimes wondered if that first analytic experience of going "deep" into himself (he had a later analysis with Herman Nunberg)—related to what Glover (1969, p. 7) characterized as an "almost penitential regard for candid confession"—at the same time that he was studying the depths of the brain, contributed to his relatively early interest in hypnosis and altered states of consciousness. In pursuit of this interest he conducted systematic research with Milton Erickson, and for several years with Sydney Margolin.

A major event, one that reinforced Kubie's interest in linking neurophysiological concepts with those of psychoanalysis, occurred in 1951. In that year he went to Montreal, accompanied by Paul MacLean, one of our Yale group working at the interfaces of psychiatry and neurophysiology. There, hidden beneath the draperies of an operating table, he, with great excitement (as reported by Paul), recorded the speech of patients undergoing electrical stimulation of the temporal cortex at the hands of Wilder Penfield. Enormously "fired up" (in MacLean's language) by this experience he elaborated his view of the symbolic process, which he had already conceived as having twin poles or anchors in the internal world of the body and in the external world of social relations (1934). Now he saw a bridge between these poles in the potentially relivable experiences stored in the temporal lobe. The profound impact of hearing these heretofore buried and now reactivated memories further enhanced his interest in psychoanalytic topography. In his teaching and supervision he regularly referred to a continuum from unconscious through preconscious to conscious states, with special reference to the preconscious flow of experience. He tied the ideas of awareness, consciousness, and attention to his concepts of psychosis and to what he called "the neurotic process." He often said that behavior could be considered abnormal when it was mainly determined by factors outside of conscious awareness and not accessible to unaided introspection. The idea that if conflicting drives or goals could only be made conscious they could be fully confronted and reconciled seemed almost an article of faith for him. In one of his last papers (1972) he reiterated this theme with renewed force: ". . . lasting and significant change requires a release of psychological processes from domination by the dictatorship of unconscious mechanisms. Only this can produce . . .

freedom . . ." (p. 31). Once, with the temerity of youth, I suggested that it might also be possible to be imprisoned by conflicting fears and desires the sources of which were consciously discernible. The intensity of his negative reaction left me feeling that I had touched a conviction that was, itself, deeply rooted.

Kubie's view of a range of levels of awareness had its counterpart in a view of potentially changing personal identity that he usually described in bipolar terms. Thus he might speak of a patient's uncertainty about whether he or she was child or adult, parent or offspring, male or female. This last theme of shifting emphases in gender identity and conflicting gender tendencies within the same person occupied him throughout his psychoanalytic career. His paper, "The Drive to Become Both Sexes," finally published posthumously (1947b), was first presented before the annual meeting of the American Psychoanalytic Association in May, 1954.

This emphasis on rapid shifts in conscious awareness, combined with the less directly expressed belief that each person contains several potential identities within him or herself, appeared to be related to aspects of Kubie's own life and personality. He was almost voraciously involved with ideas, people, and activities. He reminded me of Thomas Wolfe, who wanted to live every life, have every experience, be with every person — goals that motivated a single life of high activity, multiple associations, and rich fantasy and productivity. At times, especially in the Baltimore years when conversations were sometimes retrospective, I felt in his views a faint echo of Camus, who envied the actor his privilege of living different lives.

THE EFFORT TO INTEGRATE

The need for unification, to pull the threads of his work together, became apparent — as it does for many — in Larry's later years. This anticipated need, in fact, had been very much involved in his decision to give up his Manhattan practice and return to Baltimore. His new posts at Sheppard and at the University of Maryland allowed him to devote time and energy to the study of psychotic as well as neurotic behavior. They also permitted him the stimulation that comes from teaching students at all levels of sophistication. The last three to four years before his death, in particular, when illness and fading energy convinced him that the end was not far off, were marked by an intense concentration on thinking and writing. He seemed to have planned his life as though it were a dramatic sequence. The second scene of the last act — after he retired from Sheppard — saw a massive outpouring of revisions of earlier articles and books, final position papers, and a spate of brief communications, many titles of which began "Unsolved Problems in . . ."

The character of his last work reflected a need to be sure that his theoretical "pruning" was constructive and growth-promoting, enabling him to complete certain ideas and attain a sense of intellectual integrity. Accomplished in the face of ill health, including times of impaired memory and concentration, the work was not finished at the time of his death, but a certain plateau apparently had been reached. It is difficult not to feel that, once he had achieved a resting point, the pathophysiological events that terminated his life were facilitated by a reluctance to begin anew the fight against fatigue and pain. Syd Margolin, Larry's oldest, closest, and most faithful student and disciple, had come to visit two days before. We wondered if Larry had not awaited his arrival before he allowed himself to die.

THE NEUROPHYSIOLOGICAL BASIS OF EXPERIENCE AND BEHAVIOR

REVERBERATING CIRCUITS AND FEEDBACK

Kubie considered a recognition of the role of the central nervous system essential to the construction of psychoanalytic theory. His early paper (1930) on reverberating neural circuits in the brain was regarded by many as offering a potential link between cerebral and behavioral (including subjectively experienced) events. He believed that if spontaneous involuntary movements were due to "release from inhibition" of a usually suppressed activity, there must be some activity (without overt manifestation) always present. These ideas have a place in the evolution of the feedback concept as applied to neurophysiology and behavior. The late Warren McCulloch acknowledged this paper as the beginning of his attempt to handle information flowing in closed loops: "I had, until then, thought only of information flowing through ranks of neurons much as genes flow through generations" (1969, p. 55).

The ideas involved in the notion of reverberating circuits and "circus movements" in the brain remained important to Kubie throughout his life. Some were formalized in his paper, "The Place of Emotions in the Feedback Concept," given at a Macy Conference on Cybernetics (1952a). A central idea was that certain psychological events and their associated acts represent efforts to "close a circuit." A particular pattern of sexual behavior, for example, would not, as in the early Freudian formulations, be understood as the discharge of a drive built up to a critical intensity. The persisting pattern, rather (as discussed later by George Klein [1976]), depended upon the persistence of a cognitive state giving sexuality, under these conditions, its specific meaning(s). Sexual gratification does not terminate an anticipatory sequence but is only one link in a cybernetic chain or, as later restated by Klein (p. 98), a "series of interlocked purposes."

In one of his last writings (1974a) Kubie noted that "reverberating circuits constitute essential steps in all psychological development, both normal and pathological . . ." (p. 7). Some brains, he thought, might be so anatomically organized as to be especially vulnerable to automatic repetition, since under the influence of certain drugs "some people become automata and develop a stereotyped and unvarying repetitiveness" (p. 7). Regarding "obligatory repetition" as the *sine qua non* of all psychopathology, he suggests the possible origin of neurosis in cerebral structure or chemistry.

THE SOMATIC AND NEURAL BASE OF THE SYMBOLIC PROCESS

Another early somatic theme concerned the importance of the body as a referent for symbol formation (1934). The process begins with the infant's experiencing its psychic needs as changed aspects of its own body, so that the gradual accretion of knowledge must always be related to this initial experience (1948). Concepts and their symbolic representatives have both internal (bodily) and external referents. The symbolic process thus bridges the inner and outer worlds. "The body roots of the 'I' component of the symbol have their central representation in the more primitive archipallial cortex and its association systems [linking it] to visceral functions . . ." (1953a, p. 103). Citing MacLean's paper on the primitive "visceral brain" (1949), Kubie pointed out that olfaction seemed a possible anatomical and physiological, as well as psychological, link "between the bodily pole and the outer pole of the symbol (i.e., between the 'I' and the 'non-I')" (1953a, p. 104).

Penfield's work on the temporal lobe appeared to demonstrate a regression to an earlier period now relived vividly and literally through the reactivation of "past moments . . . permanently stored as discrete units" (MacLean, 1969, p. 40). In this connection Kubie (1953b) referred to MacLean's suggestion (1949) that the phylogenetically old temporal cortex was the "crossroads . . . for both *internal* and *external* perceptions arising from the eye, the ear, the body wall, the apertures, the genitals, and viscera" (p. 31). As he then phrased it, here is where "the 'I' and the 'non-I' pole of the symbol meet. . . . the temporal lobe complex constitutes the mechanism for integrating the past and the present, the phylogenetically and ontogenetically old and new . . . the external and internal environments . . . It is through the temporal lobe and its connections that the 'gut' component of memory enters into our psychological processes and the symbol acquires its dual poles of reference" (p. 31).

The temporal lobe was also involved in Kubie's concept (never explicated as such) of human language as having major defensive significance. Kubie described a spectrum of experiences relived with electrical stimulation ranging from the immediate and vivid to those "predominantly external . . . less a memory of a specific event than of a type of events; an abstraction or generalization from many past experiences" (1953b, pp. 47-48). The abstractions he regarded as aspects of a defensive organization: ". . . words serve as screens to cover sensory or 'gut' memories, with the inevitable consequence that every verbal memory serves to screen a deeper memory. . . . Without knowing it, this is what we have always meant when we have spoken of a patient's 'intellectualizations' as defeating insight . . . If this is true, then the ultimate answer to one of the riddles about the relation of insight to psychotherapy depends upon our ability to penetrate the smoke screen of words" (1953b, pp. 48-49). (Also cited by MacLean, 1969.) In this view rationally organized ideas, expressed in coherent language, seem always to have defensive or disavowing (in regard to "deeper" or "gut" memories), as well as communicative and expressive, functions. ". . . when the defensive functions of symbolic activities fail, the symbolic processes may serve instead to perpetuate and fixate the emotional distortions" (1953a, p. 94).

At times, Kubie conceived of preconscious experience as reflecting with minimal distortion the ongoing stream of bodily needs and processes. Thus in describing his feeling at the end of a long airplane journey, he spoke of the rich, kaleidoscopic, infinitely ranging fantasy stream that, triggered by the change in the sound of motors and the beginning descent, was gradually organized, translated into more abstract ideas and words, and made logically coherent. This process resembles that involved in the conversion of private dream experience into publicly communicable memories and statements, and is often described in terms of shifts from the primary to the secondary process. Here Kubie added his own word, "sterilize," to indicate the transformation from neurally buried "gut" experience to nonvisceral thoughts.

He also touched on a closely related theme—the neural basis of the experience of reality. This is an aspect of the idea that all symbols have an "I" pole which is internal and that the existence of the two referents or poles contributes to a failure of absolute differentiation of "I" and "non-I." Freud's (1925) essay on "Negation" provided a text here: "What is not real, what is merely imagined or subjective, is only *internal*; while on the other hand what is real is also present *externally*" (p. 183). Kubie understood this as reflecting the high precision of the neural exteroceptive as opposed to the enteroceptive apparatus (1953a). Earlier, he and Margolin (1944) had noted that the absence of data from distance receptors—to use as standards for discerning what is real and what not real—is necessary to the acceptance of dream images. Hypochondriacal illusions or hallucinations can occur in the waking state because of the lack of clear definition of proprioceptive sensations (which cannot, therefore, be similarly tested).

MENTAL ILLNESS: THE NEUROTIC PROCESS

Kubie's view of the pathogenesis of neurosis and psychosis encompassed his ideas about psychological functioning in general and fitted his conception of the "twin-anchored" symbolic process. He believed that "since the neurotic process is universal in the present state of child culture, there is no such thing as a psychotic patient who has not had a pre-existing neurosis out of which major aspects of the psychotic process will have evolved" (1953a, p. 105). The ingredients of the neurotic process, as summarized in one of his last writings (1974a), are clearly related to his general views about central nervous functioning. They include an affective potential often imposed early in life; patterns of obligatory repetition; various distortions of symbolic functions; and a consequent inability to modify one's behavior, described as a lack of "the freedom to change." These potentials, repetitions, and distorted symbolic functions exist at unconscious, preconscious, and fully conscious levels. Inability to change (i.e., lack of "freedom") may become apparent as an aspect of a neurotic state, an over-all pattern of personality functioning, or a psychotic state, all conceived as equally possible, given particular predispositions and circumstances. Furthermore, it is understood that the neurotic process is all-consuming—"an endlessly evolving chain of progressive distortions" (1967, p. 172). "A life can become so much sicker than were the initial deviations. . . . Every neurotic symptom, however simple it may seem, is a step in a long reverberating chain towards graver illness" (1974a, p. 3). Through his differentiation of secondary and tertiary life consequences which become woven into the pattern of clinical disorder he attempted to deal with an earlier concern: ". . . to avoid the confusions [between] the evolution of personality and illness, the symptoms of illness, and the immediate and remote consequences of illness" (1953a, p. 91).

THE CENTRAL AFFECTIVE POSITION

Kubie's promulgation of the idea of the "affective position" represents, in part, his effort to deal with the observations of Spitz and others on hospitalism and the consequences for infants of traumatic separation from parental figures. Since the process of cerebral myelinization is not complete during infancy, Kubie argued that at that time there can be no differentiation of conscious and unconscious and no symbolic process subject to later distortion (1953a). He did acknowledge, though, that "changes can occur on a preverbal or subverbal level . . . which seem to consist largely of the imposition of a relatively fixed central emotional position on the personality. . . . Such presymbolic changes leave residual emotional disturbances which in turn influence the symbolic aspects of all later responses to injury [and] may influence the later acquisition of symbolic functions" (1953a, pp. 94, 95). The affective position or potential may be based on precursors not only of adult rage, depression, and panic with their many intermediate shadings, but of euphoria as well. For the adult this "position" is so much a part of one's self that it is unrecognized. In this respect it might be called either ego syntonic or self syntonic (1963).

The "potential" may be established actively or passively. In the first instance "the affective color of life in general [and] the role of the affective components of psychological illness" (p. 112) arise from early developmental experiences. These "imprint" upon the personality an emotional state to which the individual always tends to return. Such "imprinting" is the universal accompaniment of pain, startle, and efforts to master one's own body regularly experienced in the earliest months of life. Subliminal stimuli that may precipitate a clinical expression of the affective potential in adulthood are pervasive.

In the second, passive, instance the central affective position or potential forms around sustained postinfantile conflicts with unconscious components: ". . . conscious conflicts can serve in a distorted symbolic form both to mask and to represent (or rather, misrepresent) a compelling inner necessity to achieve something forbidden and unattainable . . . Whenever they operate predominantly on unconscious levels, the affective potentials to which the conflict gives rise tend toward chronicity" (1963, p. 111).

An example is a patient who "Throughout his life . . . had been lost in a profound depression, of which he had remained wholly unaware until after he had been in treatment for a long time. Even then the realization came only gradually that on many occasions and under many different circumstances, no matter how trivial the event, his inner pendulum seemed always to swing back to a depressive position" (1963, p. 106). "A not dissimilar patient discovered that from the age of three he had lived his life behind a bright and active work-driven mask for a state of chronic yet unrecognized mourning" (p. 107).

Tantrums, panics, states of disgust, loathing, jealousy, and a hypomanic central position may also be chronically masked. In some respects these descriptions resemble what Freud and many of his followers labeled "reaction formations." But Kubie's affective position is not repressed or dissociated from the self. It is merely so habitual and perfectly integrated into the over-all pattern of functioning as to be out of awareness.

OBLIGATORY REPETITION

Kubie's formulations clearly follow Freud's idea of the "repetition compulsion." He writes of "compulsive masking devices" of an "insistently repetitive" (1963, pp. 108, 109) nature. But the "obligatory" repetition does not itself have defensive or undoing functions. It is "an insatiable and repetitive necessity" (1974a, p. 10), which might even evolve from a child's trivial repetitive pattern, depending upon environmental feedback. It remains insatiable and obligatory because of its association with repressed conflict. The inhibited or warded-off tendency persists and is repeated in symbolic form because it is never consummated. Neurotic behavior recurs because the goal at which it aims is never achieved. The goal is never achieved because it is unconscious, i.e., not known. Not subject to conscious control, it remains a potentially pre-emptive, though unconscious, basis of action and thought (1941). Or it is never achieved because it is one of a pair of mutually incompatible, and therefore unattainable, goals.

In personal conversation Kubie frequently utilized this theme to help one understand the behavior of people in general. He rarely described a "neurosis" or "psychosis" as something with a discrete beginning and end; rather, it was a temporary impasse in an entire life marked by blind strivings and distorted perceptions. This was true even though the ensuing activity might have been socially rewarded, as in the case of what he called a "compulsive work drive."

We may rephrase the idea to say that in such circumstances the repeated activity is usually carried out without comprehension, or the actor builds his own structure of rationalizations—which again may be socially reinforced. The repressed aims, of course, are not responsive to feedback; they are active, as Klein put it (1976), "in whichever motor channels permit . . . expression in a cognitive format that does not threaten the repression" (p. 275).

SYMBOLIC DISTORTION AND "CONSCIOUSNESS PROCESSES"

The obligatory repetition at the core of the neurotic process is involved in masking—and sometimes expressing—the central affective potential. The thoughts, feelings, and acts subject to obligatory repetition, like all other behaviors in this schema, have symbolic significance. Here Kubie is concerned (1934, 1949, 1953a, 1953b, 1974b) with the evolution of symbols from those pertaining to the diffuse body referents of infancy to the more specific abstractions, metaphors, and representatives of the unconscious found in adult life. He differentiated three types of symbolic functions: (1) abstraction from experience, as in concept formation; (2) various linguistic representations (not his term) in which, as an aspect of preconscious functioning, the relation between the original concept and the symbol remains relatively transparent; and (3) a manifest representation of an unconscious latent idea, i.e., here the link between symbol and referent remains inaccessible to introspection. The distinctions are in a sense illusory since all three are conceived as continuous: ". . . every symbol is a multivalent tool . . . simultaneously on conscious, preconscious, and/or unconscious levels every direct or indirect representation of any conceptual process will in all circumstances, if in varying proportions, be literal, allegorical, and also 'symbolic' in the dreamlike or psychoanalytic sense" (1953a, p. 97). As he said, "It is indeed difficult . . . to understand how any analyst who has analyzed the dreamlike overtones of the most mundane events of everyday life can entertain the idea that 'Ucs symbols' are anything other than one pole of a continuous spectrum . . ." (p. 97).

What Kubie called the "preconscious stream" plays a central role in his thinking about the symbolic process (1966, 1967). This stream is composed of "inner experience" reflecting, among other factors, unconscious conflict. It is constantly "processed" and "sampled" by mechanisms of "selecting, ordering, steering, and controlling which operate on conscious, preconscious, and unconscious levels." The degree to which Kubie actually conceived the "preconscious stream" as experience of which the subject could be conscious is uncertain, as he described the samples from it as "in turn represented by symbols" (1967, pp. 170-171). Furthermore, he now (1967) applied his earlier (1954a) term, "consciousness process," to the idea of samples being taken from an unceasing preconscious stream and converted into conscious symbols. This was explicit in a last posthumously published paper in which he referred to "the ability to draw statistically adequate and representative samples from the continuous preconscious stream . . . and to portray them symbolically in consciousness" (1974a, p. 9). But the "consciousness process" may be disturbed as "conflicts and affects" influence "both the sampling process and the processes of symbolic representation," distorting or disrupting the relationship between a symbol and "its roots" or its "underlying referent" (1967, p. 171). Mental illness occurs when "the symbolic process loses its ability to represent and ruminate and communicate about samples from the inner stream of preconscious mentation, along with its ability to test its relationship to reality" (1974a, p. 9). We are left with the impression of a "preconscious stream" definable only in neurophysiological terms, a level of preconscious awareness or "mentation" definable in experiential terms, and a preconscious system (Pcs.) definable according to rules for information processing or a particular type of "functioning."

Kubie did not refer to Susanne Langer's work, and I owe to Leon Wurmser (personal communication) a recognition of the similarity of his idea of preconscious fantasy to Langer's differentiation of presentational and discursive symbols. The former, metaphorical, impermanent, imprecise "abstractions made by the ear and the eye . . . our most primitive instruments of intelligence" (Langer, 1942, p. 86), are the first expressions evoked by any new experience or idea. We may regard them as possessing qualities both of the preconscious and of the Freudian primary process. The latter, discursive symbols, become pre-eminent as "Meanings become more and more precise . . . Speech becomes increasingly discursive, practical, prosaic . . ." (Langer, 1942, p. 126; cited by Wurmser, 1977). Here one can easily apply the Freudian ideas of secondary process and revision. These ideas are noted here as they seem logical aspects of a psychological-linguistic symbolic process congruent with the neuropsychological one posited by Kubie.

A PSYCHOLOGY OF CONFLICT

A view of human behavior as reflective of conflict at conscious, preconscious, and unconscious levels characterizes all of Kubie's written formulations. The elements postulated as central to the neurotic process are all involved in unconscious conflict. Kubie's psychoanalysis, like Freud's, was a psychology of conflict.

THE IDEA OF A "DRIVE"

The elements of conflict do not include the Freudian structures (id, ego, superego); as noted above, these Kubie finally dismissed as metaphors. Instead, conflict is between contradictory "drives." But the concept of "drive" itself is used in varying—although not necessarily incompatible—ways. Specifically disavowed is the use of the term as referring directly to biological processes involved in the environmental interchange necessary to survival (Kubie, 1948). Rather—in a manner congruent with Freudian theory—drives are the symbolic representations of central "biogenetic needs." These representations, variously termed "goals" or "cravings" as well as "drives," and "experienced" as "appetites," are secondary and tertiary derivatives of "primary patterns." "Experience" does not refer only to the stuff of subjectively reportable awareness. Without full explication, Kubie makes the nature of "drive" contingent in part upon the level of conscious awareness at which it (the symbolic pattern) occurs or is "experienced." The formation and expression of symbolic derivatives of biological needs differs according to the topographic "location" or mode of processing.

It is the level of conscious control itself that determines the gradation between wish and drive or compulsion. A wish, along with purpose and fantasy, is predominantly impelled and guided by conscious processes. At the opposite end of the continuum, with mainly unconscious determinants, are symptomatic compulsion, symbolic symptom, and dream. But throughout there is a mixture of conscious and unconscious, and also an intermediate range of preconscious dominance influencing metaphorical condensation, artistic creativeness, and hypnoid states. "Every human impulse, feeling, thought, act, or pattern of living may fall somewhere along such a spectrum . . . there are no acts in which any one level of processing exercises its influence alone" (1974b, p. 206).

Unconscious drives are expressed mainly in symbolic form as dreams or symptoms. Their derivative symbolic appetites (cravings, goals) have "that rigidity which . . . is the essence of all psychopathological mechanisms . . ." (1974b, p. 204).

Preconscious processes are reflected in such compromise formations as posture, clothing, and art productions. Symbolic elements at this level of awareness have simultaneous and changing multiple meanings. Kubie regarded preconscious processes as the major, if not the sole, source of creative production (1958).

Drives that exist at the level of almost full awareness are expressed through conscious, deliberate behavior. This usually, however, represents some compromise with continuing preconscious and unconscious factors.

AN ELABORATION OF "DRIVE" IN RELATION TO CONFLICT

Certain complex and lifelong behavior patterns are understood as dreamlike, symbolic expressions of multiple, irreconcilable, and unattainable "goals." Others reflect inevitably unsuccessful attempts to gratify irreconcilable "drives." Drives often appear as pairs of polar opposites, so that the gratification of one automatically frustrates its opposite, leading to insatiable behaviors. Even if a behavior pattern is successful in achieving its apparent goal—e.g., orgasm or job promotion—it may be followed by depression or a sense of emptiness and consequent compulsive repetition. This is a result of symbolic distortion, i.e., the goal for which the person strives is a symbol that does not represent its apparent referent. It represents something else, not accessible to consciousness and therefore unobtainable, and irreconcilable with its opposite, conflicting, and unconscious goal (1945, 1955, 1956, 1958, 1974b).

Kubie recognized conflicting drives to love or hate, fail or succeed, become weak or powerful, active or passive, dependent or independent. He regarded those goals, however, as adult abstractions that evolve under the pressure of social forces. He also acknowledged what he called Freud's emphasis on "the individual's struggle with his conscience . . . conscious, preconscious, unconscious, or all three" (1974b, p. 194). But most fundamental, he thought, was the child's inability to identify simultaneously with both parents, and the "stuff out of which a child's concepts of man and woman, of boy and girl, evolve" (1974b, p. 215). A central conflict to which he devoted attention throughout his career, culminating in the publication of "The Drive to Become Both Sexes," was what he called the struggle "to achieve mutually irreconcilable and consequently unattainable identities" (1974b, p. 194).

CONFLICT IN RELATION TO
SYMBOLIC DISTORTION OR DISCONTINUITY

Kubie regarded as the key issue in initiating a morbid process a conflict-engendered disturbance in the relationship of a symbol to its referent. This introduces a discontinuity, i.e., dissociation, into psychological processing. The conflicts are not between organized "psychic structures" but between "pairs or among groups of irreconcilable and often unattainable drives . . . concurrently on conscious, preconscious, and unconscious levels . . . it is only when unconscious components play the dominant role that they become neurotogenic" (1967, pp. 171-172). The discontinuity begins with repression or a process akin to it: ". . . if the underlying referent is an area of conflict, the rupture of the link between that conflict and its symbolic representatives renders the conflict inaccessible to conscious introspective evaluation, correction, or control" (p. 171). This suggests that the symbolic discontinuity itself has a repressive function, or at least interferes with the retrieval of material outside the focus of awareness. He refers to a "repressive-dissociative process which obscures the links between symbolic constructs and the percepts and conceptualizations which represent the body and its needs and conflicts, i.e., the 'I' pole of reference" (1953a, p. 106). Repression leading to discontinuity between symbols and "I" referents produces only neurosis. The processes of neurosis and psychosis can never be mutually exclusive as there is always some degree of distortion at both ends of the symbolic linkage, but the latter requires a specific distortion in the relationship between the symbol and its outer world referent, i.e., the "'non-I." Thus the difference between neurosis and psychosis lies in a dislocation of the meaning of the "non-I."

CONFLICT BETWEEN SYMPTOMS

Kubie adds to the idea of conflict between drives the observation that conflicts between symptoms further distort symbolic functions. The sequence begins with a person in an impasse, an insoluble dilemma, "trapped among irreconcilable, conflicting, and unattainable drives, one or more of which are unconscious" (1967, p. 172). This leads to the formation of primary symptomatic defenses which produce secondary distortions of life; as the initial conflicts and their continuing effects persist, insoluble conflicts among the symptoms themselves and further disruption of symbolic functions are added. It is at this point, as the meaning of external-symbolic referents is obscured, that the patient becomes vulnerable to psychotic disorganization. The phenomena of regression usually appear within this sequence, but regression as a defense mechanism is not regarded by Kubie as etiological for psychosis. The theoretical problem is to differentiate between initiating, sustaining, and feedback mechanisms involved in the appearance of symbolic distortions and to identify "changes in the relationships among the three systems of symbolic processing—conscious, preconscious, and unconscious" (1967, pp. 183-184).

Unconscious, Preconscious, and Conscious in a Psychoanalytic System

Perhaps the most emphatic and consistent aspect of Kubie's psychoanalysis is the central place accorded to levels of awareness and nonawareness.

He was progressively unequivocal in his abandonment of Freudian metapsychology, particularly the concepts of psychic energy and the psychic structures or mental apparatuses. But though he wrote at length and repeatedly about conscious, preconscious, and unconscious aspects of behavior, his attempts to relate these to a general psychoanalytic theory were limited mainly to suggesting their connection with drive, conflict, and symbol, and the central affective potential or position. The following discussion, therefore, is intended to relate his ideas about conscious awareness, in so far as possible, to those of some other contemporary psychoanalysts working without the metapsychology, and in a limited way to phenomenology, as well as to compatible aspects of Freud's thinking.

DETERMINISM AND FREEDOM TO CHOOSE

Kubie's emphasis on conscious awareness appeared to reflect personal as well as theoretical considerations. The high value he attached to confrontation was revealed in his uncompromising pursuit of the truth as he saw it and in an abhorrence of self-deception. He counted himself fully responsible for his own thoughts and acts, and did not hesitate, sometimes at socially inappropriate moments, to identify what he considered symptomatic behavior reflecting hidden or disavowed intentions in others. Consciousness was also associated with freedom. The clearest statement of his position is in the first edition of his book *Practical and Theoretical Aspects of Psychoanalysis* (1950): ". . . the man who is normal in the psychoanalytic sense can accept the guidance of reason, reality and common sense. The outside world may be unyielding; but he remains flexible, modifiable, and educable, and therefore, in a pragmatic sense *free*. This indeed is . . . the most important freedom of all, i.e., the freedom from the tyranny of the unconscious" (pp. 16-17).

Making the unconscious conscious affords liberty from potentially unmanageable drives and thus that opportunity for reflection and choice which permits personal autonomy. The idea that drives which remain unconscious (i.e., have not been made accessible to conscious control through interpretation) have the potential for creating chronic difficulties follows Freud's early thinking (1915a): ". . . the instinctual representative develops with less interference and more profusely if it is withdrawn by repression from conscious influence. It proliferates in the dark, as it were, and takes on extreme forms of expression . . . uninhibited development in phantasy and . . . damming-up consequent on frustrated satisfaction" (p. 149).

Pursuing this idea Kubie adhered to the principle that behavior dominated by the unconscious is essentially irrational, self-defeating, and maladaptive (i.e., does not take external reality into account). The therapeutic aim of psychoanalysis, it follows, is "not . . . to make pathological reactions impossible, but to give the patient's ego *freedom* to decide one way or the other" (Freud, 1923, p. 50fn). In the *New Introductory Lectures* (1933), Freud, speaking of "virtually immortal" id impulses, wrote: "They . . . can only lose their importance . . . when they have been made conscious by the work of analysis . . ." (p. 74).

In some respects Kubie's thought shares an apparent paradox with that of Freud. Both wrote of human behavior in a highly deterministic way. Freud's idea of tension discharge as a ubiquitous aim was crucial in his model of an organism functioning to prevent tension accumulation. Kubie's idea of central "biogenetic needs," expressed as symbolic "drives," "appetites," "cravings," or "trends," also implies forces passively experienced by a "driven" subject. But Kubie did not regard pure tension discharge as the primary aim of his postulated drives. Rather, he associated drives, appetites, cravings, or trends with unconscious "goals," with, in most examples (but not always explicated), some external social referent. That is, instead of drives that might be attached to a variety of objects, he seemed to conceive of specifically goal-linked intentions. The unconsciously intended goals might be, for example, changes in personal gender identity, fusion with a loved person, or destruction of a hated one. In Freudian language the object appeared to Kubie more important than the aim. But a major tenet of Freud's thought also was the idea of a purposefully operating unconscious as expressed by repressed desires (intentions) to achieve a goal. For him intention required neither the subject's awareness nor conscious volition. At the same time, though, Freud's unconscious "interacts causally (as psychic energies pushing for an outlet) . . . There is an intermediate domain in human affairs between the clearly purposive and the clearly mechanical, in which there are partial purposes, purpose in the making, precursor phenomena to full-fledged purposes" (Edel, 1974, p. 970).

Kubie appeared implicitly to recognize that the deterministic causal view was not compatible with that of unconscious intentionality, but he made no attempt to reconcile the two. Others, though (Ricoeur, 1970), recognizing that Freudian topography implies reported motivation as " 'displaced' into a field analogous to that of physical reality" (p. 360), emphasized the difference—namely, that the reduction of motives to causally antecedent or functionally dependent factors does not illuminate the concept of motive as a "reason for" action. Following Brentano, behavior becomes "the expression of the changes of meaning of the subject's history, as they are revealed in the analytical situation" (Ricoeur, 1970, p. 364). Reality is "interpreted through the intentionality of the instinctual object, as that which is both revealed and hidden by this instinctual intending . . ." (p. 371).

The writings of both Freud and Kubie imply that intending has meaning, without requiring that the intender be conscious of it. The intentional has primacy over the reflective (Ricoeur, 1970). Thus, within certain constraints, one may be said to intend and arrange one's own life. However, the idea that unacceptable intentions are automatically prevented from emerging into conscious awareness permits the disavowal of responsibility for some behavior. Thus the person can engage in activities attributable to unknown motives or passively experienced forces for which he need assume no responsibility. Disavowal of responsibility for, and the consequent refusal to reflect upon, some project or activity in which one is consciously engaged fit a definition of self-deception (Fingarette, 1969). One deceives one's self by stating that the actions one takes are not one's own but rather those of a disclaimed "unconscious."

Kubie's thought, in these respects, seems to occupy a position between that of Freud and existentialists such as Sartre. It can lead to a view similar to Schafer's (1976) emphasis on responsible action, articulated, for example, in the idea that one does not express one's (passively experienced) anger, but, instead, acts angrily. Kubie wrote (1952b) of "the symbolic process of self-deception" in contrast to "the symbolic process of self-expression in . . . language and action" (p. 48). His focus was on hiding one's "deeper" goals or memories or conflicts from one's self. In a general sense this is disclaiming meaning, which is one way of disclaiming responsibility. Unconscious intentions are, after all, accessible through interpretation of distorted meanings, themselves accessible by introspection. The distortion manifest in dreams, fantasies, symptoms, or acts represents the symbolic fulfillment or expression of, as well as a disguise for, the unconscious intention.

For Kubie and Freud the problem of free choice and determinism in psychoanalytic theory was solved through the concept of psychoanalytic change: hidden memories, wishes, drives (goals and meanings) become conscious and can be rationally dealt with. More recent theorists have faced the problem directly in terms of responsibility. Most prominently, Schafer (1976) has conceived the nature of psychoanalytic change in terms of intending and acting so as to make new arrangements. The patient lives increasingly in terms of the self as agent—doing the things from which he or she was suffering. He or she no longer suffers the effects of seemingly autonomous inner forces, but claims or reclaims as his own actions what was previously disclaimed. Schafer eschews "self-deception," however, seeing it as a misleading term for a "faulty way of observing one's own actions" (p. 238) engaged in "for reasons of personal comfort" (p. 241). But he regards these faultily observed actions (viewed, e.g., as no action at all or not one's own or the opposite) as nonetheless constituting a major category of the dynamic unconscious. The second "major referent of the dynamic unconscious . . . is the class of actions in which one *would be* engaged were one not refraining from doing so by engaging in counteractions" (p. 241). That is, the Ucs. includes both unrecognized and potential actions—each category remaining unobserved or unrealized in consequence of some counteractivity. Among the "would-be actions" the "most alarming and consequential to the analysand are those that have been maintained unconsciously since childhood and . . . never . . . assessed in the context" of the analysand's adult world view (p. 242). Schafer, then, regardless of terminology, appears to imply disavowal, specific means of reinforcing it, and refraining, as actions essential to preventing potentially realizable trends or tendencies ("would-be actions"), from becoming conscious or overt. Further, in a manner similar to Freud's anxiety reduction, these preventive maneuvers function to maintain "personal comfort."

For Sartre self-deception, perhaps as an alternative to responsibility, does not involve attribution to unconscious factors, but is rather an escape from anguish which is the experience of freedom. He conceives of a human "essence" which comes after existence and is the sum of individual actions, responsibly chosen and taken. Thus the self is reconstituted at every moment, and we even choose our past by conferring meaning on some part of it. Kierkegaard (1843), too, stressed active choice: "The ethical individual knows himself, but this knowledge is not a mere contemplation . . . it is a reflection upon himself which itself is an action, and, therefore, I have deliberately preferred to use the expression 'choose' one's self instead of know one's self" (p. 63).

The habit of disavowal is essentially self-alienating. Authentic personal choice requires reflection based on conscious awareness. Such awareness is an aspect of the "freedom to change" regarded by Kubie as the goal of clinical psychoanalysis. But though "freedom to change" might be restated as "freedom to choose," Kubie follows first in the Freudian deterministic tradition rather than in the existential one. He does not speak primarily of the choosing process or the nature of the choice that is finally made, but of freedom from the bondage of what is unconscious and thus not amenable to identification or change. Discontinuing the "obligatory" repetition of fruitless or destructive acts, or the cycle of depression and disillusionment following sexual or social "success" is primarily, for Kubie, a matter of bringing unconscious drives under conscious control. The ensuing conscious process of discrimination, inhibition, enhancement, or direction is alluded to in the concept of goal, but not explicated. A suggestion, though, about the processes of discrimination and choice lies in his idea of the scanning function of preconscious information processing, sampling unconscious material (i.e., forming symbolic representations) for revision and scrutiny.

From Kubie's position the process of becoming an agent who acts, rather than an object receiving and driven, depends upon understanding the experienced "inner force" through psychoanalytic interpretation. This includes differentiating between initiating, sustaining, and feedback mechanisms, a major aspect of the task of reducing both the initial conflict between unconscious drives and the secondary conflict between symptoms. Interpretation here designates the analyst's interventions aimed at "making the unconscious conscious." In metapsychological terms the effect is described as consequent to shifts in psychic energy. Without the metapsychology we may speak in terms of meaning, and without "drives" in terms of intention, cognition, and feedback. The formulations of the late George Klein lend themselves especially to elaborating and clarifying Kubie's thinking in these respects. Klein regarded compulsive repetition as a "manifestation of repressed ideation denied feedback from conscious organization" (1976, p. 306). He described the role of repression, precluding introspective access to the unconscious roots of behavior, in terms of meaning. Repression maintains a "gap in comprehension." Even though a "meaning schema . . . is dissociated from the person's self-conception [it] has an organizing . . . influence on conscious thought, experience, and behavior . . . of which the effects—i.e., the feedback from action—are uncomprehended" (p. 241). This is an extension and elaboration of Freud's basic idea (1926) that repression is fundamentally an "attempt at flight" from meaning (p. 153). Repression then becomes "the refusal to acknowledge the meaning of a tendency, but not the tendency itself; the gratifying aspect of the tendency has not been renounced. . . . meanings . . . are 'lived out' without comprehension" (Klein, 1976, p. 242).

The interpretation that undoes repression and hence the compelling quality of the tendency (drive) is couched by Kubie in terms of meaning. That is, interpretation is aimed at understanding, making intelligible, the conscious verbal and action forms that symbolize, i.e., "stand for," something else (usually a drive or trend), which is out of consciousness. Since he so often refers to the derivatives of an unconscious drive, it may be more accurate to suppose that he often speaks of signs rather than symbols. In any event, continued repression of the personal and social meaning of a tendency ("drive") allows it, as Klein put it, to be " 'lived out' without comprehension," or, in Kubie's words, in a "rigid" and "obligatory" manner. As it becomes intelligible and understood, the tendency is experienced, reflected upon, and acted upon as an "intention" or "choice." In this way the person becomes an agent rather than an object.

The task of interpretation becomes more difficult in Kubie's scheme, with progressive interruptions or distortions in the association between elements of the symbol and its referents. This implies, as noted above, some equivalence between "distortion of the symbolic process" and repression or resistance to conscious apprehension of the tendency, drive, appetite, or goal in question. Increasing distance between the body referent and its conscious symbolic representations predisposes to neurosis. Interruption of a linkage between symbol and the "non-I" (or "external reality") referent predisposes to impaired reality testing and, hence, psychosis. Interpretation, then, is aimed at the direct apprehension and identification of the previously obscure, indirectly expressed meanings of signs or symbolic forms. It requires tracing their linkage to particular referents and investigating the nature of the connections between them. Deliberate scrutiny and reflection then become possible about the now intelligible meanings and the patterns of which they are a part. The consequence is a more valid appreciation of one's own feelings ("internal" states) and those of others ("external reality") as a basis for responsible choice and action.

UCS., PCS., CS.: QUALITIES, DEGREES OF KNOWABILITY, SYSTEMS

Like Freud, Kubie used the ideas of unconscious, preconscious, and conscious in different ways at different times. But their adjectival use, designating degrees of knowability or conscious apprehendability, is compatible in his usage with their designation as systems of information processing, Ucs., Pcs., and Cs., characterized by discrete sets of rules or laws. The concept of the primary process was used by both men at times as virtually identical with that of the system Ucs., and of the secondary process as synonymous with the system Cs. But as Rapaport (1956; cited by Klein, 1959, p. 14) put it, Freud did not take "the next logical step . . . to state . . . that all . . . which has so far comprised the system Consciousness now becomes the function of the structure termed Ego . . ." Instead, as Freud replaced his model of a consciousness system, Cs., with the conception of an ego and an id system, conscious, preconscious, and unconscious became qualities of experience, all three of which could occur in the ego system.

Kubie's conception is not incompatible with this one. However, he went beyond Freud in regarding the systems as well as the levels of awareness as constituting a continuum, both of linguistic precision and of accessibility to consciousness. Resistance to introspective access is greatest from the Ucs., and less from the Pcs. There is least resistance to apprehending material that is in the Cs., but outside the focus of immediate attention. Others have also implied a continuum from Ucs. through Pcs. to Cs. Kris (1950), for example, conceived of unconscious impulses moving into the Pcs., becoming part of its mental process "at a considerable distance from the original impulse" (p. 306). But Kris, unlike Kubie, preferred the energic theory, as it permitted easy hypotheses of transition. Most recently Matte Blanco (1975) noted that from Ucs. to Cs. the proportion of "symmetry" (his distinguishable feature of the Ucs.) decreases. (At the deepest levels there is pure symmetry and no space-time notion.)

The dichotomy conscious-preconscious was differentiated by Klein (1959) as he expanded the area of consciousness to include the phenomena of peripheral awareness and subliminal perceptions, all involved in the nonaware registration of experience. He thought of "different states of consciousness, each definable as a distinctive pattern of experience" reflecting "the existing balance among drive, defense, and controlling structures" (p. 17). He regarded the idea of "preconscious," however, as having little value unless used with reference to a particular state of consciousness. He thought that "registrations without awareness" (p. 31) was a more useful expression, implying both a particular state of consciousness and potential elaboration in terms of primary or secondary processes.

A fuller appreciation of much that Kubie left unstated may be gained from considering the epistemological and phenomenological, as well as the psychoanalytic, aspects of the problem. The adjectives conscious, preconscious, and unconscious describe the relative capacity of a mental process or content to be directly experienced, i.e., apprehended in consciousness. What is conscious, however, is not necessarily known, i.e., it need not be ultimately true or valid. Consciousness implies only being aware of something. It is a way of relating to an object, which may include knowing, but universally implies no more than awareness—or, in Sartre's sense, being immediately and internally conscious of being conscious. The fact that one is now conscious of a mental state previously out of awareness does not necessarily mean that it does not represent, or is not, a symbol or sign of yet another underlying (still unconscious) state that has even more fundamental motivating significance for behavior. What is conscious, though, is in principle knowable. What is preconscious is in principle capable of becoming conscious and also knowable. It is not usually reflectively experienced, but can emerge spontaneously in certain forms under certain conditions in particular cultural contexts; or it is accessible with effort to aided or unaided introspection, i.e., with or without a guide or psychoanalyst.

In contrast, what is in the Ucs. (not having been repressed) is not accessible to direct apprehension. Knowledge of unconscious aims, tendencies, or, in Kubie's language, drives, is never noninferential or unmediated as in the case of conscious desires. It can, however, be reconstructed by interpretation of the presumed symbolic representations or sign derivatives of what is unconscious. This is not, after all, fundamentally different from any other form of knowing. Nothing is ever "directly" apprehended by the "mind," which can deal *only* with representations of objects—whether they are masses in the external world or feelings or ideas that occur inside one's self. But the problem of defining the conditions of knowledge of which the knowing subject is in principle capable remains unsolved. Following this question may lead to epistemological circularity, demanding knowledge of the cognitive faculty (in this case the observing psychoanalyst or the experiencing analysand) before knowledge of what is known to that faculty (see Habermas, 1968).

In Kubie's system, becoming conscious of the previously unconscious often seems equated with knowing the previously unknown within one's self. This is done by way of the Pcs., considered as an experiential stream from which more coherent and clearly defined factors can be abstracted into full consciousness. With Margolin and others, he approached the Pcs. through empirical research, on the hypnoid state and other alterations of consciousness. These altered states of consciousness revealed some of what he regarded as the often dreamlike characteristics of the Preconscious: fluidity; displacement; condensation; distortions of form, time, and space; lack of restraint by conventional logic; use of plastic sensory representations and rapid, often unintelligible, transitions from scene to scene or plot to plot. Hypnotic experimentation provided "a bridge between the laboratory and the spontaneous events of nature" (1952b, p. 71); variants such as induced hypnagogic reveries were a way of moving unconscious material into the preconscious and making the preconscious stream more accessible to consciousness (1943).

Kubie's conception is clearly in the early Freudian tradition. Freud (1905) described "characteristics of unconscious thinking," for example, as "repressed" or "alien," in contrast to "preconscious" thinking "capable of becoming conscious" (p. 161). Freud also defined the Pcs. as available to the Ucs., for example, in joke formation: "a preconscious thought is given over for a moment to unconscious revision and the outcome of this is at once grasped by conscious perception" (1905, p. 166). And dream thoughts and images freshly constructed from new day residue belong only in part to the Pcs.: since they are not easily accessible to introspection they belong to that class of fantasies that "*qualitatively* . . . belong to the system *Pcs.,* but *factually* to the *Ucs.*" (1915b, p. 191). In his last writings Freud, following Breuer, defined preconscious as what is not only "capable of becoming conscious" (1940, p. 160), but "easily, under frequently occurring circumstances" (1933, p. 71). In contrast, the transformation from unconscious to conscious "is difficult and takes place only subject to a considerable expenditure of effort or possibly never at all" (p. 71).

Kubie's thinking about levels of awareness also falls in the intellectual tradition of a number of nonpsychoanalytic authors concerned with subjective experiencing. William James (1890) in particular noted the significance of "selective attention" (p. 402) in the maintenance of awareness and a sense of reality. To call a thing real, he believed, means only that it stands in a certain relation to ourselves: ". . . the reality lapses with the attention. . . . One principal object comes into the focus of consciousness, others are temporarily suppressed" (p. 405).

Henri Bergson (1889) also conceived of a continuum of conscious awareness, from low to high, or less to more, oriented to dream or to reality. More recently, Alfred Schutz (1962) has used the term "wide-awakeness" to denote that plane of consciousness with "an attitude of full attention to life and its requirements" designating the Jamesian worlds of "attended to reality" as "finite provinces of meaning," each with its own cognitive style.

THE SYSTEMS AS MODES OF INFORMATION PROCESSING
OR ENGAGING THE WORLD

As indicated above, both Freud and Kubie at various times tended to use the concepts of Ucs. as virtually identical with the primary process, and Cs. with the secondary process. Freud (1923) implied a continuum of symbolic complexity from Ucs. to Cs.: "Thinking in pictures . . . a very incomplete form of becoming conscious . . . stands nearer to unconscious processes than does thinking in words . . ." (p. 21). Gill (1967) sees the two processes as extremes of a continuum with adaptive significance: ". . . there is a primary- to-secondary-process range from a complete ignoring of the external world to a veridical evaluation and control of thought and behavior in accord with the nature of the external world" (p. 298). It is impossible, of course, to say that one perception is more veridical than another. We can, though, agree with James that calling something "real" means that it stands in a certain relation to ourselves, and, with Schutz, that the perceived world becomes "relevant" as it is a world of interpreted facts structured by personal schemata over which we have no control.

Kubie implies alternations and combinations of primary and secondary information processing in the simultaneous apprehension of internal and external worlds. This is inherent in his idea of twin-anchored symbolic representations that permit not a concept of veridical evaluation or control, but one in which external-world perceptual referents are always linked with internal ones.

All of these thinkers share a view of conscious awareness as a continuum of planes or levels from sleeping-dreaming to alertly paying attention, adapting and coping with reality and the external world. Most relevant, perhaps, to our attempt to define the intermediate level is Langer's view of the "fabric of meaning," with a warp of "facts" and a woof of symbols. As she noted, "Out of signs and symbols we weave our tissue of 'reality' . . . But between the facts run the threads of unrecorded reality, momentarily recognized wherever they come to the surface, in our tacit adaptation to signs; and the bright, twisted threads of symbolic envisagement, imagination, thought—memory and reconstructed memory, belief beyond experience, dream, make-believe, hypothesis, philosophy—the whole creative process of ideation, metaphor and abstraction . . ." (1942, pp. 235-237; cited by Wurmser, 1977).

The idea that levels of awareness closer to dreaming (e.g., as embodied in the Pcs.) are closer to (often repressed) childhood experience and associated with the possibility of artistic creation is familiar to most psychoanalysts from the works of Freud. He also linked this level of perception and information processing to new insights, and humor. Freud wrote: ". . . the essence of the comic [is] a preconscious link with the infantile . . . enough . . . to touch upon childish nature in general" (1905, p. 225). But he went beyond the philosophers and psychologists to enunciate particular rules for information processing for each of the three levels, Ucs., Pcs., and Cs., conceived not just as qualities but as systems.

Kubie's work in these combined traditions remains compatible with his concern with the central nervous system. An examination of his version of the Pcs. suggests it as the first representation in verbal-symbolic-imagic, potentially communicable form of initially translated or transduced neurophysiological needs and impulses from the Ucs., including the "preconscious stream" from which the "samples" (to become experience) are taken. It may also be the first consciously available representation of once conscious ideas that, having been repressed, are again being apprehended. Or, as noted above, this could be the first awareness of experiences previously registered without awareness. The Pcs., in short, appears to be experience-apprehendable, but inconstant, not organized (or organized according to an unfamiliar principle), not clearly related in a logical manner to all of one's other experience and, therefore, difficult to label, classify, and interpret, i.e., to know. It is a fluid stream of images, symbols, ideas, memories, bodily sensations, impulses to act, and affective states; some, in the form of reverie, pass without volition, usually momentarily, into consciousness; others are purposefully brought into focus. Without revision, material from this stream cannot form a generally intelligible assertion. It includes affective elements as action tendencies and symbolic reflections of moods or, defensively, their opposites. These are most importantly encompassed in the concept of the "central affective potential" as a consistent predisposition based mainly on preverbal experience.

The concept of preconscious may be illuminated by noting the universal difficulty in bringing the peripheral flow of conscious experience into focus, e.g., retrieving and fixing a reverie. People who are daydreaming and admonished to "snap out of it" feel themselves "jerked back" to reality. In the process of being "snapped" or "jerked" into reality contact, significant content is lost. The loss occurs in the very act of attending to and apprehending the daydream. This act of attention-apprehension, abstracting a cross section of the stream of thought from the periphery of awareness and focusing it in the center, appears to involve a shift in styles of information processing that may account for the accompanying sense of discontinuity. The immediate memory of the focused and apprehended flow is further modified for coherence and logic (like the secondary revision of remembered dreams), and translated into public language for transmission to someone else. The loss of original experience during this process suggests again that it is not fully contained within the limits of logical verbal expression.

Something similar, but in the reverse direction, happens as psychoanalytic patients learn to free-associate. Conscious experiencing becomes less structurally organized, "reality" oriented, conventionally logical, and linguistically bounded. A reduction in specificity and precision of designation and meaning is reflected in more broadly inclusive categories, in more ambiguous symbolic designations and visual imagery that are more reflective of affective and somatic states. Conversely, the imposition of boundaries and order necessary to meet the sociocultural rules for objective communication decreases the information-carrying capacity of relatively unbounded preconscious material. It is less informationally rich, but more capable of transmission to the analyst. Klein's (1959) interpretation of Freud's (1900) observation that transient or "indifferent perceptions" may become significant day residues for dream formation suggests an expanded information-carrying capacity for preconscious symbols. Klein stated: "We can easily understand Freud to mean that incidental registrations are more easily fused into a wider orbit of meanings than is a conscious percept; they can be condensed and displaced more readily than can a consciously *intended* perception, and it is perhaps these advantages that give them a unique status in ongoing thought" (p. 9). A shift in modes of engaging the world or information processing is also implicit in Schutz's concept of "shock" experience, a radical modification in the tension of consciousness and the "accent of reality" (1962, p. 231), at moments of the emergence of a new perception or insight, or a change in a long-held opinion. In a manner reminiscent of Freud he attributed the momentary acceptance of the world of jest in listening to a joke to this kind of "shock." Here is a clear impli-cation of the sudden dominance of a different mode of dealing with information, possibly associated with a release from another, more conventional, mode associated with everyday reality.

The concept of different types of information processing may become clearer in the light of Deikman's (1971) idea of the "action" and "receptive" modes of conscious organization. "Action" is manifested by "focal attention, object-based logic, heightened boundary perception, and the dominance of formal characteristics over the sensory" (p. 68). The "recep-tive" mode, regarded as maximal in the infant state, is charac-terized by "diffuse attending, paralogical thought processes, decreased boundary perception, and the dominance of the sensory over the formal" (p. 69). While the receptive mode resembles in part the cognitive style associated with Freud's primary process, Deikman makes the point that it is not a retreat from the world (although it might be employed for that purpose) but "a different strategy for engaging the world." From our viewpoint it provides a way of "knowing" certain aspects of reality not accessible to the action mode, usually through nonverbal experience.

Schafer's (1976) concept is related, but not identical. He speaks in a manner somewhat reminiscent of James about "modes of action by means of which people can act in selectively inattentive and selectively ignorant modes, especially with regard to personal matters of great moment" (pp. 243-244). These actions, their modes, and the reasons for engaging in them are not aspects of the Pcs., but of "the dynamic unconscious" (p. 244). Conscious and preconscious are also described as modes of action.

Although Kubie writes of the Ucs., the cumulative impact of his work suggests that for him the Pcs. is the original source of the ideational-symbolic "contents" of the Freudian Ucs. This does not imply that nonconscious or out-of-awareness processes influencing behavior do not exist. But it does imply that they do not, as Freud suggested, exist in an organized, symbolic linguistic form capable of direct or disguised "upward" penetration into consciousness. Unconscious processes, then (in contrast to material which is simply out of the focus of awareness), cannot be regarded topographically as one pole of a continuum with conscious processes at the opposite pole. They might, however, be regarded as part of the continuum of receiving, processing, and reacting functions — including perhaps those involved in intentionality. They are bodily (including neural) tendencies, tensions, and expectations developed in consequence of the interaction of innate biological factors with developmental and adult experience. These tendencies may have been reinforced or aversively influenced, and may have been given symbolic significance through repeated life experience without having been transformed into verbal or imagic language. When so defined, they are highly significant determinants of behavior, and are regularly reflected in communicable ideas or images. They do not, however, fit the Freudian concept of "contents" of a dynamic Unconscious. They are, in fact, unknowable by direct apprehension, since they do not exist in the form of a language comprehensible to consciousness. "Unconscious" thus becomes a metaphor for not directly knowable.

These considerations are compatible with some of the ways in which the unconscious has been described by Matte Blanco (1975) as a "mode of being." His concept stems directly from Freud in that the Ucs. (as distinct from the repressed unconscious) is a world ruled by entirely different laws from those governing conscious thinking. Analytic work helps the Ucs. to "unfold" itself. That is, it has a "translating" function. Indirect manifestations of the Ucs. can become translated and apprehended, but not known as existing in the Ucs. The Ucs. proper can never be apprehended as such, but only through the distortions it creates in the "asymmetrical" mode of being. Consciousness selects some "asymmetrical functions" (characteristic of conscious and repressed unconscious thinking) that are a translation of some of the potentialities implicit in the Ucs. or symmetrical "mode of being."

Despite his acknowledgment of levels, Matte Blanco regards the two modes of being as essentially incompatible. What we know of and what we experience constitute a mixture. His view facilitates a reformulation of the functions of Kubie's Pcs. The Pcs. makes it possible to effect compromises of unstated needs and impulses so that they can be integrated with other aspects of experience and transformed into loosely organized thoughts, symbols, and images. This permits the eventual emergence of these latter into peripheral, and later focal, conscious awareness. Hypnoid and other altered states of consciousness facilitate registration by the Pcs., in general imagic and symbolic terms, of perceptions emanating from the external world. The translation or expression of the nonverbal substratum of behavior into linguistic form, however primitive, is essential for the later apprehension in full awareness of more complex and highly organized language designating subjective experience. This process is further facilitated by the availability via preconscious experience of memories and partly formed thoughts and images, potentially useful as construction units for the transformation of the nonstated into language.

The functions of Kubie's Pcs., then, are cognitive and symbolic-meaningful. They include sampling the not-experienced Ucs.; transforming its tendencies into experience; integrating the new experience with retained elements of conscious perception; processing, registering, and organizing these varieties of experience; and making them coherent with what has already been processed. It is a way of knowing and of engaging the world that may serve as a basis for action and provide a sense of private experiential continuity or identity. Failure to achieve this integrated experiential continuity (conscious identity) may reflect incompatibilities of the goals (objects) of the symbolized tendencies, or distortions or disruptions of the linkages between symbol, unconscious tendency, or perceived external referent. In such instances potential identities may be fragmented, split, or in conflict as "preconscious struggles" take place in an effort to achieve "divergent goals and divergent identities" (1974b, p. 200). Such preconscious pathology is the basis for personality disorganization that may be neurotic, prepsychotic, or psychotic in nature.

Conclusion

Lawrence S. Kubie was a man who could not be satisfied within the boundaries of a single intellectual discipline. His mind, wide-ranging and restless, found a natural focus in the science, art, and philosophy of psychoanalysis, which he regarded as the most significant event in the recent history of human culture. Through the profession of psychoanalysis, informed by all fields of human endeavor, he was able to express and live out many of his passionate convictions and to engage in his lifelong search for freedom from the bondage of the unconscious, a freedom which he regarded as essential to the discovery of truth. Through his person and his work he influenced several generations of clinicians and investigators in the field of human behavior. There are few aspects of modern psychiatry and psychoanalysis that do not bear some mark of his thinking, often through his friends or students. Beyond this he was a significant intellectual force for humanists and educators involved in the cultural life of his—and our—time. This volume of some of his writings celebrates him as a man who was important to us all.

References

Bergson, H. (1889), *Time and Free Will: An Essay on the Immediate Data of Consciousness,* trans. F. L. Pogson. New York: Macmillan, 1910.

Deikman, A. J. (1971), Bimodal Consciousness. In: *The Nature of Human Consciousness,* ed. R. E. Ornstein. New York: Viking, 1973, pp. 67-86.

Edel, A. (1974), Psychiatry and Philosophy. In: *American Handbook of Psychiatry,* Vol. 1, *Foundations of Psychiatry,* rev. 2nd ed., ed. S. Arieti et al. New York: Basic Books, Chapter 14.

Fingarette, H. (1969), *Self-Deception.* London: Routledge & Kegan Paul.

Freud, S.(1900), The Interpretation of Dreams. *Standard Edition,* 4 & 5. London: Hogarth Press, 1953.

———— (1905), Jokes and Their Relation to the Unconscious. *Standard Edition,* 8. London: Hogarth Press, 1960.

———— (1915a), Repression. *Standard Edition,* 14:146-158. London: Hogarth Press, 1957.

———— (1915b), The Unconscious. *Standard Edition,* 14:166-204. London: Hogarth Press, 1957.

———— (1923), The Ego and the Id. *Standard Edition,* 19:12-59. London: Hogarth Press, 1961.

_____ (1925), Negation. *Col. Pap.*, 5:181-185. London: Hogarth Press, 1950.
_____ (1926), Inhibitions, Symptoms and Anxiety. *Standard Edition*, 20:87-172. London: Hogarth Press, 1959.
_____ (1933), New Introductory Lectures on Psycho-Analysis. *Standard Edition*, 22:5-182. London: Hogarth Press, 1964.
_____ (1940), An Outline of Psycho-Analysis. *Standard Edition*, 23:144-207. London: Hogarth Press, 1964.
Gill, M. M. (1967), The Primary Process. In: Motives and Thought: Psychoanalytic Essays in Honor of David Rapaport, ed. R. R. Holt. *Psychol. Issues*, Monogr. 18/19:260-298. New York: International Universities Press.
Glover, E. (1969), In Honor of Lawrence Kubie. *J. Nerv. Ment. Dis.*, 149:5-18.
Habermas, J. (1968), *Knowledge and Human Interests*. Boston: Beacon Press, 1971.
Holt, R. R., ed. (1971), *New Horizon for Psychotherapy: Autonomy as a Profession*. New York: International Universities Press.
James, W. (1890), *The Principles of Psychology*, Vol. 1. New York: Holt, 1902.
Kierkegaard, S. K. (1843), *Either/Or*, Vol. 2, trans. W. Lowrie. New York: Anchor Books, 1959.
Klein, G. S. (1959), Consciousness in Psychoanalytic Theory: Some Implications for Current Research in Perception. *J. Amer. Psychoanal. Assn.*, 7:5-34.
_____ (1976), *Psychoanalytic Theory: An Exploration of Essentials*. New York: International Universities Press.
Kris, E. (1950), On Preconscious Mental Processes. In: *Psychoanalytic Explorations in Art*. New York: International Universities Press, 1952, pp. 303-318.
Kubie, L. S. (1930), A Theoretical Application to Some Neurological Problems of the Properties of Excitation Waves Which Move in Closed Circuits. *Brain*, 53:166-178.
_____ (1934), Body Symbolization and the Development of Language. *Psychoanal. Quart.*, 3:430-444.
_____ (1941), The Repetitive Core of Neurosis. *Psychoanal. Quart.*, 10:23-43.
_____ (1943), The Use of Induced Hypnagogic Reveries in the Recovery of Repressed Amnesic Data. *Bull. Menninger Clin.*, 7:172-182.
_____ (1945), The Value of Induced Dissociated States in the Therapeutic Process. *Proc. Royal Soc. Med.*, 38:681-683.
_____ (1948), Instincts and Homeostasis. *This volume*, pp. 52-86.
_____ (1949), The Neurotic Potential and Human Adaptation. In: *Adaptation*, ed. J. Romano. Ithaca, N.Y.: Cornell University Press, pp. 77-96.
_____ (1950), *Practical and Theoretical Aspects of Psychoanalysis*. New York: International Universities Press.
_____ (1952a), The Place of Emotions in the Feedback Concept. *Transactions of the Ninth Conference on Cybernetics*, ed. H. von Foerster. New York: Josiah Macy, Jr. Foundation, pp. 48-72.
_____ (1952b), Problems and Techniques of Psychoanalytic Validation and Progress. In: *Psychoanalysis as Science*, ed. E. Pumpian-Mindlin. Stanford, Calif.: Stanford University Press, pp. 46-124.
_____ (1952c), A Research Project in Community Mental Hygiene: A Fantasy. *Ment. Hygiene*, 36:220-226.
_____ (1953a), The Distortion of the Symbolic Process in Neurosis and Psychosis. *This volume*, pp. 87-114.

———— (1953b), Some Implications for Psychoanalysis of Modern Concepts of the Organization of the Brain. *Psychoanal. Quart.,* 22:21-68.

———— (1954a), Psychiatric and Psychoanalytic Considerations of the Problems of Consciousness. In: *Brain Mechanisms and Consciousness.* Oxford: Blackwell, pp. 444-469.

———— (1954b), The Pros and Cons of a New Profession: A Doctorate in Medical Psychology. *Texas Rep. Biol. Med.,* 12:692-737.

———— (1955), Dr. Kinsey and the Medical Profession. Review of *Sexual Behavior in the Human Female,* by A. C. Kinsey et al. *Psychosomat. Med.,* 17:172-184.

———— (1956), Influence of Symbolic Processes on the Role of Instincts in Human Behavior. *Psychosomat. Med.,* 18:189-208.

———— (1958), *Neurotic Distortion of the Creative Process.* Lawrence: University of Kansas Press.

———— (1963), The Central Affective Potential and Its Trigger Mechanisms. In: *Counterpoint: Libidinal Object and Subject,* ed. H. S. Gaskill. New York: International Universities Press, pp. 106-120.

———— (1966). A Reconsideration of Thinking, the Dream Process, and "the Dream." *This volume,* pp. 162-169.

———— (1967), The Relation of Psychotic Disorganization to the Neurotic Process. *This volume,* pp. 170-184.

———— (1968), Pitfalls of Community Psychiatry. *Arch. Gen. Psychiat.,* 18:257-266.

———— (1972), The Nature of Psychological Change in Individuals and Its Relation to Cultural Change. *Psychoanalysis and Contemporary Science,* 1:25-37. New York: Macmillan.

———— (1974a), The Nature of the Neurotic Process. In: *American Handbook of Psychiatry,* Vol. 3, *Adult Clinical Psychiatry,* rev. 2nd ed., ed. S. Arieti et al. New York: Basic Books, pp. 3-16.

———— (1974b), The Drive to Become Both Sexes. *This volume,* pp. 191-263.

———— & Margolin, S. (1944), The Process of Hypnotism and the Nature of the Hypnotic State. *Amer. J. Psychiat.,* 100:611-622.

Langer, S. K. (1942), *Philosophy in a New Key.* New York: Mentor Books, 1962.

MacLean, P. D. (1949), Psychosomatic Disease and the Visceral Brain. *Psychosomat. Med.,* 11:338-353.

———— (1969), The Internal-External Bonds of the Memory Process. *J. Nerv. Ment. Dis.,* 149:40-47.

Matte Blanco, I. (1975), *The Unconscious as Infinite Sets: An Essay in Bi-Logic.* London: Duckworth.

McCulloch, W. S. (1969), Regenerative Loop. *J. Nerv. Ment. Dis.,* 149:54-58.

Rapaport, D. (1956), The Psychoanalytic Theory of Consciousness and the Study of Dreams. Lecture to the Detroit Psychoanalytic Society, January 14.

Ricoeur, P. (1970), *Freud and Philosophy: An Essay on Interpretation.* New Haven: Yale University Press.

Schafer, R. (1976), *A New Language for Psychoanalysis.* New Haven: Yale University Press.

Schutz, A. (1962), *Collected Papers,* Vol. 1. *The Problem of Social Reality.* The Hague: Nijhoff.

Spitz, R. (1969), Aggression and Adaptation. *J. Nerv. Ment. Dis.,* 149:81-90.

Wurmser, L. (1977), A Defense of the Use of Metaphor in Analytic Theory Formation. *Psychoanal. Quart.,* 46: 466-498.

1

THE FALLACIOUS USE OF
QUANTITATIVE CONCEPTS
IN DYNAMIC PSYCHOLOGY

A system of psychological concepts merits being called "dynamic" when it comprehends conscious and unconscious motivations, and when it can demonstrate how the interaction between various psychological states can play an active role in determining the course of human life. In any effort to formulate a system of dynamic psychology it is difficult to be sure when our words describe and when they explain. Indeed, the boundary lines between description and explanation are never sharp in science. Many constant sequences are found to have cause-and-effect relationships, and many apparent cause-and-effect relationships turn out to be mere coincidental sequences. In the effort to deal with this difficulty, there is a tendency in psychology to fall back largely on quantitative concepts, that is, on the explicit or implicit assumption that a change in dimension or volume or size or strength in one or another component of the total psychological constellation is the effective variable which causes all other changes. There are some dangers in this type of formulation.

Let me begin with a quotation from Freud's (1916-1917) *Introductory Lectures on Psycho-Analysis.* This was written before 1920 when the introduction of the structural viewpoint brought far-reaching changes into psychoanalytic theory. Nevertheless, the quantitative assumptions of the earlier

First published in *The Psychoanalytic Quarterly*, 16:507-518, 1947. Reprinted by permission of *The Psychoanalytic Quarterly*.

theories were carried over without re-examination into the structural era of psychoanalytic theory.

> You will doubtless have noticed that in these last remarks I have introduced a new factor into the concatenation of the aetiological chain—namely, the *quantity*, the magnitude of the energies concerned; we must always take this factor into account as well. A purely qualitative analysis of the aetiological conditions does not suffice; or, to put it in another way, a purely *dynamic* conception of these processes is insufficient, the *economic* aspect is also required. We have to realize (a) that the conflict between the two forces in opposition does not break out until a certain intensity in the degree of investment is reached, even though the substantive conditions have long been in existence. In the same way, (b) the pathogenic significance of the constitutional factor is determined by the preponderance of one of the component-instincts in *excess* over another in the disposition; it is even possible to conceive disposition as qualitatively the same in all men and only differentiated by this quantitative factor. No less important is this quantitative factor for the capacity to withstand neurotic illness; it depends (c) upon the *amount* of undischarged libido that a person can hold freely suspended, and (d) upon *how large* a portion of it he can deflect from the sexual to a nonsexual goal in sublimation. The final aim of mental activity, which can be qualitatively described as a striving toward pleasure and avoidance of pain, is represented economically (e) in the task of mastering the distribution of the quantities of excitation (stimulus-masses) present in the mental apparatus, and in preventing the accumulation of them which gives rise to pain [p. 313].

Here are five overlapping and somewhat circular assumptions, each one of which requires critical examination. At this point, however, I want to make it clear that I do not believe every effort to explain psychological phenomena through quantitative variables is necessarily incorrect. It is my thesis, rather, that the easy assumption of quantitative variables as the only ultimate explanation of every variation in behavior is one of the seductive fallacies to which all psychological theorizing is prone. When in doubt one can always say that some component of human psychology is bigger or smaller, stronger or weaker, more intense or less intense, more or less highly charged with "energy," or with degraded energy, and by these words delude ourselves into believing that we have explained a phenomenon which we have merely described in metaphors. Grave medical pronouncements to neurotic sufferers abound in metaphors no less naïve than that of the famous internist who solemnly told all such patients they had "exhausted their nervous capital," and therefore clapped them in bed. This is not essentially different from easy statements about "depleted egos."

I am not suggesting that quantitative variations may not occur in intrapsychic relationships, but only that there is no reason to assume that every component process is capable of variations in quantity. There may well be all-or-none processes on the psychological as well as the neuronal level. As a matter of fact, the concept of quantitative variables is drawn from other sciences, and we have no right to assume a priori that they play an equally determining role in psychology; and certainly we cannot depend solely on quantity variables to make a system of psychological theory "dynamic." The issue which I am raising here goes to the heart of the problem of causation on the psychological level.

I quote from some editorial notes which Dr. Lewin and I (1936) wrote as a footnote to a paper by Dr. Hoskins:

> Psychoanalysis must be pragmatic. It describes human behavior, and in so doing must point out differences in behavior which seem, in turn, to depend upon differences both in kinds and in quantities of "energy." However, when it is observed that one patient has a greater "drive" towards a certain activity than another, it would be a most naïve explanation of this fact to deduce that the difference in the "drive" must depend solely upon differences in the amounts of specific energy invested in this direction. Such an explanation would be fallacious, just as it would be fallacious to try to estimate the amount of energy going into a machine from the amount of work done by the machine, without considering the factor of efficiency and the losses through transformations of energy into heat or other "degraded" forms.
>
> Nevertheless, in describing the conduct of two human beings, common sense alone justifies us in characterizing one man as "braver" than another, despite the fact that we are without any quantitative measurements of courage, and in face of the further fact that the energy exerted by the coward in his efforts to act bravely may be far greater than that exerted by the hero.

Similarly,in the psychoanalytic study of "drives," it is frequently necessary, for descriptive purposes, to talk in terms of quantities of "drive energy" which can be estimated only by the external results and by one's general impression. At the same time, however, there is in psychoanalysis a conscientious effort always to follow the losses of energy which occur through displacements, substitutions, and the like, and which are [or may be] analogous to the losses of energy which occur in the operations of any machine. . . .

In this respect psychoanalysis, however, is really in the same situation as the more basic sciences of neurophysiology and endocrinology. After all, it is not possible as yet to formulate such relatively simple phenomena as the nervous impulse, the factors of excitation and inhibition in the central nervous system, the variations at the synapse, or the activities of a simple reflex arc, in terms of ergs, calories, or dynes. Nor is endocrinology, as yet, in a position to apply the basic laws of thermodynamics or the fundamental, quantitative units of physical forces to the problems of the oestrous cycle. It is true that the hormonal elements can be measured with an accuracy greater than are our approximate estimates of feelings and impulses; but this is still far from the precision of physical energetics.

It is therefore scientifically necessary to keep clearly in mind the fact that the psychodynamics dealt with in psychoanalysis refers to something which is loosely analogous to, but still very far from, the exacter field of thermodynamics. These psychodynamics deal with an effort to estimate (a) the sources of energy, (b) the kinds and quantities of energy, (c) the transformations of energy, one into another, and (d) the distributions of energy. But the "energy" referred to here means not what is intended by the physicist, but *simply apparent intensities of feelings and impulses, or in psychoanalytic terms "the libido."*

Why is it that the hypothesis of quantitative variables seems to hold such a special fascination for us? This is not on rational grounds alone but on the basis of a strong emotional bias buttressed by a conviction that a science is not mature until it can count. Consequently to talk even of hypothetical and unmeasured quantitative variations gives us a feeling of scientific maturity which may in fact be premature and illusory. Perhaps it is our own process of growth which breeds in us this overvaluation of the quantitative. To the infant and child, pitting his strength against the grown-up world, relative size becomes the measure of power because size, in the end, determines the outcome of every effort which the child makes. As we struggle with the most difficult of all sciences, the science of human nature, and as we attempt to formulate psychological processes as exerting a dynamic influence on one another, it may be that thinking in terms of quantitative variables alone we are regressing to the value system of childhood. Habituation adds a further illusion of reality. Ideas and terminologies become a part of the very air we breathe, something whose truth and precision we accept without question as we become used to them through frequent repetitions. Men's minds are like rooms whose walls are lined with pictures which they take for granted because they have hung there too long. In all systems of psychology, including psychoanalysis, this human tendency has expressed itself in many ways.[1]

The problem that confronts us is one of the most difficult in the whole field of psychological theory and research. Let us first consider quantitative concepts in the description of psychological events. It is safe and easy to talk in quantitative terms when we merely describe conduct. Thus we can say of any act that it is more or less courageous, more or less angry, more or less stubborn, and we will not be misunderstood; nor will we deceive ourselves. Yet every act represents the sum of many variable forces, and consequently when we look behind the façade of behavior, merely to describe the person, we are no longer able to use quantitative terms with the same clarity. We cannot even say with accuracy that a man whose conduct has been courageous is himself courageous, or that a man whose conduct has been angry has been angry himself. We can say that the former acted as though he were courageous, when actually he may have been in a rage; or that the latter acted as though he were angry, when he may have been terrified. A man who stood up against a thousand enemies and earned the Victoria Cross may have done so for a great many reasons other than courage or freedom from fear. He may have done it because of a schizophrenic dissociation, or out of a psycho-

---

[1] Compare Rado's (1922) derivation of causality and determinism in science in general from their anthropological and ontogenetic origins, and also Reiner's (1932) discussion of Rado's paper.

pathic joy in bloodshed, or at the behest of a superego whose commands were dreaded more than the enemy. The conduct of the "angriest" patient I ever knew was always gentle. When he became angry he walked in a dainty and somewhat effeminate manner as though treading on eggs. His voice would become light, high-pitched, and childlike. Often he would then go to bed with fatigue. The more angry he became, the more timid and gentle was his conduct. If we describe this man in terms of his impact on the world, we must call him gentle, kind, and timid. If we describe him in terms of the stifled affects which are the mainspring of his life, we are justified in saying that he is in a diffuse and chronic rage.

Such observations as these are obvious to the point of banality. Even before men thought in psychoanalytic terms of unconscious, preconscious, and conscious mental processes, there were general misgivings as to the adequacy of easy quantitative formulations, some doubt as to whether they were more than descriptive metaphors. We knew that it was of little value to say that a man ran away because he was afraid, or that he was afraid because he was a coward, or that one man ran away while another stayed and fought because the first was more frightened than the second, or more afraid than the second, or more of a coward than the second. All such estimates become laden with affect. In effect they are epithets, or mere redescriptions of behavior. They are verbal circles which are devoid of explanatory value, even though they make the assumption of quantitative variables.

When we add the consideration that there are unconscious mental processes which are equivalent to conscious emotions, it becomes evident that easy assumptions about quantitative emotional variables are even more difficult to make. Thus is it accurate to assume, as do so many authors, that the subjective intensity of symptomatic anxiety is any indication of the quantity of unconscious anxiety which underlies it? The same question faces us with respect to all other affective experiences; and since there are many forces which intervene between the underlying affect and its conscious representation it is obvious that any such assumption is wholly unwarranted.

Any attempt to *explain* psychological events multiplies the difficulties many times. Since there are such intrapsychic barriers and defenses as repression, displacement, substitution, and isolation, all of which may or may not be subject to quantitative fluctuations, some of which may operate in an all-or-none fashion, no easy guesses are justified as to which varied to produce any special psychological state or action. Furthermore, whenever two forces struggle against each other until one triumphs, in order to explain what has happened one must determine whether the triumph was due to an increase of strength or an expenditure of energy on the part of the victor, or to a decrease in strength or effort or a deflection of energy on the part of the loser. Victory does not always go to the strong; sometimes it goes to the adroit; and if we are to decide which produced the victory, an accurate decision waits on appropriate indicators of change for each variable. As long as we can deal only with combined influences, quantitative guesses are misleading and lead to dependence on the easy figure of speech which implies that all differences in conduct, feeling, personality, or symptoms are due to something greater or something less. People are more or less secure, more or less rigid, more or less obsessional, more or less hysterical, more or less confident, more or less conceited, more or less domineering. All of this is verbal shorthand, not always valid even as description, and usually meaningless as explanation. To repeat, we can say of a particular moment of behavior that it is more or less something, but the minute one attempts to explain the act by going behind it to the actor, so many variable forces must be estimated that it becomes impossible to deduce from the end result which intensified and which decreased their operative force to produce the act. Especially if we try to ascribe the behavior of the individual to quantitative changes in his intrapsychic processes, in the absence of quantitative indicators, any decision as to which have varied becomes a matter of guesswork or of *ad hoc* assumption.

Let us consider how many variables there may be. (1) There are quantitative variations of external stimuli, and corresponding variations in quantities of overt responses to stimuli, or of conscious and unconscious affective responses, and variable quantities of control of these responses. (2) Presumably there are varying quantities of internal (i.e., instinctual) drives which in turn can be countered by varying quantities of inhibition, or of compulsive exaggeration (cf. Freud's "illusory strength of instinct" [1915b, p. 87]), or varying quantities of cathexes, excitation, resistance, defense, or repression. (3) In symptom formation and the processes by which symptoms precipitate out of conflict, we find assumptions as to varying amounts of isolation, repression, projection, displacement, reaction formation, rationalization, identification, compensation, idealization, sublimation, and the like.

There are still other possibilities which could be listed, but with just these in mind let me return to the quotation from Freud with which I began. There we find five hypothetical applications of the economic (i.e., quantitative) principle, each representing a possible variable.

1. That a conflict between two forces does not "break out" (probably meaning "become pathogenic") until a certain "intensity" or "degree of investment" is attained. Here in one proposition are three interdependent quantitative assumptions.

2. That quantitative differences in the relative roles of different component instincts determine the pathogenicity of a "constitution." Here certainly is a useful working hypothesis, provided that it can be subjected to experimental quantitative demonstration and verification. But no one has as yet devised any method by which we can distinguish between a constitutional hypercathexis of an instinct (assuming for the moment that such exists) and a compulsive intensification of an instinct.

3. That vulnerability to neurosis depends upon the "amounts of undischarged libido that a person can hold freely suspended." Here again are several assumptions: that libido is measurable in quantities; that its state varies between free and bound; that there is some unknown factor in an individual which makes him capable of more or less tolerance for "undischarged amounts of libido." There is, of course, the equally

plausible opposite possibility that the individual's ability to tolerate undischarged libido is the product and result rather than the cause of his neurotic processes. Here again is an intricate skein of interlocking and somewhat circular hypotheses.

4. That vulnerability also depends upon how much of the libido can be deflected from sexual to nonsexual goals. Even if we accept this as a working premise it explains nothing until we understand on what the ability to deflect libido is dependent.

5. That there is still another unknown factor in the personality which determines the ability to "master" or to "distribute" varying "quantities of stimulus," and "prevent the accumulation of stimulus masses which cause pain."

It seems to me that all of these redescribe in terms of hypothetical units of power something which is quite as adequately described by saying, for instance, that some people can endure pain or frustration and deprivation and that others cannot. To talk of the ability to master or distribute stimulus masses is not explanatory, and as a description of events it is less precise than is the simple language of the street.

Similar considerations qualify many other applications of the economic hypothesis, as, for instance, where Freud speaks specifically of hypothetical variations in the cathexes of different erogenous zones, whether these be inherited, constitutional, or acquired. A not unrelated use of quantitative concepts is embodied in such theories as Adler's concept of organ inferiority (Ferenczi and Rank, 1923 p. 35).

Further examples of Freud's multiple use of the concept of quantitative or economic variables are found in other writings. The emergence of ideas from the preconscious into the conscious is explained as due to the intensity of the cathexis (1915c, p. 126). Phobic patients are said to manifest anxiety when "the repressed impulse becomes intensified" (p. 115). Conversely, ideas are said to emerge from repression or to remain conscious if they represent "only a small amount of energy" (p. 90). Innumerable other examples could be drawn from current works, of which perhaps the most notable examples are to be found in much of the war literature, and particularly in the writings of Grinker and Spiegel (Kubie, 1946).

The introduction of the structural principle in 1920 made profound changes in certain aspects of psychoanalytic theory. The "economic principle," however, was carried over bodily from prestructural to poststructural formulations, with the consequence that the concepts of id, ego, and superego are often used as though they were autonomous entities, subject to quantitative fluctuations which are independent of one another. Recently these concepts were brilliantly reformulated by Hartmann, Kris, and Loewenstein (1946), who look upon them merely as "centers" of certain aspects of psychological activity, and without any assumptions as to quantitative changes. Their attitude, however, has not as yet permeated psychoanalytic thinking; consequently writers still do not hesitate to talk of strong and weak libidos, strong and weak ids, strong and weak superegos, strong and weak egos. Here the metaphor becomes a convenient way of begging every important question and of avoiding every difficulty in psychodynamic causation. Indeed all such *ad hoc* explanations, constructed to fit each individual clinical phenomenon, unless used to initiate research become a way of evading the hard task of searching out methods for making quantitative appraisals of the differences in psychic process and psychic constitution.

Clearly, variations in psychic processes can be described in terms of fluctuations in the intensity or dominance of any one or of any group of these variable and sensitive processes. Such descriptions are useful working hypotheses. By insidious steps, however, they lead into fallacy, the first of which is always an implication that the quantity change which has been assumed is the only such change that occurred, and that consequently this change is the effective variable which explains all.

This fallacy runs through every known system of dynamic psychological theory. Therefore two questions arise: first, whether this borrowing from physical science of the metaphor of variable quantities of energy to use in the psychological field has not actually lessened the clarity of our thinking; second, whether without this metaphor a dynamic psychological theory can be formulated. Freud's introduction of what he called "the economic principle," in addition to the dynamic and the topographical principles, may have given premature status to our human need for quantitative evaluations: ". . . beside the dynamic and topographical, we take the *economic* standpoint, one from which we try to follow out the fate of given volumes of excitation and to achieve, at least relatively, some assessment of it" (1915c, p. 114).

It is perfectly true that the analytic situation to some extent controls external variables, and permits a closer scrutiny of internal variables. But even approximate estimations of the direction of quantitative changes of individual components are never immediately possible. This is one source of the great gap that exists between clinical observation and theory in psychoanalysis.

Until it becomes possible to make quantitative comparisons of individual components in the complex stream of psychological processes, all quantitative formulations have at best only the limited value of descriptive shortcuts, and never provide a safe basis for explanations of behavior or of behavior differences. All psychological phenomena are the results of the interplay of many conflicting intrapsychic forces. Consequently any rearrangement of these forces can alter the pattern of the psychological phenomena and can release new forms of overt behavior without any increases or decreases of hypothetical charges of energy. Assumptions as to changes in quantities of energy are admissible only if alterations in the patterns of intrapsychic forces have been ruled out. A failure to realize this has made all so-called economic formulations a species of *ad hoc* speculative descriptive allegory, in pseudo-quantitative terms. This is the weakest element in all current theories of psychological causation.

2

INSTINCTS AND HOMEOSTASIS

I. INTRODUCTION

A history of the evolution of the concept of instinct would throw much light on the development of both biology and psychology. Precisely because, as Freud (1915a) pointed out, the concept of instinct stands at the border between the realm of the body and the realm of the mind, it arouses many prejudices. Consequently there is no aspect of the concept which has not been an object of controversy. The very existence of instincts has been challenged. Both in normal and in abnormal behavior instincts have been regarded as all-powerful by some observers and by others as powerless. The concept has sometimes been restricted to patterns of behavior which were assumed to be inherited *in toto* and unmodifiable by growth, development, or experience. Alternatively the concept has been used so broadly as to include every possible form of behavior. Instincts have been looked upon as nothing more than simple reflexes, or as integrations so complex as to be almost superbiological. Many enumerations have been offered, from merely one or two to large numbers, which in turn were subclassified in a variety of ways.

Out of these contradictory biases has arisen an even more confused debate about the relative importance to human behavior of what are called the "biological," "genetic," or "instinctual" forces, as opposed to "cultural" or "environmental" forces. Moreover the concept of instincts has been

---

First published in *Psychosomatic Medicine*, 10:15-30, 1948. Reprinted by permission of Elsevier North-Holland, Inc.

taken as a challenge to religion by some, and to economic materialism by others, with the result that issues that should be wholly irrelevant to objective science have intruded their influence into every debate.[1]

The aim of this paper will be to attempt to re-evaluate the concept of instinct objectively. In this attempt certain working hypotheses will be used.

1. All extremist definitions of instincts will be avoided. Thus it will not be assumed that for any instinct the entire pattern is determined solely and exclusively by inherited neuronal nets, although an inherited nucleus will be taken for granted.

2. It will be suggested that there probably are three components to every complex of instincts: i.e., a biochemical source which is clearly seen in some and less easily in others; an inherited but modifiable neuronal net; and a complex psychic superstructure of fantasies and of obligatory and phobic patterns which together shape the derivative instinctual drives.

3. Nor will it be assumed that any element in the neuronal net, whether inherited or not, is unmodifiable by growth, development, experience, and learning. Experimental evidence indicates that modifiability is possible both for the inherited nucleus and for the total pattern of adult behavior which is built around the inherited nucleus. Sherrington demonstrated long ago that even the simplest reflex is subject to continuous alteration and even reversal under the influence of activities in other areas of the nervous system. Certainly what is possible in a simple reflex can happen to more complex integrated patterns as well.

4. Biologists have objected to the use of the term "instinct" by English-speaking psychoanalysts, and these analysts in turn

---

[1] Those who are interested in this rather futile and sometimes ill-tempered controversy might find illumination in the introduction to Kelsen's (1943) *Society and Nature*. Kelsen points out that primitive man saw in nature a projection of his own experiences of retribution, revenge, reward, and the like. He anthropomorphized nature and saw it as governed by human motives and human feelings. Civilized man, on the other hand, is attempting to free himself from this "social interpretation of nature," and to emancipate "the law of causality from the principle of retribution." He thus conceives of "society as part of nature and not nature as part of society."

have answered by explaining that the word "instinct" was a mistranslation of the German word *Trieb,* which should instead have been translated as "drive" or "instinctual drive." This answer fails, however, to meet one important issue which lies behind the mere words: namely, whether there are actual differences between instinct and drive *in the human being.* Theoretically, an instinctive pattern would be one which was energized exclusively or preponderantly by biochemical processes and channeled through a fixed, inherited central network of nerve cells, fibers, and synapses. In contrast to this a *Trieb* (or drive) would be an ego-acceptable ("ego-syntonic") pattern of compulsive behavior, triggered by faint stirrings of phobic anxiety. This is the very mechanism with which we are familiar in psychopathology in the production of phobias and obsessional and compulsive symptoms. Such symptoms, however, are symbolic representations of unacceptable ("ego-dystonic") drives, whereas *drives* are compulsive mechanisms focused on acceptable acts which give some measure of direct gratification. Examples of symptomatic compulsions are compulsive counting and compulsive handwashing. Examples of compulsive drives would be compulsive eating, compulsive drinking, compulsive working, compulsive intercourse, compulsive sleeping, etc.

5. It will be shown that in adult human life the biochemical kernel out of which instinctual activity arises *never operates alone, but only as part of a complex of derivative drives.* Consequently the concept of a simon-pure instinct becomes an academic abstraction; all patterned behavior which discharges instinctual energies is seen to be the result of an integration of the biochemical nucleus with superimposed compulsions. Another way of phrasing this would be to say that the biochemical nucleus functions as though it were suspended between compulsions and phobias which form around it as their activating core. There are reasons for introducing into the concept of normal instinctual functions these terms from psychopathology.

6. In different instinctual areas the relative importance of the biochemical source and of the psychic superstructure varies widely. This results in significant differences in the

nature of the normal and pathological phenomena which can evolve within the area of each instinct.

7. If the considerations are valid, the distinction which it is customary to make between an instinctual act and a drive loses much if not all of its importance, since every instinctual act, even when it is as elementary as breathing, will be seen to contain both a biochemical core, a network of neurones and neuronal synapses, and a psychological superstructure. The difference that remains will appear as one of degree rather than of kind: i.e., differences in the relative roles of the three components.

8. In the further discussion it will become clear that all instinctual processes serve either procreative purposes for the species, or else homeostatic and self-regulatory functions for the individual. This led Orr (1942) to speak of homeostatic instincts; a characterization so all-inclusive and undifferentiating, however, as not to be very helpful. The psychological goals of instinctual processes are not their biological purposes, but either the gratification of specific appetites, or the heeding of specific warning mechanisms, or the obeying of those superimposed obligatory commands which we call "compulsions."

9. With Lashley (1928) we would point out that the crusade against instincts has failed and must continue to fail because "desires and aversions, field forces and dynamic tensions, needs and vectors, libidos and means-end-readinesses all have the same conceptual status as had the rejected instincts, and besides lack the one tie to physiological reality which the problem of genetic transmission gave to the latter" (p. 447).

10. It is hoped that this general approach to the problem will make it possible to reconcile many of the controversies which have been referred to above, and to dismiss others as irrelevant.

Those who feel that this attempt is superfluous may be interested in Freud's views on this. In "Instincts and Their Vicissitudes" (1915a, p. 67) he wrote: "I am altogether doubtful whether work upon psychological material will afford any decisive indication for the distinction and the classification of instincts. Rather it would seem necessary to apply to this material certain definite assumptions in order to work upon it and we could wish that these assumptions might be taken from some other branch of knowledge and transferred to psychology."

In the same article, Freud defined instincts as "the measure of the demand for work imposed upon the mind in consequence of its connection with the body" (p. 64), and my own study really derives from this statement. Consequently our initial task will be to describe as precisely as possible just how the various instincts "impose their demands for work upon the mental apparatus." Because of the differences in their basic chemistry and physiology, they will be seen to operate in different ways, with certain psychological differences occurring as inevitable consequences of these biochemical differences. Out of this will come a tentative classification of instincts, the lack of which Freud regretted, and which he felt sure would have to be derived from extra-analytical considerations.

That Freud himself subsequently attempted a classification of the instincts on purely psychological grounds is an interesting and possibly an unfortunate by-product of his many attempts to solve this problem. For a history of Freud's concepts of instinct and libido, see Bibring (1936) and Sterba (1931).

Recently J. B. S. Haldane (1947) and also Dobzhansky and Ashley-Montagu (1947) have stated that the most important fact about heredity in human affairs is that we inherit the capacity to change. They point out that it is the adaptive plasticity rather than the fixity of our inherited patterns which is our greatest heritage. Biologically this is undoubtedly true, but it would be fallacious to deduce from this biological plasticity that we are equally free and plastic psychologically. Unfortunately, these same human beings who have inherited this adaptive plasticity also limit their own freedom through certain rigid psychological mechanisms which closely confine their instinctual patterns. In their more symbolic forms these rigid mechanisms produce the phobias and compulsions with which we are familiar in psychopathology. Identical although subtler phobic-compulsive forces distort and restrict and guide every instinctual process in human life. This limits our freedom and plasticity almost as effectively as if we inherited unalterable patterns. In fact, it is this compulsive rigidity in human nature which has led so many psychologists to take it for granted that we inherit many fixed patterns. The difference remains important, however, since it is reasonable to expect that in the course of time it will be within our power to alter and modify our limiting compulsions and phobias by processes of emotional education, whereas the rigidity of inherited patterns could be altered only by the infinitely slower processes of evolution.

II. The Translation of Bodily Needs into Behavior

Before describing the changes in the body from which instincts are dervied, let us consider how the body's needs are converted into behavior through changes in the brain. In a recent paper on the mental and the physical origins of behavior, Adrian (1946) formulated a working hypothesis of the nature of the changes which occur in the central nervous system in response to body changes. Adrian points out that all living cells have a store of potential energy, but that it is peculiar to the cells of the nervous and muscular systems that some of this energy can suddenly be converted into other forms as the cell is thrown into activity. At the lowest level of integration, i.e., in any simple reflex system, the energy involved in the response is produced and discharged chiefly through the interaction between the stimulus and the effector organs. In so far as other parts of the central nervous system participate in the reaction, they do so solely as conducting or modifying mechanisms. They may influence both the intensity and the sign of the reflex, but the existence of the reflex is not dependent upon the existence of any central storehouse of "energy." Adrian quotes Sherrington as describing the reflex as "dead beat," meaning that it comes to rest as soon as the stimulus ceases, i.e., as soon as the body is brought into harmony with its external surroundings. That is to say, the cells and the fibers of the reflex mechanisms of the nervous system remain quiet when they are not disturbed.

This is in contrast to the cells of the brain, whose responses are not dead beat, but may continue long after the stimulus is over, even indefinitely. Furthermore, in these cells there is an incessant asynchronous flux which is based either on aperiodic discharges of stored energy or on reverberating and self-exciting circuits (Kubie, 1930), or on a combination of the two. The result is something which Adrian likens to the unorganized movements of an unruly crowd. "Thus in the brain the effect of an afferent brain message will be like that of an exhortation to a noisy crowd, whereas in the reflex pathways, it will be like that of an order to a silent and obedient regiment." According to Adrian, the afferent impulse influences the cells of the brain by synchronizing in some measure their asynchronous discharges, thus imposing an orderly pattern on their previously chaotic movements. It is this change which Adrian pictures as mediating the transformations of body energy and body need into thought and action. This is the final cerebral patterning, by which the "body imposes its demands on the mental apparatus" (Freud), the last step in the sequential processes by which the id energizes human behavior.

The instinctual messages to the brain arise from bodily changes, which generate the afferent impulses that impinge on the asynchronous dynamic processes of the central nervous system in the manner described by Adrian. A consideration of these bodily changes leads directly to the classic works of Claude Bernard (1859) and of Cannon (1932), to the more recent work of Richter (1927, 1941, 1942, 1943a), and finally to the concept of instincts put forward by the biologist Wheeler (1939).

Bernard (1859) described the internal environment of living cells, i.e., the body fluids, and the incessant efforts of the body to maintain constancy with respect to chemical constitution, acid-base relationships, temperature, etc. This was further developed in Cannon's (1932) concept of homeostasis, and his description of the self-regulating physiological processes of individual tissues, organs, and organ systems. More recently Richter (1941), in a series of careful experiments, demonstrated that the effort to maintain a constant internal environment can be carried on by activities of the organism as a whole even after the simpler physiological regulators have been experimentally eliminated. Of this he gives several examples: e.g., (a) polydipsia after removal of the posterior lobe of the pituitary, which eliminates the automatic regulating action of the antidiuretic secretions from this portion of the gland; (b) the automatic efforts of animals in a cold environment to prevent heat loss after removal of the pituitary and thyroid glands; (c) the maintenance of mineral, carbohydrate, and fat levels after various types of gland extirpations (e.g., the increase in intake of sodium chloride in adrenalectomized rats to compensate for their loss of sodium; the increase in intake of calcium in parathyroidectomized rats; the increase of intake of olive oil and the parallel decrease of sucrose intake in pancreatectomized rats). Comparable salt craving has been recorded in humans after partial or total destruction of the adrenal cortex. Richter (1942) has shown further that one possible mechanism for this is a change in the threshold of sensory discrimination in the taste buds, due to changes in the local chemistry of the tissues under conditions of specific chemical deficiencies. Thus the normal rat can recognize the difference between distilled water and salt solution 1/2,000, whereas adrenalectomized rats with desalted tissues recognize concentrations of 1/33,000. Intact taste nerves are necessary for all such compensatory diet regulation and discrimination.

On the basis of evidence from observations on domesticated animals and controlled studies on laboratory animals and on human infants, Richter (1943a) could furthermore point out the beneficial effects on growth which result from self-selection of diets in the natural habitat, and from self-selection among purified food substances in the laboratory. Self-selection experiments also proved that not only did rats choose diets which promoted growth, but that during pregnancy and lactation they chose diets particularly suitable for the chemical needs of pregnancy and of lactation. Coprophagia, infantophagia, autophagia, placenta eating, bone eating, and ouronodypsia may all serve self-regulatory functions. In some instances such self-selection appetites are so precise that they can be used for a bio-assay of preparations that influence the activities of various glands of internal secretion.

These observations are of basic importance to any concept of instincts because they demonstrate that when the simple physiological regulators are removed, the maintenance of homeostasis can in some measure be taken over by changes in the behavior of the total organism. In the intact normal animal physiological and chemical regulators and general behavior (i.e., total-organism regulators) play mutually supplementary or alternative roles (Richter, 1927, 1941, 1934b). Thus an animal living in a region in which all the available food contains inadequate amounts of salt can (a) increase its salt intake by migrating to a salt lick; or (b) the adrena cortex may conceivably become more active with a consequent decrease in salt loss in the urine. Conversely, an animal forced to live on fodder with high salt content may (a) decrease its total food intake, or (b) increase its excretion of salt by drinking large amounts of water; or (c) the adrenal cortex may become less active, with a consequent increase in salt loss in the urine.

In the interrelationship between the self-regulatory activities of simple tissues and organs on the one hand and the regulating functions of integrated behavior patterns of the whole organism on the other hand lies whatever clarification we can bring to the concept of instinct. It was on the instinct as the function of the whole organism that Wheeler (1939) laid major emphasis.

III. The Instinct as a Function of an Organism

Wheeler points out that instincts are patterns of behavior not of individual cells but of whole organisms. He then defines an organism as a system of cells, which are organized into a unit that is able to secure from the environment the substances it needs for its survival as a unit, able also to rid itself of substances it does not need, able in some measure to reproduce its own kind, and with some capacity to protect the integrity of its organized system.[2] In higher animals, Wheeler concludes, these basic purposes are represented psychologically by what we call hunger, sex, fear, and anger. To this it can be added that patterns of instinctual behavior arise out of cellular and molecular biochemistry only when an asynchronous cellular flux is brought into some degree of synchronization. It will be seen that important details of the steps by which this synchronization is imposed on cellular processes vary from one instinct to another, and that significant differences in instinctual functions result from these variations in body chemistry.

In the body, cellular processes fall into three groups: (a) those which are directly essential to the vital life processes of the individual organism (i.e., respiratory, water balance, and maintenance of tissue substance); (b) those which serve to maintain the species; (c) those which serve the other two by mediating muscular adjustments, alertness, and sleep (Sherrington, 1941, pp. 254-256). These can be used as a basis for an over-all classification of instincts into three groups: (1) the primary or vital instincts; (2) the secondary or sexual instincts; (3) the tertiary or executive instincts. Of these, the first serve homeostatic functions directly and unmistakably, the role of the second in individual homeostasis is problematical; and the third serves the first two and may in addition have homeostatic functions of its own.

IV. PRIMARY OR VITAL INSTINCTS

Within the body all vital cellular and molecular processes are continuous but asynchronous. While life exists there can be no state of absolute rest, and during what is loosely called "the resting state" the cells of the body are never in a state of inactivity but always in a continuous flux, during which biochemical processes proceed in every direction and through every intermediate phase at the same moment. The resting

---

[2] These elemental functions are found only in living organisms, of which they are inherent properties. They are not attributes imposed on the organism from without, as we impose our purposes on a complex machine and then speak anthropomorphically of "the machine's purpose." Nor does any machine possess the capacity to feed itself, to reproduce its own kind, or to protect itself.

state is therefore not a static state, but a dynamic equilibrium among continuous asynchronous biochemical processes. Examples of this are the acid-base equilibria, osmotic pressure changes, water balance, movements of electrolytes, all phases of anabolism and catabolism, oxidations and reductions, etc. When these incessant asynchronous processes approximately balance, the complex asynchronous flux produces a resting state for the body as a whole, because they leave no residual body need and consequently produce no patterns of organized behavior and no psychological "appetite." All of this changes, however, as soon as some measure of deprivation is imposed.

Respiration offers a clear example of this. As long as respiration and the gas exchanges within the body are unimpeded, some tissues will be in process of oxidation, while others are in various stages of reduction. From the point of view of the whole organism these cancel each other. If, however, the respiratory exchange is impeded, or if the oxygen-carrying power of the blood is significantly reduced, oxidations gradually become impossible everywhere throughout the body, and after intervals which vary according to characteristic rates of oxygen consumption, all of the tissues of the body are forced into a state of oxygen debt. *Thus through deprivation the asynchronous tissue respirations gradually become synchronized, with the production of a state of physiological need within the body as a whole. It is this synchronized need which is then expressed through an organized pattern of instinctual behavior, and represented by a psychological craving, which in this instance would be air hunger.*[3]

Such synchronized tissue needs can be satisfied, however, only through the active participation of tonic and kinetic muscular adjustments. These muscular activities in turn are the end result of a sequential chain of cellular synchrones: first in the respiratory needs of the cells of the body as a whole, then through synchronized afferent impulses which impinge on some suprasegmental centers in the nervous system, syn-

---

[3] Lashley (1928, p. 448) compares the significance to behavior of "reactions to a deficit" with the "reaction to a deprivation of some (anticipated) stimulus." Lashley starts to use this difference as a basis for a classification of instincts, but promptly abandons it because the phenomena overlap and their boundaries are not clear.

chronizing there the appropriate central neurons which in turn produce synchronized volleys from lower motor neurons, which cause contractions of individual fibers, to produce both tonic postural reflexes and movements. These serve the vital instinctual needs of respiration. A similar sequence could be traced for such other vital processes as drinking, eating, excreting, etc. Whether the links which mediate between the original tissue changes and the neuromuscular responses are inherited or whether they are learned through conditioning, or both, is a matter which has not yet been settled by definitive experimental investigation. Thus even in so simple an example of this process as the Hering-Breuer reflex it has not been shown whether this is an inherited or a learned (i.e., conditioned) reflex pattern. The same question remains unanswered about the salivary and gastric responses to food.

From a philosophical point of view it may be of some interest to point out that psychological processes can occur only where two time lags exist; i.e., the interval between stimulus and response, and the interval between a synchronized tissue need and its alleviation. It has been shown that where there is no interval between stimuli and response there can be no psychological process (see Kubie, 1941c, p. 81, and 1941d, p. 270). It is equally clear that where there is no interval between a tissue need and its alleviation the same thing is true. In unicellular organisms the absence of such intervals makes impossible any psychological development, because in such organisms under favorable circumstances all processes of exchange go on continuously at the surface membrane, and only unfavorable circumstances which interpose some barrier to this exchange can cause a delay between tissue requirements and their satisfaction. In differentiated multicellular organisms, however, even under optimal conditions such a delay must always occur, since it takes time to gather in the essential substances from the environment and to distribute them through the body, and since it takes additional time to gather up tissue waste, transport it, and get rid of it. Thus in the higher organisms structural complexity interposes unavoidable delays which make possible the entire superstructure of psychological evolution.

In each primary or vital process there is a time-consuming series of overlapping component steps:

   a. Intake of raw material;

   b. Assimilation and temporary storage of raw material;

   c. Release of raw material from body reservoirs;

   d. Transport of raw material throughout the body;

   e. Neutralization and destruction of metabolites, in so far as possible; and/or the production of specialized tissue products;

   f. Transport of waste;

   g. Storage of waste;

   h. Evacuation of waste.

The term "primary or vital instincts" can correctly be applied only to those patterns of behavior which are built upon the intake and/or the output ends of this series, since only the first two steps and the last two can give rise to behavior which is goal-directed toward the external world. Consequently only these initial and terminal steps are subject to psychological representation and elaboration, the intermediate phases being wholly internal.[4]

V. DIFFERENTIATING ASPECTS AMONG THE THREE PRIMARY INSTINCTUAL PROCESSES

Some degree of homeostatic or homeodynamic equilibria must be maintained among many biochemical processes in order to preserve body structure and function. Among these are the transfer of electrolytes, the acid-base equilibria, all of the intermediary processes of carbohydrate, protein, and fat metabolism, and many more besides. In the service of all of these, however, the organism as a whole carries on three basic

---

[4] There are physiological processes which are essential to homeostasis but which are entirely internal to the body (e.g., bone-marrow function). These cannot be influenced by behavior directly, do not create organized body cravings, and therefore are not susceptible to psychological representation. Consequently they cannot properly be included among the instincts as here defined. Cf. Pearl (1933) and Kubie (1944). Similarly Sherrington (1941) writes: "In short where the act of the integrated individual can do no more about it, mind forsakes the act" (p. 207).

processes which relate it to the outside world. These are the three primary instinctual processes: to wit, gas exchange, water balance, and the maintenance of tissue substance. Like all chemical processes in the body, these are interrelated and interdependent. Thus gas exchange cannot proceed normally in the absence of proper water balance, and the same is true for water balance and the normal utilization of food stuffs, etc.

Furthermore, they overlap with respect to the organs which they employ. Not all gas loss is through the lungs. Fluid loss occurs through the lungs, skin, and bowels, as well as via the bladder, etc. In an unpublished paper ("Some Physiologic Considerations concerning Inhibition"), Dr. Melvin R. Somers has recently described another aspect of this overlapping. He points out that the intake of air is accomplished by muscles which must be stabilized in order to hold the breath when swallowing. If this fails to occur and food is aspirated into the respiratory passages, then muscles are called into play for expiration, for forcible coughing, and for gagging, which are the same muscles as those involved in the explusion of all abdominal contents (e.g., urine, feces, vomitus). Thus respiratory and gastrointestinal or abdominal muscular synergies are not completely differentiated from one another.

Nevertheless, there are physiological differences between the three basic processes which cause them to play quite different roles in our psychic lives. These differences are with respect to:

a. The duration of the period of deprivation which is compatible with life;

b. The duration of the period of deprivation before synchronization of tissue processes occurs;

c. The duration of the interval between the intake phase and the output phase;

d. The speed of transport in the body, both on the intake and on the output sides;

e. The storage, neutralization, and buffering capacity of the body for raw materials, intermediate products, specialized products, and waste products.

In the duration of these time intervals, respiration (i.e., gas exchange) stands at one end of a scale, the maintenance of water balance next, and the maintenance of tissue substance third. In respiration, synchronization of tissue chemistry begins within a few seconds of the onset of deprivation, and is complete within a minute or so. There is a minimal gap in time between intake and output, which together form a single, rapidly oscillating mechanism. Both in the lungs and in the tissues gas exchange and transport are rapid, and the body possesses only a minimal storage capacity and limited power of neutralization.

Water balance comes next in all of these respects. Here deprivation can exist for hours before body stores are depleted and tissue needs become sufficiently synchronized to make themselves felt. The gap in time between intake and output is usually a matter of hours. There is moderate storage capacity in the gastrointestinal tract and in body tissues and fluids, and on the outgoing side in the bladder. This longer interval between intake and output provides an opportunity for each of these two phases to become a nucleus for separate patterns of behavior and of psychological elaboration. Consequently two separate psychological superstructures are built around the body's need for water: one around intake, and one around output.

These differences are even more marked in the processes by which tissue substance is maintained. For food stuffs the deprivation must last for days or weeks before tissue needs are synchronized. There is a large storage capacity both in the tissues and in the bowel, and the gap between intake and output is a matter of hours or even days. Consequently the physiological and psychological elaboration of the intake and output phases is quite separate; and again two behavioral superstructures are built on the biochemical basis of the complex requirements for tissue maintenance.

It is important at this point to emphasize the fact that the biochemical need of tissues for any chemical substance is unconditional. As far as the body chemistry is concerned, nothing can substitute for water or for oxygen or for the primary food stuffs. On this level, therefore, there can be no divergence between instinctual aim and chemical object, although the role of mediating human objects varies in a significant fashion which will be discussed in section IX. At this point, however, let us consider the warning mechanisms with which the body anticipates its primary needs, their nature and function and their relation to the problem of instincts.

VI. THE ROLE OF WARNING MECHANISMS IN THE PRIMARY INSTINCTS

There is a warning mechanism for every instinct, and each warning mechanism operates through the sensory component of the neuronal pattern of the instinct (Lashley, 1928). This in turn will be seen to have a direct relation to the mechanisms of anxiety.

Even in the primary instincts which are built around respiration, water balance, and tissue maintenance, the relationship between the underlying biochemical processes and their psychological representation is neither direct nor simple. Although the synchronization of tissue requirements under the influence of deprivation provides the fundamental source of energy out of which appropriate behavior evolves, in each of these primary instinctual functions the body has developed a warning mechanism which is called into play before the occurrence of actual tissue depletion. Thus under ordinary circumstances all of the psychological cravings which we speak of as "instinctual" are set off by the appropriate warning mechanisms and not by the tissue needs which were their original sources. It is only after sustained deprivation that tissue depletion enters into the pattern of instinctual behavior as a direct biochemical instigator of psychological craving.

In a personal communication, Karl S. Lashley has emphasized a point of great interest in this connection: namely, that alone and of itself deprivation is not always an adequate stimulus. For instance, where oxygen deficiency is not accompanied either by an accumulation of CO_2 or by alterations in the acid-base equilibrium, the warning mechanisms may not be activated. This is seen in severe anemias, in the low oxygen tensions of high altitudes, and in carbon monoxide poisoning. Through an evolutionary process the protective warning mechanism seems here to have become almost compeltely dissociated from the elementary organic need. In lesser measure the same thing can be observed in hunger. Lashley refers to his early experiments, in which rats fed on an inadequate standard diet showed a great increase in measured activity, whereas rats fed to repletion on a diet which lacked adequate nutritional values showed no increase of activity in spite of a weight loss equal to that of the first group. Evidently in hunger too the warning mechanism can become dissociated from the organic need. Evolution has placed the warning mechanisms in a key position in setting off patterns of instinctual behavior.

In respiration, for instance, we do not normally experience air hunger. Nor is there a state of oxygen want in the tissues at the onset of each normal respiratory cycle. This occurs only in states of acute or chronic interference with the exchange of gases in the body. Therefore lack of oxygen is not the immediate stimulus which sets off the normal respiratory mechanism. This is done rather by the accumulation of carbon dioxide and the attendant ticktock oscillations of the acid-base equilibrium, which set the threshold of the respiratory center for its response to proprioceptive impulses from vagus endings in the lungs (the Hering-Breuer reflex). Consequently it is not strictly accurate to say that we breathe because we need oxygen, but only that we breathe because if we did not breathe then we would very soon begin to need oxygen, whereupon we would have to breathe or else die.

Actually, in normal life we breathe for psychological reasons before we have to breathe out of physiological necessity. There is a faint phobic stir underlying every breath we take, as the breath-holding Yogis well know. *Even in this most elementary of the instincts, therefore, no absolute distinction can be made between instinct and drive.*

The same thing is true of our need for water and for food stuffs. Here too a warning mechanism precedes tissue change as the instigator of appetite. In the case of water, a sense of dryness and consequent thirst may antedate by hours the occurrence of any generalized tissue dehydration throughout the body. It is not surprising, therefore, that the warning sensation can be dissociated from the tissue change, making it possible to hallucinate thirst as in social drinking, or for the patient to feel thirsty after intercourse or masturbation; or that we can develop such compulsive symbolic oral activities as finger-sucking, smoking, and kissing. Similarly in the case of food stuffs, it is well known that "hunger pangs" occur in irregularly periodic waves, without relation to tissue depletion, except for the occasional specific stimulus of hypoglycemia.

It is important, then, that the warning mechanism always precedes tissue depletion, and that in the different primary instincts the intervals between the activities of the warning mechanisms and the onset of any degree of underlying biochemical depletion vary from a matter of a few seconds in respiration to hours in water balance or days in the maintenance of tissue substance. The longer this gap, the greater are the psychological complications which can be developed. Therefore this homeostatic device which protects tissues from the cumulative injury which would result from recurring moments of tissue depletion, at the same time creates an opportunity for many psychological complications, since all such warning mechanisms, like the boy in the fable, are capable either of total inhibition or of constantly crying "wolf, wolf."

Here again, therefore, simple temporal differences among a group of physiological mechanisms have psychological consequences. The longer the interval between deprivation and synchronization, or between deprivation and death, the more complex is the psychological superstructure which can be built upon a particular body need. Contrariwise, the shorter the interval between the warning mechanism and the onset of true tissue depletion, then the more urgent, immediate, and inflexible are its demands, and the more limited is the potential psychic superstructure. This is because the point at which psychological forces operate to influence either the intensity or the direction of instinctual drives is either these warning and preparatory mechanisms, which intermediate between basic tissue changes and the resultant instinctual drives, or else the neuromuscular apparatus which executes the drives. There is no clear evidence that psychological processes alter the basic underlying tissue requirements themselves.[5]

A second difference which is psychologically important arises from the fact that there are wide variations in the extent to which the warning mechanisms can be inhibited or reversed on the one hand, or exaggerated on the other:

a. The respiratory warning mechanism can be slowed down to our basic metabolic needs, as with Indian mystics, but only to a relatively slight extent. On the other hand, it can be exaggerated widely, as in hysterical dyspnea.

b. In water intake, the warning sense of dryness in the mucous membranes of the throat induces an energetic psychic need which is essentially unquenchable by psychic processes. Men who are dying from lack of water are said never to cease to suffer from thirst. Perhaps this is because "inhibition" of thirst would depend upon an overactivity of the secretory cells of the mucous membrane which might be impossible during a period of actual tissue dehydration.

c. In starvation, tissue depletion occurs slowly from our relatively abundant body stores, and the "warnings" of periodic hunger contractions are almost wholly independent of immediate tissue needs, except for the occasional correlation with hypoglycemia. It is known that even in extreme starvation, "hunger" can be inhibited. Evidently it is easier to inhibit gastrointestinal motility when "hungry" than it is to overwork the secretory cells of the mucous membranes of the mouth and throat when "thirsty." In the case of food the

[5] There is some evidence that the respiratory tide may serve as an activating or energizing force in the psychological apparatus as a whole, influencing profoundly the processes of sleeping and of waking (Kubie and Margolin, 1944). In this connection it is of interest that patients tend to drift into states of sleeplike or semihypnoidal immobility and apathy when they are placed in alternating pressure chambers, so arranged that continuous oxygenation and removal of CO_2 can occur without apparent respiratory movements (Barach, personal communication). This may in turn be related to the hypnoidal trances achieved by the Yogi mystics through their control of respiration. (See also Thunberg, 1926.)

greater dissociation between the underlying chemical process and the psychic appetite, the ease with which the warning mechanism can be either inhibited or exaggerated, the complete temporal dissociation between intake and output, and the large storage facilities in tissues and bowel provide opportunities for especially extensive psychological superstructures, both normal and abnormal.

As we have already pointed out, whenever there is a wide separation between the biochemical processes of intake and output, independent warning mechanisms develop for the phases of ingestion and excretion. This is true both in water balance and tissue maintenance. Thirst and the need to void have no direct linkage, and a similar independence exists between hunger and the need to defecate. Notwithstanding this, psychological processes can create artificial linkages which have no physiological purposes and may thus distort the underlying biochemical and neuronal patterns. As an example, when trying to explain the processes of ingestion and excretion to his five-year-old son, a physician drew a diagram which showed morsels of food dropping into the upper end and bowel movements dropping out of the lower end of a schematized human figure and gastrointestinal tract. The five-year-old child studied this diagram with great interest and care, and for some months thereafter could not be dissuaded from leaping from the table to rush to the lavatory as he neared the end of each meal.

The warning mechanisms within the bladder and bowel are subject to multiple psychological influences and alterations. They can be inhibited to the point of reversal (as in hysterical retention or obstipation), or exaggerated to the point of compulsive overdrive (as in frequency or colitis). Either tendency may or may not be accompanied by hallucinatory or pseudohallucinatory sensations arising from the warning apparatus itself. Thus with or without peristaltic movements or tonic disturbances we may feel the need to urinate when the bladder is not distended, or to defecate when the bowel is empty, etc.

It is evident that the extent to which psychological processes can influence the various warning mechanisms varies widely.

Thus although in respiration and in fluid needs some measure of inhibition of the activity of the warning mechanism is possible, it can never go far without causing death, and can never reach the point of complete reversal. On the other hand, exaggerated air hunger and compulsive water drinking can arise either on the basis of an organic disturbance (as in postencephalitic respiratory disturbances or in diabetes insipidus) or as a psychogenic manifestation. In these two basic instinctual processes pathological disturbances of instinctual behavior are largely confined to exaggerations and "addictions."

In the case of food, inhibition of appetite is a matter of everyday experience in the lives of all children and adults, with phobic and disgust reactions and pseudohallucinatory disturbances of smell and taste. Conversely, insatiability, over-valuation of certain foods, symbolic eating, food infatuations, and food addictions are equally familiar.

In general, therefore, we may say that where a warning mechanism cannot be reversed or inhibited (as with respiratory and fluid needs) the possible reactions to frustration or deprivation are limited largely to panic and rage. Concerning fluid intake there is some evidence that in prolonged thirst there is a slow internalization of the reaction with a gradual lapse into a depressionlike state. On the other hand, where actual reversal of sign of a warning mechanism or its intensification are equally possible (as with food and sex) a correspondingly wider diversity of reactions to deprivations and frustrations can occur.

The warning mechanism is interposed between the biochemical process and its expression in behavior. Because it can be subjected to variable degrees and combinations of inhibition and compulsive exaggeration, it is impossible from habitual behavior to draw any conclusion about quantitative variations in underlying biochemical needs. Instinctual behavior always represents the algebraic sum of many forces and is never a direct indicator of tissue needs alone. Therefore all talk of quantitative variations in libido is premature until we are able to measure the several component forces independently of one another. This is equally true whether we are describing the human being or the experimental animal (this volume, Chapter 1).

Warning mechanisms operate through a phobialike anxiety, in that that anxiety is triggered by specific situations which, as with every phobia, must be dealt with by some obligatory act (i.e., an ego-syntonic compulsion). It is in this sense that every instinctual drive has a compulsive component, and that every instinct functions between the pressure of normal phobic and normal compulsive psychological processes which are the anlage of all pathological distortions.

VII. THE SECONDARY INSTINCTS
(SEXUAL OR PROCREATIVE INSTINCTS)

Our knowledge of the physiological changes which presumably generate and implement sexual need is limited. Descriptively, however, it is possible to see that in the series of instincts which derive from biochemical tissue needs the sexual instincts stand at the opposite pole from respiration.

In the first place, intake from the outside world seems to play no direct or specific role in sex. Indeed, we cannot even say to what extent sexual instinctual behavior depends upon the synchronization of asynchronous cellular processes, whether under the influence of deprivation or of other forces. Nor is it clear whether "deprivation" in a tissue sense exerts any physiological influence on sexual matters. Certainly complete abstinence is wholly compatible with the life of the individual, if not with the life of the species, and there is no known limit to the maximum period of deprivation which is tolerable either psychologically or physiologically. Consequently the relationship between sexual abstinence and bodily need or its psychological representation is undetermined, and sexual deprivation seems significant primarily as a psychological rather than as a physiological experience.[6]

---

[6] See Lashley (1928, p. 448) on the role of "reactions to a deprivation of some [anticipated] stimulus," and also his summary (p. 454) of the experimental work which demonstrates that while patterns of sexual craving and of sexual behavior can be set off by means of several sensory pathways, no one of them is physiologically essential.

To begin with, the biochemical substrate of sexual behavior has not been determined either for the male or for the female. One hypothesis has been advanced which derives from a characteristic of the germ plasm which differentiates it from cells of the soma. It is known that mitotic division gradually ceases in cells of the germ plasm when conjugation with a cell of the opposite sex fails to occur. Presumably this must result in a continuous slow accumulation of germ cells whose vital functions are diminishing, or which are slowly dying. According to this hypothesis it then becomes at least conceivable that the accumulation of such cells in areas of storage (e.g., *vas deferens* and epididymis of the male, or periodically in the ovary of the female) might lead to the secondary physiological changes in the tissues of the reproductive system, such as local vascular engorgement and secretory activity, which in turn could give rise to erotic tension and the preparatory mechanisms of erection. Or, alternatively, such accumulations of dying cells might produce chemicals which could directly activate the cells of the central nervous system.

Against the validity of any such hypotheses is the fact that deafferentation of the entire reproductive tract has little or no effect upon coital activity in the estrous rat, and that normal copulatory behavior follows the injection of ovarian hormones in female rats which had been surgically deprived of ovaries, tubes, uterus, and vagina. Furthermore, castrated male rats mate under the influence of testosterone propionate, even though the vesicles, coagulating gland, and prostrate are removed (Frank Beach, personal communication).

Birds confront us with similar perplexing problems. In a personal communication, G. E. Hutchinson writes:

> The whole sexual cycle consists ot a number of phases: e.g., migration, territory occupation, prolonged courtship, actual coitus, nest building, incubation, and care of the young. In such cases it seems reasonably certain that the males are sexually active early in the courtship period but that the female is not yet receptive. As far as can be judged from the material published on the histology of the gonad, it is very unlikely that in such a case the male could be excited in the way suggested.

Hutchinson adds his own conviction that the biochemical basis of excitation must be essentially uniform for all vertebrates, and suggests that some pituitary function is involved.

Investigation of this problem is further complicated by the fact that the basic neural patterns for sexual behavior appear to be inherited in a relatively undifferentiated form throughout the vertebrate series; and that on this inherited pattern hormones exercise a decreasing influence as one ascends the evolutionary scale, while in this same evolution the patterns of sexual behavior become increasingly modifiable by intricate and subtle psychological influences.

Franz Alexander (personal communication) makes the interesting suggestion that the growth process itself and/or the replenishing and replacing of body cells which goes on continuously throughout life may be the source of some biochemical surplus, some by-product, which can activate the inherited neural patterns of psychosexual craving. No evidence for or against this notion exists at present, but such a mechanism would explain the persistence of sexual need in the absence of the gonads and of all erectile tissues of the genital and reproductive organs.

If it is true, however, that some chemical by-product of the continuous process of cell replacement serves as a biochemical stimulus to a hereditary neuronal pattern of psychosexual behavior, then it could be that the primacy of the genital zone in the normal adult represents a periodic synchronization of activities in various areas of the nervous system, which in turn represent the various erogenous zones. This in turn may be subjectively experienced in the completed orgasm.

All that we may conclude from available experimental evidence is that the biochemical basis of states of sexual excitement, and the physiological meaning of gratification and of deprivation, have not yet been ascertained. Therefore it is not possible at this time to include sexual behavior in the general law that biochemical deprivations transform the random biochemical activities of the body tissues into synchronized and coordinated body needs. Whether or not this basic principle will some day prove to be applicable to sexual behavior, as it is to what we have called the primary instincts, must wait on new experimental evidence.

In summary, it may be said that biochemical, physiological, and temporal differences in these four instinctual functions (to wit, gas exchange, water balance, tissue maintenance, and species maintenance) cause inevitable differences in the psychological superstructure which can be built upon them. At the same time, almost nothing is known about quantitative differences between the biochemical tissue requirements of different individuals within the same species. What evidence exists seems to indicate that wider differences may ultimately be found in the biochemical components of tissue needs with respect to sex and food than with respect to water balance and respiration.

VIII. The Tertiary or Executive Instincts

The warning mechanisms which have been discussed above arise out of afferent impulses which are generated by a series of local changes. The first of these constitute a group of biochemical changes in the tissues themselves, with respect to such things as hydration, salt balance, hydrogen ion concentration, carbohydrate metabolism, oxidation and reduction, etc. Both by local effects and by reflex paths these produce local vascular, glandular, and secretory changes, and ultimately smooth and skeletal muscle adjustments. Thus, as an example, the afferent impulses from the bladder depend not on the amount of urine held in the bladder, but rather on the relation of that amount to the tonus of the bladder muscle. This in turn leads directly to the executive act of voiding with all its attendant afferent and efferent impulses. Thus in all of the primary and secondary instincts there is a close integration between the warning mechanisms and the executive functions.

In this way cellular processes which have been synchronized by deprivation are then organized into patterns of total behavior through the mediation of warning mechanisms which call upon the body musculature to go into action. The axial-skeletal musculature of the head and trunk is directly involved in breathing, sucking, chewing, and swallowing, and the smooth muscles of the bladder and gut are coordinated with the skeletal muscles of the trunk and perineum to implement basic excretory needs. Moreover, the axial-appendicular muscles are brought into the total pattern quite early, as in reaching for food or holding a bottle or squatting for excretion. These neuromuscular synergies are intimately related to the primary instincts, and since they are played upon by psychological forces these in turn enter into the effectiveness with which primary and secondary instinctual needs are served.

Ultimately the axial-appendicular musculature is used in all of the elaborate patterns of activity which make up the total complex of instinctual activity. This includes the over-all drive to activity as a nonspecific means of externalization or discharging central energetic processes and alternatively the relinquishing of all such activity in sleep. These patterns of behavior, which subserve both the primary and secondary instinctual processes, we have called tertiary executive instincts, meaning thereby all of the complex derivative states of coordinated neuromuscular activity of the body as a whole. These make the difference between total sleep and total alertness, between passive submission and active aggression, and in the nervous system the difference between, on the one hand, a maximal degree of asynchronous flux and, on the other, synchronized, coordinated, and rhythmical volleys of neuronal discharges. These synchronized and coordinated volleys constitute the physiological mechanism for the discharge or externalization of central energy of which Sherrington (1933, 1941) writes, and for what Freud (1920) calls the discharge of psychic tension. For the relationship of this to the physiology of anxiety, see Kubie (1941d).

Sherrington's own words in this connection are of considerable interest (1941, pp. 254-256): "In a nerve center, tonus carries with it, besides its overt discharge, a fringe of subliminal preparation which is favorable for ensuing change, whether of increment or of decrement. More than that, the subattentive or subconscious fringe of mind which takes such a share in the management of our motor acts is not 'aware,' even subattentively or subconsciously, of a muscle which has in it no action at all." It would seem, then, that tonic vigilance of this kind guards against the more explosive anxiety which occurs in flaccid and atonic neuromuscular states. This point of view is elaborated further on p. 255, where Sherrington writes: "This vigilance of the roof brain is suspended in sleep . . . The desistance of 'action' is profound slumber . . . Like the vigilance of tonic muscles, the background activity of the roof brain, which persists in our waking state and even in light sleep, can be regarded as a 'tonus' of the roof brain (Bremer). Deep sleep is a lapse in that tonus. . ."

It has not yet been possible to isolate any specific biochemical process underlying the aperiodic cycle between activity and sleep. Perhaps this is because in spite of the experimental work on so-called "sleep" or "wakefulness" centers, neither in laboratory animals nor in man has it been possible to differentiate that activity or sleep which arises out of biochemical necessity from that which is the result of a superimposed psychological necessity. All that can be said with confidence is that the body seems to require both states, that anatomically and physiologically they involve every body function, that it seems certain that they must have some biochemical foundation, that the nature of this has not yet been discovered, that it is hidden under an especially complex psychic superstructure, and finally, that as with all other instinctual needs both activity and sleep are woven into an intricate pattern of compulsions and phobias.

In certain ways our state of ignorance about the instinctual nature of the activity-sleep cycle resembles our ignorance about sex. In the case of sex, as we have seen, we are ignorant of the nature of the underlying biochemical process and of its physiological reaction to deprivation; but at least something is known of the nature of the "warning" mechanisms. In the case of the activity-sleep cycle, we know nothing of either.[7] This makes it difficult to say just where to place this behavior in the

---

[7] Consider our ignorance of the meaning and mechanism of yawning and of that painful eyelid-drooping sleepiness which can be dispelled in a moment by alarm or interest; and also the uncertainty concerning the basic mechanism of anxiety (Kubie, 1941d).

over-all category of instincts as we have defined them. Never
theless, it is obvious that this sleep-activity cycle, which derives
from hypothetical underlying biochemical tides, plus hypothetical warning mechanisms, is interwoven with every other
instinctual process. The balance between activity and sleep
enters into every act we do or leave undone, and into the
responses to temptation and gratification, and deprivation
and frustration. Yet the behavior which derives from sleep-
activity cycle differs from all primary instinctual patterns in
the fact that it cannot be arranged in a bipolar dichotomy. We
eat or starve, drink or thirst, breathe or suffocate. But we are
never either totally awake or totally asleep. These are relative
and not absolute terms. Parts of us are asleep in our waking
moments, and awake in our sleeping moments, and in between lie all gradations of states of activity and inactivity;
investigation and pursuit; assertion, aggression, and destruction, or defense, withdrawal, and fight, or silence, inactivity,
dreaming, and sleep. These in turn are represented psychologically by restlessness, curiosity, eagerness, impatience,
boastfulness, anger, rage, fear, self-depreciation, depression,
fatigue, etc. And all of these states of activity, of thought, and
of feeling play into the patterns of our instinctual activities.

IX. AIMS AND OBJECTS, AND THE LINK TO HIGHER PSYCHIC ELABORATION

All instinctual activities are aimed at external objects,
which may be animate or inanimate, or both. In the evolution
of the different patterns of instinctual behavior, the inanimate
or chemical objects — because of their relative constancy — play
less of a role psychologically than do the human beings who
mediate certain of the instinctual gratifications and therefore
play a large role in the concurrent conscious and unconscious
fantasies. In respiration and water metabolism these are
simple and elementary, but they are increasingly elaborate in
food, sex, and general activity. Psychologically, our instinctual processes are oriented not toward the inanimate chemical

substances on which our lives and our species depend, but rather toward these interposed fantasies.

In the hierarchy of the instincts, one further difference remains to be considered which is psychologically the most important. This is the difference in the role other human beings play in facilitating, guiding, educating, correcting, or obstructing the gratification of the various instincts.

We are never separated in space or time from the air around us. Therefore no human aid is needed to bring us and the air together. Once a baby is born, and once his respiratory functions have been established, no other human being plays a role in this most basic gratification. Furthermore, because all can breathe their fill simultaneously, there can be no such thing as respiratory rivalry.[8] In fact, with respect to respiratory functions the only feelings which other human beings can arouse are fear and anger, by acquiring the threatening significance of strangling and smothering. This is an additional reason why anxiety and rage play a dominant role in the psychic superstructure which is built around the respiratory function. It is of considerable interest that the above statements would have to be qualified in the description of the instinctual activity of cetaceans, since the adult porpoise will when necessary boost the newborn baby to the surface for breathing.

In the other instinctual processes, the human being as an animate instinctual object plays a role whose importance increases and whose functions become more complex as we ascend the instinctual scale.

Thus with respect to the other two primary instincts (i.e., water and food) a distinction must be made between the roles played by the human object on the intake and output sides. On the intake side, in contrast to the independence of the infant with respect to respiration, the infant can neither drink nor eat without the aid of nurse or mother, who is therefore essential for the gratification of the instinctual need. Consequently the instinctual goal is less the needed chemical substance than the smell, the taste, the sight and sound, the feel,

---

[8] Nevertheless, after the birth of a baby brother a five-year-old child was heard to wonder whether or not there would be enough air to go around.

and the warmth which together make up the sentient presence of the human being without whom the instinctual gratification is impossible. At a later stage, however, this same person acquires other meanings. She teaches manners and cleanliness in eating. She imposes restrictions on the spontaneous appetite, and at the same time teaches the child to feed himself in pursuit of an "independence" which often becomes emotionally synonymous with rejection. It is precisely here that in every human life the struggle begins between impulses toward passive dependence and aggressive self-determination; and here too is laid the ground plan of sibling rivalry, since, unlike air, food and drink are not free and limitless goods.

On the output side, no human agent is needed for the primary function of urination and defecation. Here, then, the role of the human object in the primary instincts resembles somewhat his role in the respiratory cycle. Praise and blame soon enter the picture, however, and the human object is wooed with excretory gifts, especially if cleansing is made a pleasant occasion. Subsequent education in cleanliness, however, gives the adult a nuisance value and brings on again the profound struggle between submission and rebellion, with discipline and punishment coming to the fore. One might summarize this by saying that on the intake side the adult human being gives or withholds love in the form of water, food, the breast, and his very presence, and on that basis starts to train and educate; while on the output side, the same human object gives or withholds approval, or disapproval, acceptance and rejection, and on that foundation educates through discipline and punishment.

Thus the human instinctual object plays an active and complex role in all of the primary instincts except respiration. He not only supplants the chemical object as the psychological object of the instinctual pattern, but feeds back responses which create new demands that have their roots partly in instinctual need and partly in the adult's attitudes. For example, at first an infant may cry for food and water without guilt or anxiety. Soon, however, this cry may be an appeal not for the needed chemical substance but for the loving presence of the human agent. Thereupon it must often be suppressed, lest the nurse or mother become angry, and lest this anger deprive the infant both of the loved presence and of the food. Later, as the executive functions are mastered, the need may be expressed in more angry forms, or the anger may lead to an impulse to run away, which in turn must also be suppressed lest the child lose the mother's love and therefore end up hungry both in a physiological and in an emotional sense. Here occurs the fusion of what we have called the primary and tertiary instincts.

Furthermore, sibling rivalry finds a sharp focus on these levels of primary instinctual function. As we have said, there can be no rivalry for air, but there can be rivalry for the warmth and feel and taste and smell of the parent's body which betokens nourishment, for the smile or the sound of the voice which means favor and therefore the gratification of nourishment itself, of for cleansing attentions, etc. These elementary rivalries are the roots of adult competitions, ambitions, and jealousies, of angry and destructive rages, and of guilt. In this way the whole complex superstructure of personality has its roots in primary instinctual nuclei, and the vicissitudes of instinctual object relations are so great that they give rise to many conflicting forces which in turn feed back into the central organ to produce new and complex derivative demands.

In the secondary or sexual instincts, and also in the tertiary or executive instincts, it is obvious that the role of the human object is subject to even greater variation, a detailed description of which lies beyond the scope of this paper. From this general point of view, all human instinctual drives are viewed as composite resultants of the interplay of obligatory ego-syntonic needs and ego-syntonic inhibitions. In essence these are truly compulsive and phobic in nature, but they are regularly rationalized as voluntary moral or esthetic choices. In this sense all instinctual drives are as compulsive as a hand-washing compulsion, with the difference that the compulsive nature of instinctual necessities is masked by their individual and cultural acceptability and by their biological usefulness, as a result of which we do not try to dissociate ourselves from them as something alien.

Parenthetically it should also be noted that if this point of view proves to be valid, it will necessitate a significant alteration in Freud's original formula. It would then no longer be possible to say that a neurosis is "the negative of a perversion" (1905, p. 87). One could say only that a perversion is itself a specific neurosis: i.e., a compulsive deviation of sexual aims and/or objects, against which, as with any other neurotic drive, secondary neurotic defenses may be erected. Clearly, these secondary defenses are at the same time efforts to gratify the very drives against which they are erected. In this sense their dynamics are identical with those of any simple hysterical symptom formation, since they represent both the unconscious compulsive purpose and the defense against it.

X. SUMMARY

1. There are no absolute distinctions between instincts and drives. The nucleus of each is a neuronal pattern which is partly inherited and partly acquired and modified through learning and conditioning.

2. The instincts can be ranged in order in a hierarchy of increasing complexity. In this hierarchy there is a gradual shift from a preponderance of biochemical influences on the neuronal pattern to a preponderance of psychological influence. In varying proportions both types of forces operate on the central neuronal pattern of every instinctual process, and their relative roles will be different in different species.

3. The primary instincts which serve the basic biochemical needs of the individual organism are called into action by warning mechanisms. These warning mechanisms anticipate any actual tissue depletion, but when such depletion does occur as the result of deprivation, it energizes behavior by synchronizing the chemical processes of body tissues.

4. The psychological influences arise out of an unstable dynamic equilibrium between compulsive and phobic mechanisms which alternatively exaggerate or inhibit the underlying instinctual demand.

5. There is no such thing as a simon-pure instinct, devoid of

the influence of psychological forces. The relative role of the nuclear biochemical source and of the psychological superstructure varies from one end of the hierarchy to the other. In that complex constellation of biochemistry, neuronal pattern, and superimposed phobic and compulsive processes which we call "instincts," the biochemical component plays the predominant role at one end and the psychological processes a minor role, with the converse relation true at the other end of the scale. Therefore there would seem to be no gain in clarity by substituting the term "instinctual drive" for the term "instinct" at any arbitrary point. Indeed, this becomes a purely verbal issue. It is probably better to call them all "instinctual drives," so as to indicate that the differences are relative and not in kind.

6. In this hierarchy, in order of complexity are respiration, water balance, and maintenance of tissue substance (all vital to the biochemistry of the individual), with a widening temporal separation of the intake and output phases in water balance and tissue maintenance so as to produce two separate groups of instinctual derivatives. The secondary instincts serve to maintain not the individual but the species and involve increasing complexity and lengthening intervals, and consequently greater susceptibility to psychological elaboration and distortion. The third order of instinctual processes has to do with the general level of neuromuscular activity, which operates primarily to implement and support all instinctual acts, and also determines the general level of alertness and of total neuromuscular activity, and the aperiodic cycle of sleep and wakefulness, of aggression and submission.

7. The role of the human being as the animate object of the instinctual pattern varies from one end of the hierarchy to the other. At the simplest (i.e., respiratory) end of the series, the human object plays a role which is limited almost wholly to primitive fear and anger. At the other end, the human being plays an indispensable role in the instinctual pattern and becomes the major, complex objective of all the psychological needs which are rooted in the instinct.

8. Many questions are not yet understood clearly, such as the precise role of learning and of inheritance at each link in

these complex patterns, the true meaning of the concepts of libidinal fixation and of libidinal regression, and especially the different factors which determine the modifiability, the distortions, and the therapy of instinctual drives in the hierarchy which we have described. It is to be hoped that in the course of time these issues will be subjected to investigation instead of to controversy.

Conclusions

1. Thus we find that in discussing instincts Freud made two important points which have been very largely neglected, partly by himself, and partly by other workers:

a. That a classification of instincts must rest on a physiological rather than a psychological basis;

b. That instincts represent the demand which the body makes on the mental apparatus.

Our discussion supports Freud's position.

2. All instincts consist of (a) the direct or indirect expression of biochemical body processes, through (b) inherited yet modifiable networks of neuronal synaptic patterns, which (c) are molded in turn by superimposed compulsive and phobic mechanisms. These are seen to operate in normal psychology as in psychopathology. The relative roles of the three components of instinctual activity vary in different instincts and in different species.

3. Therefore it is impossible to make any absolute distinction between instinct and drive (*Trieb*). The differences are quantitative rather than qualitative, and are due to the different roles played by the three components mentioned above.

4. In many of the instinctual processes the biochemical source of energy is converted into behavior through deprivation, because deprivation synchronizes the continuous asynchronous flux which in states of rest goes on in body tissues. The biochemical processes, however, are linked to warning mechanisms, which under ordinary circumstances come into play before any actual tissue deprivation occurs. In

higher animals instinctual patterns are therefore triggered by warning mechanisms rather than by tissue hungers.

5. Therefore, on the psychological level, instinctual aims and objects are also built around the warning mechanism.

6. This point of view about instincts, if correct, has certain consequences both for theory and for research. Research on the relation of instincts to the neuroses would focus on various interrelated problems: (a) species and individual variations in underlying biochemical processes; (b) species and individual variations in the inherited and/or acquired networks of neuronal and synaptic patterns, and variations in their modifiability; (c) variations in the constellation of superimposed compulsive and phobic mechanisms which exploit the biochemical and the neuronal core; (d) the role of fixation, displacement, regression, and dissociation with respect to (a), (b), and (c).

3

THE DISTORTION OF THE SYMBOLIC PROCESS IN NEUROSIS AND PSYCHOSIS

I. Basic Principles and Some Current Fallacies

This paper will describe briefly what seems to the author to be one of the key differences between pathological and normal psychological processes in human beings, and more particularly between psychotic and neurotic processes. The problem will be approached not from the standpoint of variations in psychoanalytic theory, but from a more general consideration of fundamental psychoanalytic and psychological principles. In the recent history of psychiatry there have been many descriptions of differences between sickness and health, and between different forms of illness. Each such attempt has had partial validity, yet none has clarified the essence of these differences. Such attempts have fallen into three general groups.

1. The older distinctions of "classical" psychiatry were clinical and phenomenological. That is to say, they were based on the presenting symptoms and complaints of patients. Certainly any such distinction should be able to account for differences in superficial symptoms and complaints; yet these manifestations of illness do not in themselves constitute the essential difference between sickness and health, or between

First published in *Journal of the American Psychoanalytic Association,* 1:59-86, 1953. Reprinted by permission of the Editor of *Journal of the American Psychoanalytic Association.*

different forms of sickness. It is therefore valid to use symptoms and complaints as a test of a formulation, as we will do below, but it would be fallacious to use them as a basis for classification, just as it would be fallacious to use debility, fever, or a rash as a basis for a classification of organic disease, although any significant classification would ultimately have to provide an adequate explanation of these end products of the pathological process.

2. Secondly, there have been attempts to differentiate the various forms of mental illness in terms of their practical consequences. Here again no satisfactory differentiation can rest solely on the effects which a psychopathological process has on behavior and adaptation. Because I have already discussed at length the fallacies, contradictions, and inadequacies of this approach, especially with respect to the difference between normality and neurosis (Kubie, 1949, 1950b, 1951), I will not repeat that argument here. In passing, however, I will emphasize the fact that efforts to find the essence of psychopathology in its consequences have led to serious theoretical confusions, especially in the consideration of the effects of the psychopathological process on human relations. It has become almost a fashion to substitute for this older and descriptive phase the more pretentious words "interpersonal relations." Not only has this substitution added nothing to our understanding of the process, but the phrase itself has acquired question-begging implications in current debates over the relative roles of biological and cultural factors in the genesis of psychopathology. Furthermore, as so often happens with terminological innovations, the term "interpersonal relations" is no longer used merely to describe one of the consequences and manifestations of neurotic difficulties. Insidiously, it has been invested with a causal magic, so that now one often reads of psychopathological states as being "due to" disturbances in interpersonal relations, the cart thus pulling the horse as neatly as may be (cf. Cobb, 1950).

Similar confusions exist with respect to the characterization of the consequences of the psychotic process. Here a major emphasis has rightly been on disturbances in the psychotic's ability to relate himself accurately to the outside world and to discriminate between reality and fantasy, either on the perceptual or on the conceptual level, or on both. Certainly everyone will agree that difficulties in both of these psychological functions are essential elements in any psychosis, and that in turn these difficulties have secondary consequences of their own which further complicate the later evolution of any psychotic state. Yet to describe the consequences of a process does not reveal its essential mechanism; and the essence of the neurotic process cannot be differentiated from the essence of the psychotic process merely by describing differences in their end results. To say that in the psychosis there is a disturbance in object relations and in reality testing, and that the libidinal object in the psychosis is essentially narcissistic, characterizes certain attributes and consequences of the psychotic process but not its essential nature, nor that which distinguishes it from the neurotic process.

If we are to understand the intrinsic mechanisms of psychopathology, we must indicate specifically at what point in the psychic apparatus key distortions arise. It is only when we have reached agreement on these basic differentiae that it will become possible to begin the attempt to explain *how* it is produced.

3. The third approach to this problem has been ontogenetic: that is, through tracing the life histories of individuals who ultimately develop either neuroses or psychoses or both. This is the "How did they get that way?" approach, and it has taken three major forms:

a. In keeping with his essential bias, the orthodox Kraepelinian psychiatrist attempted to do this by reconstructing the history of a patient's symptoms.

b. The Meyerian psychobiologist gathered a more intimate anamnesis, based largely on the conscious life history of a patient. He attempted to understand illness by tracing the development of the personality and of the general life adjustment. This was an important if limited advance, in that it implicitly recognized the continuity of the forces which produce both personality and illness. This carried the further implication that one can neither understand nor modify illness without understanding and altering personality. At the same time, however, it insidiously treated personality development from a moralistic bias. Personality was "to blame" for illness; but the patient was "to blame" for developing a blameworthy personality. His "habits" were bad, and he had to be urged and trained to change them.

c. In place of the Meyerian conscious history of the personality as a whole, the analyst has attempted to trace the ontogeny of illness in terms of the evolution of various Cs and Ucs part components of the personality. Thus the analyst traces the history of instinctual, superego, and ego developments, and he studies the interaction of these three converging streams as they are altered by the incessant flux of fixations, regressions, identifications, incorporations, and other psychological processes. Again this marked an advance; the analyst's developmental approach will ultimately throw light on the genesis of the differences between normality and the neurotic and psychotic processes. Before we can explain the genesis of differences, however, we must know *what* differences we are explaining. For lack of clarity on this point, our efforts at ontogenetic explanations have proved to be largely premature, both from the theoretical point of view and from the point of view of concurrent, step-by-step, clinical and experimental verification. I would repeat that our primary deficiency has been our failure to define with precision the essential nature of the critical changes whose development our ontogenetic theories have attempted to trace.

This criticism applies equally to all analytic schools: i.e., to both the so-called cultural and to the biological or genetic approaches. Each such hypothesis will in the end make its contribution, but it will be possible to evaluate them only when they can be considered in relation to a clear understanding of what they are attempting to explain.

It may give point to my criticism of these various attempts to characterize the essential nature of psychodynamic illness if I revert to the analogy of organic disease. There we recognize chains of etiological factors: i.e., social, economic, community hygiene, nutritional, hereditary, epidemiological, infectious, biochemical. We set up no either-or dichotomy here between cultural and biological, nor do we confuse any set of causative forces with the disease itself. At the same time, we include in the spectrum of illness its general and also its specific consequences: i.e., individual suffering, debility, crippling, death, family injury, social injury, etc. Yet these also are not the disease itself. In between the causal chains and the consequences we recognize specific pathological processes within the body, which are set in motion by the causative chain and which ultimately mediate the end results. It is this peculiar constellation of pathological processes with its own idiosyncrasies which is "the disease entity," and it is this which I am here trying to characterize for neurotic and psychotic illness.

I want to repeat that it is only when we can characterize some specific deformation of the human psyche as pathognomonic for the neurosis or psychosis that we will be in a position to consider systematically how that deformation is produced through different types of instinctual (id), ego, and superego development; or through the influence of specific phases of conflict (e.g., genital, Oedipal, pregenital, pre-Oedipal, etc.) with consequent fixations, regression, etc.; and finally through different cultures. In any final picture of the phenomena of health, neurosis, and psychosis, these issues must all be included, but it is not possible to consider them clearly until we have succeeded in describing the central deformation. The lack of this has been a hampering gap in basic psychoanalytic theory, which this paper is an attempt to fill.

In this communication I will therefore confine myself exclusively to a description of the essential nature of a change which subsequently must be explained. In this way I hope to avoid the confusions which have arisen in previous theoretical formulations from mixing together into one composite hypothesis considerations of the evolution of personality and illness, the symptoms of illness, and the immediate and remote consequences of illness. I repeat that ultimately all of these must be fitted into the complete picture, but for the purpose of this communication, I will limit myself to asking: (1) Where is the human psychic apparatus most vulnerable in a specifically human way? (2) How is this vulnerability manifested? (3) What different kinds of distortion can result? and (4) Do these differences illuminate the contrast between normality, neurosis, and psychosis? I will *not* ask, how do the various forms of vulnerability arise?

II. ESSENTIAL THESIS

Ego functions can be variously characterized. One useful descriptive grouping is into perceptual, conceptual, executive, defensive, and integrative (or synthetic) activities. Yet all ego functions are so interdependent that no one of them can ever occur alone. Even so simple a perceptual act as hearing is synergically dependent upon executive motor adjustments (e.g., in the muscles of the neck and scalp). Integrative activities begin with the perceptions of infancy, and from early childhood no perceptual act can occur without conceptual reverberations. Nevertheless, in different settings the relative roles of these functions vary. There is, however, one feature of ego functions which is found in its every aspect, and which at the same time is peculiar to the psychological processes of the maturing human animal. It is therefore precisely in this feature of ego activities that I will seek that aspect of psychopathology which is peculiarly and exclusively human. This is in the *symbolic process,* using the concept of *symbol* in a broad and inclusive sense, which will be explained below. In essence, my thesis is that in all forms of adult human psychopathology, distortions of symbolic functions occur which cannot occur in the human infant before symbolic functioning begins, nor in animal forms which are not capable of a high degree of symbolic thinking, feeling, and behavior.

This thesis raises two important subsidiary issues. Can the concepts of neurosis and psychosis be applied to subhuman forms without introducing anthropomorphic fallacies? Second, can these concepts, derived as they are primarily from the clinical study of adults, be applied to infants at an age before they are capable of at least a rudimentary form of symbolic thinking, feeling, and behavior? This, in turn, calls into question the entire structure of Melanie Klein's theory of infantile psychopathology, which implicitly and explicitly adultomorphizes the infant. Klein invests the infant's unmyelinated cerebrum and his partially myelinated afferent and efferent pathways with adult conscious and unconscious symbolic perceptions, conceptions, and fantasy formations— in short, with the full complement of adult psychic equipment. (This Kleinian fantasy hardly seems to meet the requirements of rudimentary common sense, and is character-istic of her uncritical if inventive world of science fiction.)

The flat statement of the thesis, as presented above, gives me an opportunity to discuss at once an apparent objection which will occur to everyone. I hope that at the same time this will make clear the usefulness of the distinction which I have already emphasized repeatedly: i.e., the distinction between descriptions of causal sequences and the characterization of resultant changes.

Thus as an objection to my thesis one thinks at once of Spitz's (1945, 1946; Spitz and Wolf, 1946) impressive demonstrations of the fact that during the first year of human life unduly prolonged separation from the mother and a lack of adequately concentrated contacts with a substitute mother can produce permanent and disastrous effects on the neurological and psychological development of infants. Evidently such separations can release forces which profound-ly influence the later emotional and symbolic development of the infant. Therefore my thesis cannot be that nothing which happens to an infant in its presymbolizing phases can influence its later psychological development. That would be patently absurd. It is equally fallacious, however, to call the separation which induces later illness a disease, or to make the retroactive, adultomorphic error of characterizing the upset which the separation produces in the infant in terms which are borrowed from adult psychopathology. To speak of "primal depressions" or "infantile psychoses" is a confusing use of words. There is no possible evidence that the primal reaction to deprivation has a Cs and/or Ucs content comparable in any way to that of those later adult disturbances of which it is suggestive and to which it undoubtedly contributes. It is therefore not justifiable to do more than describe the infant's reaction to separation in terms appropriate to infancy, and then to trace its consequences. This stricter use of concepts and terms has the value of putting us in a position in which we can characterize first the sequence of pathogenic experiences, and then the essential qualities of the specific distortions which they can induce. We need not then go on forever confusing in our terminology the bacteria with the disease.

For an orientation toward a future study of this problem, it may be helpful to emphasize the fact that I am not arguing that human psychopathology consists *exclusively* of a disturbance in symbolic functions. That is not the point of this article. The work of Spitz and of others indicates that changes can occur on a preverbal or subverbal level, changes which seem to consist largely of the imposition of a relatively fixed central emotional position on the personality. Despite the importance of this question it has not been studied sufficiently. The role of pleasure and of displeasure, the conditions under which emotions become fixed, the role of physiological changes in fixing them, the influence of subsequent evolving symbolic functions both preverbal and verbal, and the influence of pregenital object relations—all of these require further critical analysis. This in turn leads to a second important issue: namely, the role of symbolic functions in the defense against such emotional centers, and how, when the defensive functions of symbolic activities fail, the symbolic processes may serve instead to perpetuate and fixate the emotional distortions.

For the time being, however, there remains one basic reason for making a clear-cut distinction between psychopathological processes, the essence of which consists in the distortion of symbolic functions, and on the other hand those psychopathological processes which arise through the distorting impact of highly charged emotional experiences occurring at an early age, before symbolic processes are established. These latter can be induced experimentally in preverbal animal species, which are capable of a limited degree of symbolic function at most. They can also occur as a response to primitive emotional stresses when these occur in preverbal stages of human life, while the capacity for symbolic function still remains similarly limited. Such presymbolic changes leave residual emotional disturbances which in turn influence the symbolic aspects of all later responses to injury. Furthermore, as Spitz and others have shown, they may influence the later acquisition of symbolic functions. But it is the disturbance in the symbolic function itself which characterizes adult human psychopathology in a pathognomonic fashion. Ultimately it will be necessary to work out in detail the interrelations of these two fundamental aspects of psychopathology. In this communication, however, I will limit myself to a consideration of the significance of disturbances in the symbolic sphere alone.

III. The Symbolic Function — Cs, Pcs, Ucs

With these introductory considerations, let me return to my thesis. In the following exposition I will use the word "symbol" to characterize three closely related processes which are not ordinarily brought together under one heading, although each comes under the general category of symbolic function.

a. There is the symbolic function by means of which in thought and in speech we represent abstractions from experience. Here the term "symbolic function" is coextensive with all higher psychological functions, and especially with concept formation.

b. There is the symbolic function with which we are all familiar in figures of speech, metaphors, slang, poetry, obscenities, puns, jokes, and so forth. Here the concept behind the symbol is translated into some other mode of expression, but the relation between the original concept and the symbol remains relatively transparent except where it is obfuscated in varying degrees for "artistic" purposes, as in the more obscure realms of modern art and modern verse. This use of the symbolizing capacity of the human psychic apparatus characterizes that type of function which Freud called *preconscious* or the *descriptive subconscious*. It reaches its most systematic development, of course, in the intuitive processes of the creative artist and scientist.

c. Finally, there is the more limited psychoanalytic use of the term "symbolic function" where the symbol is a manifest representation of an unconscious latent idea. Here the link between the symbol and what it represents has become inaccessible to conscious self-inspection.

For *symbol* in the psychoanalytic sense we might reserve some special term; but since all three are aspects of the symbolizing capacity which is the unique hallmark of man, and since the three merge and overlap one with another, not to have one generic name for them would obscure the essential continuity of all "symbolic functions" from one end of the spectrum to the other. Furthermore, the distinction between "indirect representation" and "symbolization," as originally propounded by E. Jones[1] and recently given tentative support by Rapaport (1951) remains to me a distinction without an essential difference. Indeed, it may be positively misleading. It would hardly seem necessary to remind ourselves that there are no such discontinuities in nature as those who put the symbolism of dreams in a category of its own seem to imply. Furthermore, it is important to recognize the continuity of these three kinds of symbolic function, since it is because of

---

[1] The characteristics which are advanced as distinguishing true symbolism from "other indirect representations" are: "representation of unconscious material, constant meaning, independence of individual conditioning factors, evolutionary bases, linguistic connections, and phylogenetic parallels in myths, cults, religions, etc." (This is Rapaport's [1951, p. 237 fn.] approximate quotation from Jones [1916], and from Rank and Sachs.) It is quite obvious that not one of these factors is an exclusive feature of literal, allegorical, or unconscious symbolism. Each of them operates in all three. Furthermore, it turns its back on Freud's own statement that the idea of symbol "cannot be sharply delimited at all times—it mingles with . . . substitution, dramatization, [and] even approaches allusion" (quoted by Rapaport, p. 283). The conception of the continuity of the symbolic process in no way contravenes the fact that the symbol in the dream is used in a selective way for certain selective purposes. Similar considerations can clarify and dispose of Schilder's effort to set symbolism aside as "preparatory stages of thought development." And to state, as did Betlheim and Hartmann (1924), that a certain type of symbolism is "the language of the unconscious" (p. 306) is merely to state that if the unconscious is to be represented at all, it has to be represented by a special type of symbol.

this continuity that every symbol is a multivalent tool. That is to say that simultaneously on conscious, preconscious, and/or unconscious levels every direct or indirect representation of any conceptual process will in all circumstances, if in varying proportions, be literal, allegorical, and also "symbolic" in the dreamlike or psychoanalytic sense. Consequently, in actual daily use symbols are simultaneously charged with meaning in all three ways and on all three levels. This makes of every symbol a chord with a potentiality of at least nine simultaneous overtones.

This continuity will be clear if we consider the various ways in which the symbol SNAKE can be used. First, it can represent a real snake, or the species snake as a whole. Here it does not matter whether the spoken word or the written word or a drawing or model of a snake is used as the symbol. Second, the symbol SNAKE can be the snake of the Garden of Eden, or the traditional snake-in-the-grass of melodrama. Such an allegorical reference to external evil and to conscious conflicts over instinctual problems will be clear to everyone. Finally, however, there is the use of the same symbol as the manifest representative of some unconscious latent idea, of which "penis" would be a typical clinical example, plus all the urges and conflict-laden struggles which center on this latent idea. There can be no hard and fast line between these three major types of symbolic usage, and whenever we use the symbol SNAKE at all, there will be a simultaneous excitation of all three levels of meaning in varying proportions. In other words, every moment of thought and feeling involves simultaneously the activation of a literal, an allegorical, and a dreamlike meaning of the symbolic representative of all of the percepts and concepts which are relevant to that moment of psychic activity. It is indeed difficult for me to understand how any analyst who has analyzed the dreamlike overtones of the most mundane events of everyday life can entertain the idea that "Ucs symbols" are anything other than one pole of a continuous spectrum, or that they fail to play a role in the very least of our daily thoughts, feelings, and actions. (Cf. Jones, 1916, and also Rapaport, 1951.)

IV. The Bipolarity of All Symbolic Function, Cs, Pcs, Ucs

I believe that up to this point most analysts will find themselves in essential agreement with me. But whether they are or not, from this as my premise I derive my major thesis, which I will summarize in a series of propositions:

1. The capacity to make abstractions from disparate, concrete experiences and to represent those abstractions by various symbolic devices is the *sine qua non* of man's highest psychological and spiritual capabilities. Without this capacity it would be impossible for man to have any psychological processes more complex than the sensory afterimages of prior experiences. In the waking state, these would be simple wish-fulfilling sensory reverberations, essentially identical with the well-known phenomenon of the phantom limb. In sleep, these would be simple, childlike dreams of gratifications. In the absence of a matured symbolic function, this level of psychic life would mark the outer limits of man's capacity for psychological development. (Cf. Freud [1900a, pp. 535-536]: "All thinking is merely a detour from the memory of gratification . . .")

2. His ability to isolate fragments of his experiences and to represent them separately makes it possible subsequently to synthesize new psychological concepts out of fragments of earlier sensory events. Each such construction implies, however, a symbolic representation both of the prior percepts and of their synthetic abstractions. Such syntheses of new conceptualizations out of memories of earlier percepts make use of all of the devices which are characteristic of the primary process, such as condensation, displacement, substitutions of various kinds (e.g., *pars pro toto*), and reversibility through the pairing of opposites. Although often overlooked, it is an elementary fact that each of these economizing devices can occur consciously, preconsciously, or unconsciously, and that where they occur predominantly on either a conscious or preconscious level, they mediate abstract thought and language (i.e., our ability to communicate our experiences to one another); whereas where they occur predominantly on an

unconscious level, in sleep they determine the shapes of our dreams, and in the waking state the shapes of our illnesses.

3. Several years ago (Kubie, 1934a), I pointed out that in their early developmental phases our concepts are vague, broad, and overlapping, but that with maturation they gradually become more discrete and distinct. The same steps are observed in the evolution of the symbolic representations of concepts, i.e., in the drawings of children and in their acquisition of language. This was represented schematically in Figure 1.

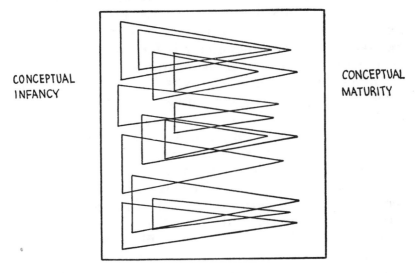

CONCEPTUAL INFANCY   CONCEPTUAL MATURITY

FIGURE 1

In all dissociating processes (such as sleep, the hypnagogic state, toxic states, and fatigue) we drop back from mature levels of conceptual development (in which concepts and their symbols are relatively distinct one from another) to earlier levels (in which concepts and their related symbols overlap). This is an inevitable ontogenetic basis for certain of the characteristics which are common to the language of the dream and to psychopathological phenomena in general.

4. In that same paper (Kubie, 1934a), I alluded to one other fact which is relevant to this thesis, and which I am here developing more fully: namely, that early in its formative

process every concept and its symbolic representatives develop two points of reference, one internal with respect to the boundaries of the body, and one external (see examples on p. 97 and p. 101). This dual anchorage of every symbol in the constellation "I" and in the constellation "non-I" is inherent in the process by which we acquire knowledge and by which we orient ourselves both to ourselves and to the outer world. It is also a key to an understanding of the process by which psychological tensions and experiences can acquire somatic representation. These later complications, to which further reference will be made below, only serve to accentuate this function of the symbolic process as a bridge between the inner and outer world. One consequence which is of immediate importance to my thesis, however, is that the differentiation of the "I" from the "non-I" is always relative and never absolute.

In outline, the argument runs as follows. (Here I can no longer limit myself strictly to a consideration of ego functions alone, since these never operate in isolation.) As with the establishing of all new conditioned reflex connections, the acquisition of any new knowledge depends upon the prior existence of a state of instinctual tension and deprivation: i.e., we learn both at the behest of id pressures and under the influence of superego pressures. In earliest infancy, however, cravings arise exclusively in body tensions. This is true only briefly, however; that is to say, only until the inevitable and universal superstructures of compulsions and phobias gather to deform the pressures which arise out of our underlying biogenetic requirements (this volume, Chapter 2). During this brief initial period, however, the infant experiences his psychic needs as changes in his vague sensory percepts of the parts, the products, and the requirements of his own body. These are the larval experiences out of which "I" concepts start to form, even before the infant can differentiate any of it clearly from the "non-I" out of which his object relations will gradually be constructed. New units of experience subsequently enter into the budding psychic life only by hitching on to what is already present (i.e., William James's "apperceptive mass"). Therefore, as any new unit is apperceived, it comes into relation to previously experienced percepts and to the immature concepts which are forming around them; and at the outset these prior psychic events to which new knowledge of the external world must be related are in every instance concerned with the body. These considerations can be summarized by saying: (a) that the first learning concerns itself entirely with bodily things; and (b) that at this stage all expanding knowledge of the nonbodily world must relate itself automatically to what has already been experienced in the bodily world. As a consequence of this characteristic of the evolving learning process, before there can be a sharp differentiation between the "I" and the "non-I," all percepts of the outer world must establish points of reference to inner bodily percepts and concepts. Consequently, every evolving conceptualization of the outer world comes into relationship with evolving conceptualizations of the body world, creating new conceptual gestalts, in which the bodily world and the outer world establish specific symbolic relationships to each other, *such that each can be and is used to represent the other.* At first this relationship is conscious, and we encounter it in the language of the games and songs of early childhood (e.g., "This little pig goes to market"; legs are "dogs"; the female genital is a "pussy"; the male genital is a "bunny" or a "cock"; the whole body is a horse; etc., etc.). Later in life, however, the dual relationship becomes unconscious, and is found chiefly in the manifest symbolism of dreams, in hypnagogic reveries, in delirious states, in art and literature, and in the symptom formations of the neuroses and psychoses.

At this point it is well to remind ourselves of a later complication in the process by which knowledge is acquired, concepts formed, and symbols established. This complication has already been referred to as the bridging function of symbolic thinking. The "I" which begins with the body alone gradually comes to include all internalized and unconscious external objects and relationships. (It is immaterial here which metaphor we use to characterize this process of internalization, whether introjection, incorporation, or identification, since these are overlapping metaphors by which to characterize various aspects of the same fundamental process.) At the same time, the "non-I" comes to include all externalizations (projections) of internal experiences, including many bodily concepts which originated as parts of the "I." Actually, it is this very dual anchorage of the symbol of which we are speaking that is the bridge over which these processes take place: i.e., internalization and externalization, introjection and somatization. *Without the dual anchorage of the symbolic process, these familiar transmutations of experience could not take place either consciously or unconsciously. This is another reason why the effort to set the dream symbol of psychoanalysis in a category apart from any other form of "indirect representation" (E. Jones and others) is not only intrinsically fallacious, but also irreconcilable with the implicit requirements of psychoanalytic psychology.*

5. In summary, then, every symbol refers simultaneously to concepts derived from body needs and images and to concepts derived from percepts of the outside world. Consequently every symbolic unit hangs like a hammock between two poles, one internal or bodily (the "I") and one external (the "non-I"), so that whenever we consciously think and speak of the outer world we are wittingly or unwittingly thinking and speaking of the inner world; and similarly, when we are consciously thinking and speaking of the inner world, whether we realize it or not we are simultaneously thinking and speaking of the outer world. This relationship can best be illustrated by a simple diagram, which indicates that on different occasions the same symbol will carry emotional and conceptual connotations which are weighted with different percentages of these two component elements in the symbolic process: i.e., the internal and external poles of reference (Figure 2). In this sense, the Cs, Pcs, and Ucs "meanings" of any symbol can be represented most accurately by points along a continuous spectrum.

6. Furthermore, these considerations have a firm grounding in physiological and anatomical facts. As I have indicated, every symbol has simultaneous poles of reference to the "I" and to the "non-I" worlds, the "I" having its origins in proprioceptive percepts of the body, and the "non-I" in exteroceptive percepts of the outer world. Thus the symbolic process is itself the bridge between the "I" and the "non-I" on

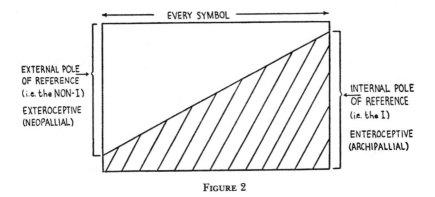

FIGURE 2

both a perceptual and a conceptual level. For this bipolar (or multipolar?) reference of all symbols on the psychological levels, there is also a neuroanatomical and neurophysiological basis through their bipolar (or multipolar?) representation in the central nervous system. In its full development this anatomical and physiological basis for the bipolarity of the symbolic process may be as uniquely characteristic of the human brain as is the symbolic process for human psychology. The body roots of the "I" component of the symbol have their central representation in the more primitive archipallial cortex and its association systems.[2] This links the "I" component of the symbolic process to visceral functions, through the autonomic tie-up of the archipallium, with direct expression via the effector system of the hypothalamus, and

[2] "I wonder if your use of the term 'archipallial' is not a little too confining since it does not include other primitive cortex such as the so-called 'paleopallium' and the transitional (or 'meso-') cortex. The total mass of such cortex is considerable in all mammals. All the foregoing terms are, however, in my mind, rather unsuitable because they carry with them so many misconceptions regarding the location, origin, and cytoarchitecture of the cortex they refer to. *Primitive cortex,* on the other hand, is a term which is all-inclusive and yet dodges some of the misconceptions, particularly the cytoarchitectural ones based on Nissl preparations. The work of Lorente de No is pretty persuasive that any attempt to designate the degree of organization of cortex on the basis of cell layers seen in Nissl preparations is entirely unrealistic. It is probable that the niceties of distinctions between primitive and neocortex can be made only by the use of staining methods (such as the Golgi-Cox) which allows a finer differentiation of the types of cells, as well as their connections" (Paul D. MacLean, personal communication, July 9, 1951; see also MacLean, 1949).

finally through its special relation to the olfactory system. In this way, the "nose brain" constitutes a link between the archipallium or visceral brain (MacLean, 1949) and the neopallium, the latter with its primary relation to distance receptors and their specific and highly differentiated association systems. Anatomically and physiologically, therefore, as well as psychologically, olfaction is an intermediate link between the bodily pole and the outer pole of the symbol (i.e., between the "I" and the "non-I"). These relationships parallel the evolution of nonosmatic primate life from osmatic lower forms: i.e., the erect arboreal primate forms from the ground shrew, "poking away among the grass roots and living largely in the world of smells" (Cobb, 1950, pp. 38-40). It is conceivable that this may have something to do with the special role of olfactory phenomena both in hypnagogic reveries and in hallucinatory and delusional constellations. At all events, it is of prime importance that every *symbol* has at least a bipolar psychological reference, and at the same time at least a bipolar central representation in the nervous system. Because of this the symbolic process is vulnerable to organic and to psychodynamic injury at both poles.

7. What, then, is the nature of this vulnerability? We will consider this primarily on the psychodynamic level. Both the internal and the external connections of a symbol can be conscious, but whenever for any reason either link becomes distorted, a psychopathological process is set in motion. In other words, a pathological distortion of psychological processes must ensue whenever there is any distortion of the relations of a symbol to its substrate at either the "I" or the "non-I" pole of reference: i.e., to the world either of internal percepts and concepts, or of external percepts and concepts, or both. Thus, whether the cause is some organic disruption of brain function or a disruption caused by psychological forces, psychopathological processes arise whenever there is a disturbance in one or more of the links between a symbol and some component of the complex constellation or gestalt which it represents. *Psychodynamic injury begins with the process which in analysis is called "repression." This can take place at either pole, but we will see that which pole becomes the major*

focus of the repressive process is the factor which determines the nature of the ensuing illness. This formulation constitutes a return to the full implications of Freud's original position: namely, that (a) without a dynamic unconscious there can be no psychological illness (none, that is, which is psychodynamic in origin); and (b) that without repression there can be no dynamic unconscious.[3] Freud subsequently modified this formulation, but for many reasons I believe that we will soon find ourselves returning to his earlier formulation. In the meantime, let me emphasize again that this is why it would be impossible for man to develop either a neurosis or a psychosis without those very symbolic potentialities which are essential to his highest psychological development.

V. Relation of Bipolarity of Symbolic Functions to Neurosis and Psychosis

Let me return now to my original question: Does this hypothesis throw light on the old and baffling problem of the nature of the essential difference between the neurotic and the psychotic processes? (Note that this is not the same as asking what is the difference between a "neurotic" person and a "psychotic" person, a question which is rooted in several ancient fallacies.) I will assume the truth of something that seems to me self-evident: namely, that since the neurotic process is universal in the present state of child culture, there is no such thing as a psychotic patient who has not had a pre-existing neurosis out of which major aspects of the psychotic process will have evolved. If this is true, the specific question which must be answered is: What does the psychotic process add which is not present in or different from the neurotic process, qualitatively and/or quantitatively? We are not asking what are the differences in the *effects* of the neurotic and psychotic processes, nor in their symptomatic manifestations, nor in their ontogeny. We are asking: What is the essential change which is peculiar to each?

[3] Because neither issue is relevant to my thesis, I will bypass the problem of inherited unconscious processes, and the related question of what can be Ucs which has never been Cs.

I submit that this difference has to do primarily with the point at which the relation of a symbol to its substrate is disturbed. As analysts we take it as axiomatic that in every psychogenic psychopathological process the symptoms and the symptomatic behavior of the patient constitute an unconscious symbolic language for the expression of repressed intrapsychic conflicts. The conflict, however, is not the illness. Psychopathological illness begins as the conflict engenders a repressive-dissociative process which obscures the links between symbolic constructs and the percepts and conceptualizations which represent the body and its needs and conflicts, i.e., the "I" pole of reference. *This is the primary point of rupture in any psychopathological process.* Alone, however, this produces only the neurosis. In the psychotic process there is an additional specific distortion in the relationship between the symbol and its pole of reference to the outer world, i.e., to the "non-I." In varying proportions, there is always some degree of distortion at both ends of the symbolic linkage concurrently, which is why the processes of neurosis and of psychosis can never be mutually exclusive, although one or the other may predominate. (Parenthetically, it is worth mentioning that organic disease or injury in the archipallial and/or neopallial systems has effects on the symbolic process which are characteristic of organic disease of the nervous system, and which parallel in certain ways the differences between the consequences which are characteristic of psychodynamic repression of the "I" and "non-I" linkages respectively.)

VI. Some Tests of the Useful Applicability of This Hypothesis

As already mentioned, one of the tests of the usefulness and validity of any such formulation is the extent to which it can account for the characteristic clinical manifestations of illness, in personality, symptomatic behavior, and symptoms. Let us apply this test to my hypothesis.

a. There is general agreement that clinically one of the major differences between a neurosis and a psychosis has to do with a clinical consideration, which is variously spoken of as reality testing, object relation, object cathexis, narcissistic libidinal investment, etc. It is characteristic of the looseness of our theoretical formulations that these terms are sometimes used as though they were the names of causative processes, and sometimes as though they were the names of symptomatic end products and reaction formations in the psychotic process. Actually they are the latter, and exercise causative influences only in relation to secondary and tertiary consequences of illness. It is precisely here that the bipolarity of the symbolic process makes the essence of the psychotic change understandable. When the major emphasis of repression is on the link between the symbol and the "non-I," a disturbance must occur at one or all of the three stages or levels of the perceptual-conceptual functions of the ego: to wit, in the patient's ability to *perceive* external stimuli undistorted, and/or in his ability to build undistorted concepts out of these percepts, and/or in his ability to represent these concepts in precise and translatable symbols. Clinical experience substantiates this deduction. The difference between neurosis and psychosis is *not* found in the *appropriateness* of the emotional responses, whether to percepts or to concepts, or to language symbols. The emotional responses to a cat on the part of a patient who suffers from a cat phobia may be quite as "inappropriate" as are the emotional responses to a cat on the part of a patient with a delusion about cats, but in the former there will be no distortion of the patient's understanding of the meaning of CAT, whether as percept, concept, or language symbol. In the psychotic process, however, one or more of these components of the symbolic process will have been dislocated from its relationship to the presenting object, so that a CAT and its symbolic derivatives actually mean to the patient something other than itself.

Such dislocations can occur at one of several points, or simultaneously at several of them. These too can be ordered in a series from those which are less malignant to those which are more malignant in their significance: i.e., in illusions percepts themselves are distorted; in hallucinations percepts are manufactured; in delusional confusion percepts and concepts are misrepresented. In the laboratory of nature (i.e., in actual illness) these disturbances occur in varied mixtures.

b. I will attempt to trace ceratin intricate implications of this formulation, having to do only with the *perceptual* component of the psychotic process. This should not be read to mean that I hold "hallucinations" to be the paradigm of the psychotic process or state, nor that clinical hallucinations are always present in psychoses. On the contrary, I will point out that the hallucinatory process is far more universal than that, that it constitutes a potential out of which the psychotic process can arise, but that there are hallucinatory processes which for definable reasons are devoid of psychotic implications, and that this difference depends specifically upon which pole the symbolic process is predominantly involved.[4]

This point arises out of the fact that disturbances, whether at the perceptual end of the series or toward the conceptual superstructures, can center predominantly on either the proprioceptive (archipallial) system or on the distance-receptor system in the neopallium, with a corresponding emphasis respectively on distortions of the inner somatic world and its derivative "I" concepts, or on the external world and the "non-I" derivative concepts. As a consequence, differences arise which have dynamic implications that are at the same time both physiological and psychological. In the study of the psychotic process, two facts are generally overlooked: (1) the hallucinatory manufacture of *certain kinds* of percepts occurs

---

[4] The relationship of this concept to Freud's statement that what is inside me (and therefore *me*) is unreal when compared to what is outside me (and therefore *not me*) as developed in his paper on "Negation" (1925) will have to be discussed on another occasion. It is relevant here, however, to point out that Freud recognized the difference of the quality of reality with respect to what was internal as opposed to what was external, a distinction which is important in the evolution of my whole concept of the difference between neurosis and psychosis. Thus Freud said, "What is not real, what is merely imagined or subjective, is only *internal*; while on the other hand what is real is also present *externally*" (p. 183). This obscure statement becomes transparently clear if one takes into account the difference in the precision of the exteroceptive as opposed to the enteroceptive apparatus. This is why in the pages which follow I lay stress on the disturbances in the perceptual ingredient in the psychic process for our understanding of the difference between neurosis and psychosis.

all the time as a natural and inevitable psychophysiological function, and is devoid of psychotic significance; (2) of these nonpsychotic hallucinatory percepts, one type occurs regularly in the waking state and another type in the dreams of sleep. Thus the ordinary dreams of sleep are nonpsychotic hallucinatory experiences, in which distance receptors (predominantly visual) are used almost exclusively. Let me quote what I have already written on this topic:

> Many special features of the thought process in dreams are a direct result of the fact that in the dream we think primarily by means of visual images. In this respect dream thinking resembles the thought process of the human child, and probably that of all lower animals. Certainly most of us recall the look of things more readily than we can recall their sound or taste or smell or feel. This is partly because form and color remain relatively constant, whereas other modalities of sensation are transitory experiences, which can less readily be re-experienced unaltered. Furthermore, vision is the only sensation which during sleep can be completely eliminated at the level of the sense organ, that is, at the source. This is done through darkness and by shutting the eyes. Sound, taste, smell, the various forms of touch and internal bodily sensations can never be excluded to the same extent during sleep. At best they are diminished by rendering them more or less constant and by a process of central muting in the brain (which is called "Inhibition"). As a result, sounds are rarely heard clearly in dreams, but are usually represented by a thought of the sound; and taste and smell and bodily sensations are seldom experienced as such in dreams. None of these is totally excluded, but their roles are quite secondary to visual imagery, which is the principal language of the dream process. This is why the dream is predominantly a visual hallucination. Furthermore, for most people the visual images of dreams consist largely of black, white, and grey. Colors appear relatively rarely, and are usually limited to one color, which picks out some particular object for special emphasis. The physiological reasons for this are not known [Kubie, 1950a, pp. 70-71].

In contrast to this, in the waking state of any and all of us, nonpsychotic hallucinatory experiences occur which involve exclusively the proprioceptive somatic receptors. Of these, the commonplace sensations of pain, itching, sleepiness, heat and cold, and the innumerable other body hallucinations which we accept in daily life are examples. Both of these hallucinatory processes entail some degree of disturbance in object relationships and in reality testing, but in neither case does the hallucinatory experience or the implied impairment in reality testing indicate that we are dealing with an active psychotic process. This is precisely because in these two situations no reality testing is possible with respect to the sensory modalities which are involved. In sleep, for example, the visual fantasies which constitute the language of the dream can run riot in the dark, where it is the one sensory modality which is completely eliminated from perceptual stimulation. In other words, in the dreams of sleep we can accept these visual pseudo percepts complacently as though they were real, precisely because no comparisons with "non-I" reality are possible. Therefore their acceptance implies no general breakdown of the capacity to test percepts by considerations of reality, and consequently their acceptance does not carry the implication of psychosis.

Let me quote again:

> For instance, in daily life the degree of organization of sensory data constantly delimits the boundary between imagery and hallucination, which is another aspect of Ego functions. In dreams we accept as normal the occurrence of visual and auditory images of hallucinatory vividness; but it is in sleep alone that it is "normal" to have such hallucinations—to wit, only when the corrective and comparative data from distance receptors are not active. In contrast, during waking states even the most normal individuals can have varying degrees of hypochondriacal illusions or hallucinations; because proprioceptive sensations from the body lack the clear definition of those which are mediated by the exteroceptor apparatus, and therefore are less able to correct the pseudosensory creations of the imaginations [Kubie and Margolin, 1944, p. 613].

To repeat: in sleep (i.e., in the dark and with closed eyes), the opportunity to test the reality of visual images is of necessity in abeyance. Therefore, although the dreamed image of a lion is a projection of conflict-driven intrapsychic processes, and in spite of the fact that it can have hallucinatory vividness for the dreamer, there is no way of comparing it with a real lion or for that matter with any other actual visual perceptions. Awake, however, and with eyes open, and in the light, that same lion could be "seen" in the same sense only if there had been a breakdown in all of those comparative processes by means of which we distinguish between external reality and our waking daydreams. In the waking state, the ability to check on the reality of pseudo percepts in the sensory modalities which are served by distance receptors is essential to maintain the boundaries between reality and conscious and/or unconscious fantasy. In the waking state any impairment of this function carries psychotic implications. But note that even in the waking state this applies only to the exteroceptive modalities, and note further that this capacity depends in its essence on the relation between symbolic processes and their "non-I" poles of reference.

Reality testing for proprioceptive percepts contrasts sharply with this. Neither asleep nor awake do proprioceptive percepts have the degree of precision which characterizes the percepts produced by our exteroceptive equipment. Nor is there any way of comparing directly our proprioceptive percepts with pseudo percepts (as we can with vision, hearing, etc.). Therefore even in the waking state, within wide limits somatic hallucinations or illusions are compatible with nonpsychotic functioning; it is only when the conceptual superstructures depart far from reality that the somatic distortion acquires psychotic implications.

We may summarize this by pointing out that the language of the dream depends almost exclusively on the use of the most sharply discriminating of our distance receptors (i.e., vision) which therefore constitutes the primary agent of reality testing and our first barrier against psychosis. In the dreams of sleep, auditory, olfactory, gustatory, tactile, and proprioceptive sensations play progressively diminishing roles in approximately that order. (Even in somnambulistic dreams, active kinesthetic stimuli from muscles and joints fail to produce conscious awareness of movement any more clearly than they do as we walk around in the fully waking state.) Therefore we can conclude that, in dreams, that form of exteroceptive imagery which depends predominantly on the activity of those central cortical areas which are linked to distance receptors (neopallium) constitutes the major mechanism for the manufacture of symbolic representatives of our conceptual abstractions. In the dreams of normal sleep our conflictful psychic life is represented by projections which utilize predominantly the external pole of reference of the symbol, while body imagery is strikingly scanty. In this quite specific sense the sleep dream is always a transitory and benign psychosis. (No adequate comparison has been made of dreams whose effects terminate on waking with those which launch enduring psychoses.) If, on the other hand, the same process occurs when we are awake, it indicates that the external pole of the bipolar symbolic process is being used to represent internal psychological conflicts. When this occurs, we find ourselves confronted with the essence of the psychotic process.

On the other hand, in the waking state it is an everyday occurrence unconsciously to represent conflicts by proprioceptive hallucinations. These are familiar to us as aches and pains, itches, and sensations of heat and cold and of movement, etc. All of these come within the scope of every man's daily experiences. They are not psychotic in their implications for the simple reason that it is impossible to subject proprioceptive sensations to precise reality testing by any process of comparison and contrast.

What does this mean? It means first that, whether awake or asleep, disturbance in the relation of the symbol to its substrate at the "I" pole of the symbolic process must impair reality discriminations about the body and its sensations (as evidenced by somatic hallucinations), yet is consistent with the absence of psychosis, although it is a regular ingredient of the neurosis. It means secondly, and on the other hand, that in the waking state any disturbance of the relationship of the symbol to its substrate at the "non-I" pole of the symbolic process must impair reality discriminations about the external world, thus giving rise to a loss which is inherent in the psychotic process. It is noteworthy that it is only when a somatic hallucination is elaborated into a somatic delusion, and thus constitutes a psychic self-mutilation through a basic alteration of the externalized body image (as though the "I" had become part of the "non-I"), or else where it imposes itself in fact on the external world by actual self-mutilation (i.e., by an active attempt to alter the body as though the body were part of the outside world), that the waking body-dreams of the neurotic acquire psychotic implications.

SUMMARY

I have attempted to explore the implications of a new hypothesis concerning the distinction between normality and psychopathology. In doing so I have artificially segregated into two groups the forces which are at work: those forces which arise primarily through the impact of early emotional stresses on presymbolic stages of human life, and those which arise through a distortion of the symbolic process itself. I have not discussed the first group of forces beyond pointing out that they characterize the psychopathology both of subverbal animal forms and of preverbal stages of human life, whereas the second characterizes the psychopathology which is distinctively human, whether of the child, adolescent, or adult. I have presented some evidence for the hypothesis that every unit of symbolic thinking has both an exteroceptive and an enteroceptive root: i.e., that each has a link both in the *"I"* world and in the *"non-I"* world, and that the major distinction between the neurosis and the psychosis depends upon whether the distortion of the relationship of the symbol to what it represents is primarily at the "I" or at the "non-I" end of the symbolic linkage, respectively. I traced certain consequences of this for that disturbance of psychological function which is called a "hallucination," and I presented reasons for the generally overlooked fact that under appropriate circumstances certain types of hallucinatory processes fall within the realm of normal psychological functions, while others have neurotic and still others psychotic implications. The reasons for this are correlated with the underlying thesis.

To some critics it may seem strange or even misleading that I should have focused so much of my discussion on the hallucinatory process, since in its full-blown clinical form hallucinosis is one of the relatively rare manifestations of the psychotic process. I have done so *not* because I believe that all psychotics hallucinate, nor that all hallucinations are psychotic, but rather because I believe that there is an unbroken continuity among all psychological manifestations, a continuity between normality, neurosis, and psychosis. If this is true, then it follows that precisely because hallucinations are one of the more extreme manifestations of the fully developed psychotic state it became essential to test my hypothesis by seeing whether it was possible to recognize and demonstrate the existence of this continuum in the hallucinatory process of normal psychology, the hallucinatory process which can occur in the neurotic, and the hallucinosis of the psychotic. Here again a close scrutiny of the more pathological processes of psychotic hallucinations throws light on the essential nature of the psychotic process itself and on the related processes of the normal.

4

THE CENTRAL REPRESENTATION OF THE SYMBOLIC PROCESS IN PSYCHOSOMATIC DISORDERS

How tensions which originate on the level of psychological experience convert into somatic disturbances has long been a mystery. This paper will present logical, anatomical, and physiological data which suggest (1) that it is the symbolic process itself which makes this transmutation possible, and (2) that this aspect of symbolic function is mediated through an area of the brain which MacLean (1949, 1950; MacLean, Alejandro, and Arellano, 1950) has called the "visceral brain." In developing and considering this thesis, it will be helpful to keep in mind the various ways in which the body can be represented in conceptual symbols on conscious, preconscious, and unconscious levels, as a whole and in its parts and processes. For, as has been demonstrated elsewhere, the ontogeny of speech, and indeed of all symbolic processes, has some of its roots in our evolving percepts and concepts of the body (Kubie, 1934a).

In 1933 the late Raymond Pearl, in discussing the relationship of the classification of diseases to "the innate biological worth or value of certain organ systems," pointed out that some organ systems establish a direct contact with the external environment, whereas others fail to, and that from this fact alone stem quite varied physiological and psychological consequences.

First published in *Psychosomatic Medicine*, 15:1-7, 1953. Reprinted by permission of Elsevier North-Holland, Inc.

Ten years later, with this observation as well as related psychoanalytic findings in mind, the suggestion was made (Kubie, 1944) that out of an elaboration of this principle a useful basis might be found for an ultimate classification of disorders from a psychosomatic standpoint. (I would underscore the fact that this was offered as one possible basis for classification, not as a definitive classification in itself.) Four general categories of body organs and processes were described, which differed in their accessibility to symbolic representation and therefore in the ways in which they can become involved in psychological conflicts.

I. Organs Which Implement Our Relationships to the External Environment

These primarily involve the exteroceptive sense organs, the striated muscles with their proprioceptive controls, and the organs of speech and their central representation—in short, the organs which subserve the external relationships of the individual, his orientation in space and perhaps in time, his ability to communicate with others, the sensory impressions which reach him from the outside world and his ability to organize them, and his conscious orientative faculties. These are essentially the organs of the ego, as the term is used psychoanalytically. In current idiom, disorders of these functions are ordinarily classified as conversion hysterias. The organs themselves occupy a clearly defined place in conscious and preconscious thought, and are objects of complex ideational processes. On the conscious level they belong to the original body "I"; but because they mediate our relationship to the "non-I" world around us, they can also merge with and represent the "non-I" world on an unconscious level.

II. Organs of Internal Economy

These organs lie deep within the interior of the body, and consequently are hidden from the individual's capacity for direct knowledge of himself. Furthermore, even though some of these organs have indirect connections with the outside world, our subjective awareness of them is absent or limited, with a parallel limitation of their psychological representation. In 1944 I included the terminal segments of the gastrointestinal tract, the respiratory tract, and the urinary apparatus in this category. These might better have been listed either in the next category or in an intermediate position, an ambiguity which illustrates the fact that all such categories are at best only approximate nodal points on a continuum. Disturbances in the organs of internal economy are usually spoken of as "organ neuroses" and have sharply differentiating physiological consequences, which are fully discussed in the original paper. A major psychological consequence of the hidden position of these organs is their limited and often ambiguous or paradoxical symbolic representation: physiologically they are an essential part of the "I" world, yet psychologically they can never play that role on a conscious level. Unconsciously they are sometimes viewed as "I" and sometimes as an alien and hostile "non-I."

III. Organs of Primary Instinctual Functions

I am concerned here with the primary instincts alone, whose associated organs have direct apertural connections with the outside world (this volume, Chapter 2; Pearl, 1933). These organs serve the intake and output of air, water, food, food wastes, and external secretions. They are organs of appetite, swallowing, excretion, and genital function. Between such an internal organ as the uterus and the instinctual organs of genital function there is a graded transition, just as there is between the stomach and the mouth or between the small bowel and the anorectal segment. This transition is reflected in the symbolic representation of these organs and their functions.

It is necessary to explain why the apertures are the focal organs around which primary instinctual functions are built (this volume, Chapter 2). In the first place, biologists and experimental psychologists agree that the definition of instincts as "hereditary forms of behavior" is not an adequate characterization, since there are both hereditary and learned components in all behavior, from the simplest reflex circuits to the most complex patterns which are ordinarily subsumed under the concept of instincts. For this reason some biologists would abandon the term altogether. Most, however, feel that the concept is needed nonetheless. In "Instincts and Homeostasis" (this volume, Chapter 2) it is applied to constellations of behavior which evolve in a specific way out of biochemical processes in the body that cannot be maintained in dynamic equilibrium without continuous or periodic exchanges of actual substances with the outside world. These complex biochemical processes go on all the time. The state of so-called rest is actually a continuous asynchronous flux, a dynamic equilibrium in which the "pluses" and "minuses" cancel each other out, leaving no unbalanced need for either intake or output for the body as a whole.

Synchronization of the biochemical processes is imposed upon the asynchronous flux of the "resting" state in one of two ways. On the intake side, the synchronization is imposed by deprivation. On the output side, it is imposed by accumulation and, in certain instances, by the distension of a storage or passageway organ. Certain psychological differences among the instincts result from the fact that the rate at which synchronization occurs, whether in response to deprivation or to accumulation, varies for the different instinctual processes according to the nature of their biochemical origins. But as these processes are synchronized, whether by deprivation or by accumulation, a need arises, first in cells, then in the tissues and organs, and finally in the whole body. This is expressed through patterns of neuromuscular and glandular behavior, which are in part hereditary and in part learned, and which involve both the somatomuscular and the autonomic nervous systems. It is through these patterns of neuromuscular and glandular behavior that the necessary exchanges are effected with the outer world. In turn, these patterns are shaped and deformed into appetites and "drives" as we know them by superimposed compulsive and phobic psychological mechanisms. *This final shaping involves the use of conscious and unconscious symbolic processes.* When instinctual behavior is viewed as serving the body by effecting the necessary interchanges of substance with the outside world, the organ and function around which all psychological representation focuses must be the appropriate aperture; the symbolic representation of all primary instinctual functions is concerned primarily with the apertures, their function, gratification, frustration, and control. (I would repeat that this description is purposely limited to the primary instinctual processes.)

IV. Involvement of the Body Image as a Whole

Here the representation of the body is diffuse and not confined to any one organ group. Patients whose somatic disturbances fall into this group are, in general, the chronic invalids and the so-called neurasthenics; but among them will be found many who, during the evolution of their illness, pass through phases in which one or another of the other groups dominates the clinical picture.

As has been indicated, the psychological representation of these four categories of body image and body function varies. The organs of Group I are sometimes treated as part of the "I" world and sometimes as though they were part of the world around us. The organs of Group II are often unknown and unrepresented until the organ is brought into our conceptual scheme by some illness, accident, or special circumstance (such as an illness or accident to someone with whom we have close conscious and unconscious ties). The organs of Group III play an important role in our symbolic processes, between Groups I and II. The fourth group constitutes a special problem, with special kinds of symbolic representation. Fuller development of these differences will be considered in another paper.

In a paper entitled "The Problems of Specificity in the Psychosomatic Process" (Kubie, 1953b), I pointed to one other distinguishing feature of all primary instinctual functions which is relevant to the function of symbolic processes in psychosomatic disturbances. This is the fact that the relative roles of the somatomuscular systems on the one hand and of the autonomic nervous system on the other differ significantly among the four categories.

In the first group, the primary function of each organ is innervated predominantly by the somatomuscular and somatosensory apparatus, with the autonomic system playing only a secondary, synergic, or supportive role.

In the second group (the organs of internal economy), the autonomic nervous system functions almost alone, with the somatomuscular and somatosensory systems playing a secondary, supportive, or adjustment role.

In the third group (those of instinctual function), the patterns of instinctual behavior are always *initiated* as somatomuscular activity under the guidance of the voluntary nervous system, but end up as almost purely autonomic action. As each individual instinctual act gets under way, there is a graudal increase in the participation of autonomic function until finally, at the critical point, the autonomic nervous system takes off on an independent jet-propelled flight of its own. One sees this most clearly in swallowing, urinating, defecating, and, of course, in sex, but it is true in subtler ways in every instinctual act (this volume, Chapter 2).[1]

In the fourth group, where there is a diffuse involvement of the body as a whole, the somatosensory and higher conceptual and symbolic systems play the dominant role, with little effector activity, whether somatomuscular or autonomic. The differences among the four basic categories in the relative roles of voluntary and autonomic nervous functions must be included in any consideration of the central mediation of psychosomatic relationships through their symbolic representation.

[1] This critical transition from somatomuscular and somatosensory control to autonomous autonomic control is a basic characteristic of instinctual (apertural) functions on both the intake and output sides. Yet to the best of my knowledge it has never been adequately explored in terms of its organic or psychological mechanisms. The study of the artificial aperture, which in a sense creates an artificial new "instinct," would seem to be the natural point of departure for such an investigation (Margolin, 1951).

First, however, one other general consideration. One of the perplexing facts about theories of psychosomatic disease has been the existence of a tendency to revert to the concept of organ disease, which in general medicine was discarded long ago. There was a period in which the influence of gross pathology led investigators to think of individual organs as the site of discrete and independent disease processes. Then came a period when tissues were singled out for emphasis (Bichat). This was followed by a similar emphasis on individual cells and membranes (Virchow), and finally by the modern period in which all structures are regarded as foci of an incessant flux of biochemical and biophysical changes which involve not merely the tissues alone but all body fluids as well (Lewin and Kubie, 1951). Thus the progress of our medical thinking has been away from the concept of isolated organ diseases. How then does it happen that in psychosomatic medicine there has been this reversion to an outgrown concept of organ disease? I believe that this has occurred because even organs which are physiologically interwoven into one indivisible whole may be singled out psychologically to play artificially isolated roles in our conscious and unconscious processes. Consequently the central representation of components of the body image can be isolated in psychosomatic disorders even when the same organs are physiologically completely interdependent (Kubie, 1953b).

This leads us finally to a consideration of the symbolic process by which the body image, both as a whole and in its parts, is represented consciously and unconsciously, and how this symbolic process is in turn subserved by the central nervous system (Kubie, 1953a; this volume, Chapter 3).

Under ordinary circumstances emotional tensions which are generated through psychological experiences are expressed through the symbolic processes of speech, language, and sensory imagery. This is true whether the tensions are acute or chronic, conscious or unconscious, or a mixture of the two, as is more usual. These tensions can also be expressed through "the language of the body," that is, through some disturbance of sensation or somatomuscular or vegetative functions, or through distorted combinations of these processes. It has perplexed investigators and theoreticians alike to understand how tensions which are generated on the level of psychological experience can be expressed in two such different ways. Many words have been applied to this phenomenon, such as conversion hysteria, somatization, and organ neurosis, but these metaphors evade rather than face the essential question by providing us with the illusion that we have solved the problem when we have only redescribed it with a new figure of speech. The words also imply an unproved assumption: namely, that tensions are always expressed first by psychological means and only subsequently in somatic language. There is no evidence that this is the invariable sequence. Instead, this paper will suggest that the two may often be concurrent, since symbolic representations of every conceptual process are rooted in both the body and the outside world (this volume, Chapter 3).

The world which is external to the boundaries of the body is perceived by means of our exteroceptive sensory apparatus and through those proprioceptors by which we recognize the external parts and implements of our body, such as our limbs, faces, distance receptors, and organs of communication. This is the original "non-I" world, even though it gradually comes to include some elements of the body image. At the same time there is an internal world which is rooted originally in the dimmer, less sharply localized, and less clearly discriminated subjective sensations from the body. This is the "I" world of internal somatic sensations, mediated by enteroceptive and deeper proprioceptive experiences.

It is not necessary here to trace the changing content of these two worlds or their areas of overlap, but it is possible to demonstrate that every conceptual unit is rooted in both the "I" and "non-I" worlds. Indeed, it may be that every conceptual until has at least a triple linkage, in the "I," the "non-I," and an intermediate world. In this way the symbol itself may constitute the bridge between these alternative and often simultaneous channels for the expression of internal tensions. In other words, it is the symbolic process, with its multipolar conscious, preconscious, and unconscious linkages, which provides us with projective pathways for language and distance imagery at the one end and introjective pathways for somatic dysfunction at the other.

I have described the multipolar anchorage of symbolic functions in two previous papers (Kubie, 1953a, this volume, Chapter 3), to which I must refer the reader for a full development of this thesis. Here, I would underscore only one essential element: namely, that every concept and its symbolic representation must, inevitably, develop through an interplay of meanings which begins internally and subsequently extends to include external points of reference (Kubie, 1934a). Since in intrauterine life internal perceptions ontogenetically precede external perceptions, all new units of external experience must enter into the evolving psychic life by hitching onto what is already present. Thus the earliest learning builds on intrabodily experience, and the expanding knowledge of the external world relates itself automatically to those body impressions which have already been experienced internally (Kubie, 1934a). The multipolar anchorage of concepts and symbols is represented in the games, songs, and dreams of childhood, and is carried over into the dreams and symptom structures of adult life. It is this which gives to the symbolic process its bridging functions; and no matter what metaphorical term we use to describe it, whether we speak of it as internalization and externalization, as introjection, incorporation, identification, or projection, without the multiple anchorage of the symbolic process none of these familiar transmutations of experience could take place at all. This remains true whether the transmutations take place consciously or unconsciously, on a purely psychological level or with the body involvements of the psychosomatic process.

Modern knowledge of the organization of the brain recognizes a neuroanatomical and neurophysiological basis for this multipolar function of the symbolic processes. The multipolarity of the symbolic unit was dramatically demonstrated during a recent visit of mine to the Neurosurgical Service of Dr. Wilder Penfield at the Montreal Neurological Institute (Kubie, 1953a). In his operating room it was possible to find objective confirmation of this theoretically derived conception of the symbol as a multivalent link between the "I" and the "non-I" world. The external convexities of the temporal lobes of patients with psychomotor epilepsy were exposed under local anesthesia. In the search for epileptogenic foci, the temporal lobes of such patients were systematically explored by electrical stimulation. In the course of this exploration the patients named objects in response to visual stimuli, and often spoke spontaneously. On the operating table, this speech was recorded on a Dictaphone. Even a cursory review of the material provided repeated examples of the use of symbolic language, with the same transition between internal and external reference that one finds in the games and songs of children and in the dreams and symptom formations of adults.

For example, during operation an Iowa farm girl was shown a series of simple line drawings of familiar objects which she was asked to name. This she did quite readily, until Dr. Penfield stimulated an area in the lobe which caused a temporary arrest of speech. This occurred just as she was shown the drawing of a human hand. At the moment of stimulation her speech ceased as though she were frozen into immobility. Then, when the current was turned off, she began first to make mouthing movements, and then slowly and hesitatingly said in sequence: "Five, five, five, five horses, five horses, five pigs, five pigs, five fingers, fingers, hand." In other stages of exploration, both of this patient and others, stimulation deep in the temporal lobe produced visual images of animal figures and human figures, musical sounds and body sounds, external and internal smells, and gastrointestinal sensations almost interchangeably; in short, a broad array of extero- and enteroceptive data.

Penfield's evidence is largely derived from the temporal cortex, and predominantly from its external convexity (1952; Penfield and Rasmussen, 1950). It is complemented by Dr. Paul MacLean's neuronographic and electroencephalographic studies of the basal areas of the brain and of the structures which lie deep within the temporal regions (the more medially placed temporal cortex, the basilar cortex under the frontal lobes, the insula, and possibly the buried cortex of the hippocampus). In other words, MacLean explored a more primitive and transitional cortex. It had long been known that the premotor cortex exercises an influence on various autonomic functions in a circumscribed, point-for-point relationship. MacLean's work indicated that the deeper areas of the temporal lobe and its connections represent complex autonomic functions in a more organized manner (1949, 1950; MacLean, Alejandro, and Arellano, 1950). Basing his studies on the work of Elliot Smith, Herrick, Papez, and others, MacLean points out that there is an ancient part of the forebrain which has been called the rhinencephalon or great limbic lobe, and which includes the so-called archipallium, paleopallium, and mesopallium. MacLean assigns the descriptive name of "visceral brain" to it. C. J. Herrick indicated years ago (1933) that the old rhinencephalon or nose brain is not merely a central receptor for smells, but a "non-specific activator for all cortical activity, memory, learning, and affectivity." It becomes clear from MacLean's work that this ancient brain, much of which lies in the depths of the temporal lobe, has an extensive relationship with both the neopallium and the hypothalamus; in this way it constitutes a crossroad or association area for both internally and externally derived perceptual processes: that is, for those arising from the eye, the ear, the body wall, the apertures, the genitals, and the viscera, all reaching the temporal lobe via the diencephalon. (Smell, on the other hand, reaches it directly.) Here, then, in the depths of the temporal lobe with its intricate connections (the "visceral brain"), is a crossroad where the multipolar functions of the symbolic process can be integrated. This does not mean that the temporal lobe alone mediates all symbolic functions, but rather that the "visceral brain" constitutes a mechanism for integrating the external and internal environments of the central nervous system, the past and the present, the phylogenetically and ontogenetically old and new. Thus it is through the "visceral brain" that the "gut" components of memory are able to enter into our psychological processes, and it is precisely here that the multipolar areas of reference of symbolic function can be served. It is through these mechanisms that we are able both to project and to introject, and it is because these central structures serve the multipolarity of symbolic function that the central nervous organ can mediate the translation into somatic disturbance of those tensions which are generated on the level of psychological experience. It is this "visceral brain," then, which may be essential for psychosomatic relationships, as they confront us clinically.

5

THE FUNDAMENTAL NATURE OF THE DISTINCTION BETWEEN NORMALITY AND NEUROSIS

INTRODUCTION

The present paper offers a hypothesis concerning the essential difference between normal and neurotic psychological processes. I have made several previous attempts to present this hypothesis, but unfortunately those earlier formulations contained ambiguities which caused the hypothesis to be misunderstood. I have, however, profited from the resulting discussion and correspondence with my colleagues, and I hope that the hypothesis has similarly benefited. I therefore begin by acknowledging my indebtedness to colleagues upon whose kindness I have imposed with reprints, manuscripts, and lengthy letters, and whose friendly, challenging, and skeptical comments have been invaluable. Among these are Frank Beach, John Benjamin, Margaret Brenman, Merton Gill, Molly R. Harrower, Heinz Hartmann, Robert Knight, Ernst Kris, Bertram D. Lewin, Rudolph Loewenstein, Sydney Margolin, David Rapaport, Fredrick C. Redlich, and René Spitz. There are others, of course, but these are the ones I have pestered with least mercy, and who have been endlessly patient in giving me the benefit of their criticisms. I cannot ask them to share responsibility for any of my suggestions, but certainly they have contributed greatly to any value the hypothesis may have.

First published in *The Psychoanalytic Quarterly*, 23:167-204, 1954. Reprinted by permission of *The Psychoanalytic Quarterly*.

In later papers I will trace the implications of this hypothesis for various related problems, such as the genetic
hypothesis, the neurotic distortion of instinctual sources of
behavior, the neurotic distortion of the emotional components
in psychopathology, the neurotic distortion of the symbolic
process itself, and the secondary variations in the neurotic
state as it occurs in the adult human being. Here, however, I
will limit myself to a presentation of a conception of the
essential difference between health and neurosis in general.

I. A COMPARISON OF THE NUCLEAR AND HOLISTIC
APPROACHES TO THE DISTINCTION BETWEEN
HEALTH AND ILLNESS

Understanding behavior, whether sick or healthy, implies
an understanding of all the many forces that converge to start
it, to keep it going, to steer its course, and to obstruct or stop
it—plus an understanding of all its consequences, primary,
secondary, and so on. The pursuit of such an all-embracing
goal, however, would carry us away from and not toward the
object of this inquiry. Here we are asking not what are all the
differences between sick and healthy human behavior, but
which among these is the essential difference, the quality the
presence of which is the *sine qua non* of health, and the
absence or distortion of which is the *sine qua non* of illness.

This question is equally important in distinguishing between organic health and organic illness in which, as in the
neuroses, an inclusive characterization of illness requires more
than a list of symptoms. It reaches back into the origins of
illness; to the variations, for example, in vulnerability among
different individuals, and the influences of socioeconomic and
biochemical factors on such vulnerability. It includes states of
potential and subclinical illness, during which even for years
there may be no external manifestations of the disease. At the
other pole, it encompasses the secondary and tertiary consequences of illness for the patient, for his family, and for society, including the results not only of the active process, but
also of the residual defects that may follow the active phase of

disease. Although this inclusive concept of disease embraces every sociological implication, we cannot substitute such considerations for a precise understanding of the specific nature of disease. Indeed, although culturally useful, the holistic approach makes scientific precision difficult. For instance, is a patient who suffers from subclinical hypothyroidism sick or well? What of a man with a minor insulin deficiency which has not yet produced manifest symptoms and who does not yet need insulin from external sources? What about someone who is incubating an infectious disease, before the symptoms of illness appear? He may feel well, yet be more dangerous to others than when his illness finally becomes manifest, so that one could say that he is individually well and socially sick. What about someone who cannot develop a lasting immunity to a particular strain of pneumococcus or streptococcus, and who may suffer from repeated attacks of scarlet fever or of pneumonia? Between the episodes of acute infection, and while he carries in himself the potentiality of specific and perhaps even fatal illness, is he sick or well? Is a man sick or well while he has a subclinical tuberculosis, without manifestations of active infection, which may have been latent for twenty or thirty years? Or what of the man with a healed tuberculosis, with a reduction in pulmonary capacity and limitation in general freedom in life, but without active infection; or of the residual paralyses of poliomyelitis?

These examples imply distinctions among the vulnerability to illness, the potentialities of illness, subclinical processes of illness, illness as a dynamic process, the many secondary symptoms of illness which in turn have tertiary and quaternary individual and social consequences, and the relatively inert residual symptoms which in turn have their own consequences. All along the road, moreover, are consequences not only for the patient but for the patient's family and for all whose lives touch his, consequences which in turn depend upon his position in the family group and in the community, and which ultimately touch the welfare of society as a whole. All of these constitute part of the total picture of disease. In the multifaceted concept of disease are many phenomenological or symptomatic differences in the concurrent biogenetic, ontogenetic, and sociocultural forces; yet none of these reveals the heart of the distinction between organic sickness and organic health.

This is recognizable as a truism for organic disease; yet analogies to each of these considerations can be recognized in the various efforts to characterize neurotic illness, in which, if we are not to become lost in a sociological fog, the same principle should govern our thinking. Indeed, precisely because psychoneurosis is the most ubiquitous of all diseases, with highly complex sociological interrelations, we have a special scientific obligation to isolate the essence of the neurotic process for study. There are complex circular relationships between neurotic symptoms and the society in which we live. These relationships produce consequences of a secondary and tertiary order without illuminating the essential distinction between psychological health and neurotic illness. I must repeat that in the present state of our knowledge the attempt to include every one of these variables in the characterization of neurotic illness will be merely confusing. As in all science, we begin by isolating the essence of what we are investigating. Ultimately, we must take all aspects of the neurotic process into consideration, but before attempting this we need a precise understanding of its intrinsic nature. Perhaps one reason why there have been so many confused and purely verbal controversies about etiology and therapy is that we have included too much in the concept of the neurotic process, before a clear working hypothesis about its essence has been accepted. We have propounded explanatory theories before deciding what we are trying to explain.

II. THE RECENT HISTORY OF EFFORTS TO DISTINGUISH BETWEEN PSYCHOLOGICAL HEALTH AND ILLNESS

PHENOMENOLOGICAL DISTINCTION

Orthodox psychiatry distinguished neurosis from health by the presence of symptoms, the "phenomenology" of the neurosis. The limitation of this differential criterion was that it overlooked the most widespread neurosis of all, namely, the neurosis expressed not in overt symptoms but in subtle distortions of character. It failed, moreover, to recognize that many diametrically opposite symptoms with dramatically contrasting consequences were remarkably interchangeable, so that the clinical appearance of a patient could change from one extreme to the other, or from symptomatic to asymptomatic forms and back again. If we fail to recognize that compulsions and phobias are reverse sides of the same medal, we shall naïvely assume that they are separate diseases with separate etiologies. The same is of course true for compulsive eating and anorexia nervosa. Or if we fail to recognize the compulsive elements in a hysterical paralysis, we shall treat a conversion symptom and a handwashing compulsion as independent and unrelated processes. If we do not realize that the symptomatic interludes between manic-depressive states, or anxiety states intervening between hypomanic attacks, can be different phases of one process of illness, we shall classify these states separately and be misled in our search for the essential differences between health and illness, and for the differences among forms of illness.

We know that a young adolescent with an obsessional inhibition toward work pays an immediate price for his neurosis, and accumulates at compound interest an increasing debt until he breaks. His brother, with an almost identical underlying neurotic process, may develop a compulsive drive to work which from early life wins him praise, distinction, honors, and an open door to many fields of activity. He will not be called upon to pay the price of his neurosis until his thirties or forties or fifties or later. The secondary differences between the consequences of these two forms of a single illness are so great that it is easy to lose sight of their essential identity.

In evaluating whether an act is a healthy one, statistical norms are of no help. It is a semantic misfortune that the word "norm," used in statistics, and the word "normal," used in speaking of health, have a common root. Cavities in the teeth and colds in the head are universal, but they are not therefore normal; nor is health itself abnormal because it is rare. It is never sufficient for the physiologist to say of the heartbeat, "I do not need to explain it, because everybody's heart beats." Similarly, it is no explanation of human behavior to say "Everybody behaves that way." Such a statement merely raises the further questions, "Does *everybody*? And if so, why *everybody*? And if not, why do some deviate?

Nor is the conformity or nonconformity of an act to any culture a differential criterion, since under appropriate circumstances both healthy and neurotic processes can produce conformity or deviation, defiance or submission. Nor is it the utility of the act, since everyday experience indicates how frequently the useful, the useless, or the destructive act can serve healthy and neurotic purposes equally. The criterion is not the comfort of the act, nor the temporary gratification derived from it, whether a simple instinctual gratification or a more complex ego satisfaction, since many patently neurotic acts can for a considerable time be both comfortable and highly gratifying. Nor is the yield in terms of pain, frustration, and deprivation a sure indication that an act is neurotic, since human beings are often called upon to face and accept and endure these for healthy reasons. It is not the pleasantness to others of an act, since amiability can be among the subtlest of neurotic symptoms. Neurotic behavior is not invariably associated with disturbances in interpersonal rapport, for the neurotic process may manifest itself in an assiduous cultivation of human ties. Certainly it is not success or failure, both of which can be determined by neurotic forces, and both of which can end in depression. It is not the sense of moral responsibility, nor the awareness of consequences, since the psychotic can be as aware as the preacher of moral issues and of the consequences of his actions. Above all, it is not a question of weakness or of strength, whether of the whole personality or of any part of it. In this connection I cannot emphasize too often a fact which ought to be obvious: that among sufferers from neurosis are those whose every moment requires a degree of self-discipline, high purpose, and courage which the healthy person is rarely called upon to exercise. Many psychologically ill human beings struggle along from moment to moment only by the expenditure of heroic strength; yet, when viewed from a distance, these same lives

may seem to be the embodiment of timidity. I frequently recall with humility and respect the little figure of a woman
whose life was so beset with multiple masked phobias that she
scurried along the street, clinging to the walls, keeping her
eyes averted from every passer-by lest she look where she
should not, haunted by fear and anxiety, her every step an act
of major heroism. In forcing herself out into the world at all
she exercised a courage I have rarely seen equaled, although
she looked and acted the role of the "wee cow'ring timorous
beastie." In our scientific formulations, therefore, we must be
constantly on guard against the clichés of those hostile to
psychiatry, who express that hostility by looking down their
noses at all who suffer from neurotic disabilities. When we
employ pseudoscientific, pseudoquantitative epithets about
strength and weakness, we are unintentionally feeding the
vanity, prejudice, ignorance, and hostility of these persons.
And certainly, in this question of "strength" we shall be far
from the essential criterion of health we are seeking.

As we proceed with our analysis of the problem, we shall
find ourselves forced to conclude that no symptomatological
differences between neurosis and normality, whether these are
described in terms of current manifest symptoms or in terms of
their consequences, can clarify the essential distinction.

Such misinterpretations of the varied consequences of different secondary symptoms of an illness have often misled
organic medicine in its efforts to isolate essential disease processes. It is quite natural, therefore, that they should confuse
both descriptive psychiatry and psychoanalysis. This is another
example of a danger to which I have already referred, the
danger of attempting to explain before we know what are the
units that require explanation.

SOCIOLOGICAL DISTINCTION

Another effort to define neurosis was in terms of its social
consequences. This might be called the "epithet" phase in the
study of the neuroses. It recognized that patterns of disturbed
behavior had many social implications. It failed to recognize
that many neurotic activities, because they are socially useful
and socially approved, or because they directly satisfy instinc-

tual hungers, may mask their neurotic nature for long periods of time and pass as "normal." Here our thinking is full of contradictions. We know that much of the valuable work of society is done by people who are sick organically or emotionally. We do not deny the existence of organic disease in a patient because he is a creative writer or painter or lawyer. But we tend to deny the existence of neurosis when the neurotic mechanisms energize socially useful activities, even though in the end the man himself, his family, and society as a whole will pay a high price for the neurotic components in his life and works. The masked neurosis, which may have seemed well tamed for years, ultimately turns to destroy us, as the animal in a circus cage may turn on his keeper (Kubie, 1951). Innumerable tragic examples of this are to be found in science, literature, art, politics, and economics. Indeed, it happens subtly every day in times of peace. In war it happens with melodramatic impact. Concealed neuroses have enabled and sometimes forced sick men to wear the mask of heroism, flying when this meant the destruction not only of themselves and of their planes, but of their companions as well (Kubie et al., 1946). Their masked neuroses have often compelled sick men in the merchant marine to go back to sea, even when they had been assured that they had already done more than their share, and even when going back to sea meant that they would endanger not only their own lives but also the lives of others (Margolin et al., 1943; Margolin and Kubie, 1944). In peace and in war there are as many sick ways of being a "do-gooder" as of being a "do-badder," of being a clergyman as of being a criminal, and although the consequences to society are different, the consequences to the individual and to his family may be surprisingly similar. Therefore the fact that work and its products have value, or that men are "brave" or "virtuous," should never be confused with the nature of the dynamic processes within the individual that ultimately determine the health or sickness of an act or of a whole life.

The distinction is between the manifest clinical neurosis and the neurotic process, which can be concealed "asymptomatically" within the personality as a whole. It should not be forgotten that of these two it is the second that in the long run is usually the more destructive. The clinically manifest neurosis hurts chiefly the patient, and consequently he himself usually seeks help without outside pressure (Kubie, 1951). For this reason he is accessible to efforts at therapy. But that aspect of the neurotic process that is concealed in the personality tends to cause suffering chiefly to others. Therefore such a person usually tries to defend the aspect of his neurosis that is expressed in his whole way of life. In such a case, it is society or the person's family that tries to maneuver the reluctant patient into therapy in an effort to protect itself from the destructive effects of his concealed character neurosis. Precisely because such a neurosis causes pain to others rather than to himself, the person rarely seeks treatment for it and, once in treatment, he is most resistant. Clearly, therefore, mere acquiescence in treatment is a useful distinction between two forms of the neurotic process, but it is not (as Redlich has suggested [1952]) a criterion for a distinction between neurosis and health. A man with a hand-washing compulsion seeks treatment. A man with a compulsive drive to work rejects treatment, yet in spite of outstanding contributions and success may end in depression and suicide. From the social point of view the first is sick, the second well. From the point of view of scientists who are trying to understand the essential mechanisms of human conduct, the second is as sick as the first. Many lives could be used to demonstrate that neither the social value of a life nor its accessibility to treatment contributes to our understanding of the essential distinction we are seeking.

ONTOGENETIC DISTINCTION

A third approach to this distinction has been ontogenetic or historical. This approach has passed in recent decades through three periods, the Kraepelinian, the Meyerian, and the psychoanalytic (this volume, Chapter 3).

1. The Kraepelinian psychiatrist concerned himself primarily with an attempt to reconstruct the history of a patient's symptoms. The fallacy of this approach has already been indicated.

2. The Meyerian psychobiologist assembled a more inti-

mate and more inclusive history of significant milestones and patterns in a patient's life. This inquiry included in its scope the personality as a whole, but it was based almost solely on anamnestic material of which the patient and his family were conscious.

3. The analytic approach added the history of the patient's unconscious as well as conscious psychological development; it attempted to trace the ontogeny of health and illness through the development of various components of the personality and its psychic processes, emphasizing especially those of which the patient was unconscious. At different stages in analytic theory, the analyst has emphasized the developmental history of instincts, of the superego, and of the ego. These types of development came to be treated as converging streams, altered by their own interactions and by the constant interplay of such processes as fixations, regressions, identifications, and incorporations. This approach has marked a significant advance, but it has suffered from the same basic limitation as beset the two less sophisticated preceding efforts: it failed first to establish as its working hypothesis a recognizable distinction between psychological illness and psychological health. That is precisely what I will try to do in this paper; I will attempt to characterize that deformation of psychological processes which I believe to be the essence of nonorganic, dynamic psychopathology in the adult human being. I must also point out that in this communication I will not try to explain how or why this deformation occurs.

III. A Review of Previous Steps in the Development of the Hypothesis

To eliminate earlier ambiguities and to make clear the present form of my hypothesis, it will be necessary to trace briefly the steps by which it developed.

In "A Critical Analysis of the Concept of a Repetition Compulsion" (Kubie, 1939), I summarized the internal contradictions in the concept of the repetition compulsion as it was understood at that time. I asked whether an initial or primary compulsion which leads to a neurotic act can be distinguished from a hypothetical compulsion to repeat, which presumably has an independent existence apart from the original neurotic impulsion toward the specific act. In attempting to answer this question, I pointed out (a) that in any behavior the mixture of conscious and unconscious forces that determines the form in which gratification is sought determines at the same time the flexibility or inflexibility of the behavior, and (b) that inflexibility is the essential characteristic of all neurotic manifestations in contrast to the essential flexibility of normal behavior (especially pp. 397-399). This was related to an observation previously emphasized by Brickner and Kubie (1936) that the repetition of neurotic symptoms results automatically from the fact that neurotic symptoms are in part substitutive (i.e., symbolic) gratifications which never gratify, with the inevitable consequence that *no neurotogenic conflict can heal itself merely by reaching satiation.*

The thesis was carried further in "The Repetitive Core of Neurosis" (Kubie, 1941b). Here I emphasized specifically (a) that in the human being all normal physiological and psychological processes are repetitive, (b) that such repetition is necessary primarily for survival and secondarily for all processes of learning, and (c) that neurotic repetition is distinguishable from normal repetition by the fact that neurotic repetitions are automatic and obligatory. Consequently the so-called obsessional or compulsion neurosis, and the perversions as well, can be viewed merely as transparent and self-revealing examples of the distortion of repetitiveness that characterizes all neuroses (p. 24). The paper includes a speculation about how the obligatory repetition that characterizes the neurotic process is established. I attempted to describe the differences in secondary symptoms, which result from differences in (a) the phase of development at which the obligatory mechanism is established, and (b) the primary focus of the repetitive mechanism; this focus may be the instinctual processes themselves, their secondary derivatives, or their affective reactions.

In "The Neurotic Potential and Human Adaptation" (Kubie, 1949), I challenged the sociologist's attempt to use "adaptation" to differentiate between neurosis and normality, and made an effort to distinguish primary (i.e., essential) from secondary differences between psychological normality and psychological illness. I pointed out that everything characteristic of the neurotic process can be deduced as a consequence of the domination of behavior by unconscious processes. "Whenever most of the determining psychological forces are conscious, the resulting conduct will merit being called normal.... On the other hand, where unconscious processes dominate or where conscious and unconscious forces pursue incompatible goals, then the behavior which results will deserve to be called neurotic . . ." (p. 91). It is unfortunate that I mentioned only conscious and unconscious processes, and made no reference to the role of preconscious processes; yet even in this initial incomplete formulation the fallacy usually attributed to it does not appear. The formulation makes no claim that "conscious behavior is normal and unconscious behavior neurotic." It is concerned exclusively with the accessibility to consciousness of the forces that produce behavior.

In the third chapter of *Practical and Theoretical Aspects of Psychoanalysis* (Kubie, 1950a), the formulation is again confined to the dichotomy between the relative roles of conscious and unconscious processes in the determination of behavior.

In "The Neurotic Potential, the Neurotic Process, and the Neurotic State" (Kubie, 1951), the theoretical formulation took several steps forward. (a) For the first time it was explicitly stated that at the present stage of our understanding we should limit ourselves to an effort to characterize the state of health of a single act or moment of life, and not the normality or neurosis of an entire personality. (b) Those characteristics that are not universally present in normality, or that do not characterize all neurotic processes, were contrasted with those features that are universally characteristic either of the one or of the other. (c) Again it was emphasized that every act is a mixture of both the normal and the neurotic, in that every act results from a mixture of psychological forces, that is, from a "continuous interplay of conscious and unconscious forces." There it was explicitly stated, however, that this is a deliberate oversimplification, and that preconscious forces also play an important role in all psychological processes, especially in the economies and intuitive leaps of mental processes. (d) Another consideration introduced briefly and for the first time concerned the role of the symbolic process, using the concept of the symbolic process in a broadly inclusive sense. It was pointed out that in the creative uses of symbolic processes, preconscious and conscious forces play the dominant role, whereas in the neurotic distortions of the symbolic process, unconscious forces play the dominant role. (e) All human beings who are not mentally defective are capable of making condensations of experience, of developing abstractions from these condensations, and then of representing these abstractions by appropriate symbols. Because the symbolic process is vulnerable to distortion through processes of repression, these two processes together constitute the essence of the neurotic potential universal among human beings. Out of this universal neurotic potential the neurotic process evolves gradually and progressively, and in turn the fully developed neurotic state crystallizes out of the neurotic process episodically under circumstances of special stress.

Thus the neurotic potential is a universal and inevitable human phenomenon highly charged with possibilities of good and evil. The neurotic process, which arises out of this inescapable neurotic potential, has affective components which man shares with lower animals. Peculiar to man, however, is the symbolic process in its full development and with its specific distortions. It is the symbolic process that makes possible our highest cultural and creative potential; yet at the same time it is through a distortion of the symbolic process that the neurosis evolves. For the most part this neurosis is subtly concealed and disguised until some situation or event arises which unmasks it and precipitates the fully developed neurotic state.

This thesis was further developed in "Problems and Techniques of Psychoanalytic Validation and Progress" (Kubie, 1952b, pp. 48-52, 91-99). Here I drew attention to the fact that every symbolic unit represents simultaneously an inner and an outer world, so that the symbol itself forms the essential link between these two psychological worlds, a fact which in turn has a profound influence upon all neurotic, psychotic, and psychosomatic developments (this volume, Chapter 4).

Finally, in "The Distortion of the Symbolic Process in Neurosis and Psychosis" (this volume, Chapter 3), I summarized earlier psychiatric and psychoanalytic approaches to the distinction between normality and neurosis and between neurosis and psychosis, and gave a more detailed discussion of the differences in the roles of conscious, preconscious, and unconscious symbolic processes in the production of neurotic, creative, and normal behavior. Here the bipolarity of the symbolic process was used as the basis for a distinction between neurosis and psychosis, and for an explanation of psychosomatic phenomena.

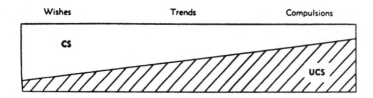

FIGURE 1 (from Kubie, 1952b, p. 93). Every human thought or feeling or act or pattern of living falls somewhere along such a diagram as this. The technical and quantitative problem is to determine where. It will be noted that the diagram indicates that there are no acts in which Ucs. processes play no role, and none which are devoid of Cs. determinants. If this is true, then in all probability the ends of the scale are theoretical abstractions.

These diagrams are not to be taken literally. They are designed, rather, to illustrate, and I hope to clarify, the evolution of a concept. Figure 1 is an artificially oversimplified picture of the concurrent interplay of conscious and unconscious processes in any one moment of experience and behavior.

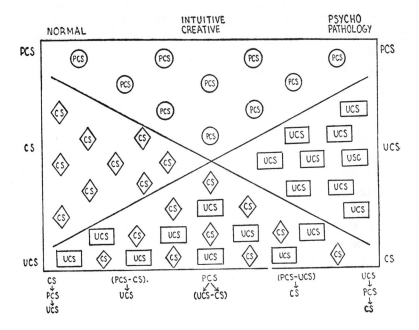

FIGURE 2. Figure 2 is an effort to present diagrammatically the subtle and complex state of affairs as they probably exist in the state of nature; i.e., human nature, in which the concurrent role of preconscious processes frees our psychic apparatus and more specifically our symbolic processes from their rigid anchorage. At the conscious end this anchorage is to fixed and literal relationships to external reality. At the unconscious end there is if anything an even more rigid anchorage to unreality, i.e., where unconscious symbolic relationships predominate and as long as they remain under repression are unmodifiable even by experience. The flexible and creative contribution from the concurrent play of preconscious processes is illustrated in this diagram, which has an unavoidable complexity reminiscent of the Nomograms which the late L. J. Henderson used to represent the concurrent change of many mutually interdependent constituents of the blood stream.

IV. The Essential Difference between Health and Neurosis

Every human act, thought, feeling, and impulse can, under appropriate circumstances, be normal or be neurotic. What difference, then, can indicate when an act is the one and when it is the other? I emphasize that only after this differentiation can be made with respect to single moments of human behavior will it be possible cautiously to apply the same principle to patterns of general conduct, then to personalities as a whole, and finally perhaps to whole cultures.

Let me repeat what I have previously emphasized. Not one of the qualities popularly associated with the idea of neurosis is an invariable concomitant or cause or result of the neurotic process (Kubie, 1949). One quality, however, is constant and sets a normal act apart from one that is a manifestation of the neurotic process. This is not a judgment of value, but rather a clinical description of that one attribute of behavior common to every neurotic action and absent from every normal act. If we are to understand the difference between the two, it is essential to keep this characteristic clearly in mind. This clinically derived distinguishing trait centers on the freedom and flexibility to learn through experience, to change, and to adapt to changing external circumstances. Thus the essence of normality is flexibility, in contrast to the freezing of behavior into patterns of unalterability that characterizes every manifestation of the neurotic process, whether in impulses, purposes, acts, thoughts, or feelings. *Whether or not a behavioral event is free to change depends not upon the quality of the act itself, but upon the nature of the constellation of forces that has produced it. No moment of behavior can be looked upon as neurotic unless the processes that have set it in motion predetermine its automatic repetition irrespective of the situation, the utility, or the consequences of the act.* This may be the most basic lesson about human conduct that has been learned from psychoanalysis. Let me repeat: no single psychological act can be looked upon as neurotic unless it is the product of processes that predetermine a tendency to its automatic repetition. Whenever this occurs, under whatever culture or circumstances, the neurotic process will be found at work.[1] This, then, is my working hypothesis concerning the

---

[1] Certain organic deformations of the central nervous system can determine automatic repetitiveness (Brickner, 1940; Penfield, 1952; Kubie, 1953a); furthermore, biochemical processes may contribute to stereotyped repetitions or may release latent repetitive patterns. One can cite the tedious repetitive liturgies of the

essential distinction between an act that is healthy and an act that is neurotic. In the unstable equilibrium among the many psychological and physiological processes that determine all psychological functions, what types of disturbance can determine this tendency to stereotyped and automatic repetition?

The answer I suggest is that wherever an alliance of the conscious and preconscious systems predominates in the production of behavior, the resultant behavior will come to rest either when its goal is achieved and satiety is attained, or when the goal is found to be unattainable or ungratifying or both, whereupon the effort ceases. Thus such behavior never becomes either insatiable or stereotyped. It can be altered by the experience of success and failure, of rewards and punishments, of pleasure and pain. It can be used to test reality and it can be tested against reality. It is therefore anchored in reality, yet it remains freely flexible. On the contrary, whenever the unconscious system (or perhaps an alliance between the preconscious and unconscious systems) predominates, the resultant action must be repeated endlessly. This occurs because its goals are predominantly unconscious symbols, and unconscious symbolic goals are never attainable. Since the predominant forces are unconscious, they will not be responsive to the experience of pleasure or of pain, or to rewards and punishments, or to logical argument — neither to the logic of events nor to any appeals to mind or heart. The behavior that results from a dominance of the unconscious system has the insatiability, the automaticity, and the endless repetitiveness that are the stamp of the neurotic process, whether this expresses itself through overt neurotic symptoms, or through art forms, or through subtle deformations of those general patterns of behavior that constitute the personality.

If we generalize from this to a concept of health in a still broader sense, extrapolating from isolated moments of

---

alcoholic, and the similar actions that occur under the influence of barbiturates and in hypoglycemic states. Such clinical phenomena indicate that automatic repetitiveness is a disturbance of function in which organic and psychological processes converge. This interaction of organic and psychological processes constitutes a crossroad which merits more systematic interdisciplinary investigation than it has ever received.

behavior to patterns and to personalities, we may say that a state of greater health is achieved whenever those areas of life that are dominated by inaccessibly unconscious forces are shrunk, so that a larger area of life is dominated by conscious or preconscious forces, which can come to awareness when necessary. This is a reasonable concept of health and a reasonable formulation of the goal of therapy, leaving ample room for the creative economies of intuitive, preconscious functioning. This conception makes it possible to understand how psychoanalytic therapy may enable the preconscious processes of the artist and scientist to operate freely and creatively, since with successful therapy they will no longer be warped and blocked by forces that emanate from unconscious conflicts. In this way the hypothesis makes clear how unconscious conflicts (that is to say, neurotogenic conflicts) distort both conscious and preconscious functions in all creative processes, whether scientific, literary, artistic, or humorous, and in dreams and psychological illness.

To recapitulate, I should say that on pragmatic grounds we are justified in calling "normal" any act in the determination of which the alliance of conscious and preconscious forces plays the dominant role, that is, forces that are accessible on need; whereas on the same grounds we are justified in calling abnormal or unhealthy or neurotic any act in the determination of which unconscious processes are dominant (whether alone or in an alliance with the preconscious), because such forces will predetermine its automatic repetition irrespective of its suitability to the immediate situation or its immediate or remote consequences. I repeat that this is not to say that the conscious or preconscious process in itself is normal and the unconscious process in itself abnormal, any more than one can say that a pathogenic bacterium is in itself either normal or abnormal. We deal here with a complex constellation of biological, psychological, and cultural forces, all operating on conscious, preconscious, and unconscious levels, in a state of continuous unstable equilibrium. On different occasions any one act may be precipitated out of this dynamic and unstable equilibrium as the expression of endlessly varied mixtures of forces, which are both cultural and instinctual in origin. It is

the composition of the mixture that determines whether the
resultant act will meet our pragmatic criterion of health or
illness.

V. What This Hypothesis Does Not Mean

So that we can approach a consideration of this hypothesis
free from past misunderstandings, let me list some of the
implications it does *not* entail.

1. It does not imply that a psychological act that is conscious is normal and one that is unconscious is abnormal.
Indeed, since we can never be conscious of more than a small
fragment of what we are doing at any moment, such a statement would constitute a misuse of the terms. Around the
fringes of consciousness there is an incessant play of symbolic
automatisms. These are the economizing psychological processes by which we execute all the shortcuts that are essential
to thinking and feeling. They are not merely the seven-league
boots by which we take rare, inspired, intuitive leaps; rather,
they constitute a major component in any moment of thinking, talking, feeling, and action. Consequently, although it is
never possible for us to measure precisely how much of any
psychological moment is taking place on a conscious, preconscious, or unconscious level, we can be sure that the conscious
part is never more than the public representative of a background of mental activity which includes a broad but dimly
perceived preconscious fringe; beyond this in turn hangs the
iron curtain that obscures all concomitant unconscious component processes. This fact is well known, generally accepted,
yet often overlooked. The implication relevant here is that the
distinction we are drawing between normal and neurotic
depends not on the level of consciousness on which an act
occurs, but on the level of consciousness on which those forces
operate that determine the act. An act may be normal or
neurotic whether it occurs in a state of full consciousness, or in
sleep, or in any other state of partial or dissociated consciousness, such as a trance. The distinction depends not upon
whether the final act is conscious, preconscious, or uncon-

scious, but on whether the processes that in alliance determine the act are preponderantly conscious and preconscious, or preponderantly unconscious. The distinction is thus dynamic and not purely descriptive.

This use of the concept of levels of consciousness is an extension of Freud's earlier concern with conscious, preconscious, and unconscious "levels" as organized systems. It implies that within each of the systems, conscious, preconscious, and unconscious, there is a tendency for all the component processes, whatever their various origins, to combine and operate together. In itself this assumption constitutes an important starting point for objective investigations.

2. Related to this is another misunderstanding, the implication that our hypothesis leaves out of account the importance of all intuitive, economizing, "preconscious" functions. I grant, of course, that this misunderstanding arose partly from the ambiguities of my earlier formulations, since I omitted from some of them any reference to the role of preconscious processes. I did this partly to simplify the presentation, and partly because I assumed that it would be obvious that when I spoke of conscious processes I had in mind the conscious-preconscious alliance. As a result of this omission my early formulations sounded as though I had in mind a simple interplay of conscious and unconscious forces. Certainly no one interested in the creative process, whether in science or in the arts or humanities, could leave preconscious processes out of consideration (Kris, 1952, especially Chapter 14).

3. The hypothesis does not assume a homogeneous determination of any moment of behavior. For instance, it allows for the observable fact that even when someone is functioning under the domination of unconscious forces, conscious and preconscious processes are helping to shape many of the secondary symptomatic manifestations of the neurosis. It recognizes similarly that when conscious processes alone or a conscious-preconscious alliance dominates, unconscious processes play a significant subsidiary role in the energizing and shaping of behavior. Consequently, an implication latent in Freud's original formulation becomes explicit in this hypothesis: unconscious forces become destructive only when they play a preponderant role in the determination of behavior.

4. Our hypothesis implies neither that an obsessional, introspective self-consciousness is a prerequisite for normality, nor that the well-analyzed initiate is entitled to look down his well-analyzed nose at the rest of the world from Olympian heights, with a preposterous assumption that he has full insight into his every motivation at every moment. Rather, it implies an analytic humility based upon a full acknowledgment of the impossibility of knowing one's own unconscious to such an extent. The implicit ideal of normality that emerges from this hypothesis is a person in whom the creative alliance between the conscious and preconscious systems is not constantly subjected to blocking and distortion by the counterplay of preponderant unconscious forces, whether in the prosaic affairs of daily life, in human relations, or in creative activity. Here is no unreal fantasy of a "normal" person out of whom all the salty seasoning of secondary unconscious motivations has been dissolved.

5. Nor does the hypothesis imply that in order to be healthy we must be self-consciously aware either of our every act or of our every purpose, but rather that the predominant forces must be accessible to introspection on need. To paraphrase what Freud said about the therapeutic shift in the relationship between the id and the ego, where the unconscious was, there the conscious and the preconscious must be. What was unconscious, whether from the first or as the result of repressive processes, must become accessible enough to self-inspection to become conscious when needed. This implies a change from the repressed, dynamic unconscious to the preconscious fringe. The healthy integration of psychological processes requires that they should be accessible to self-inspection on need, and not that they should be continuously in the center and forefront of consciousness.

6. Previous misunderstandings on this point force me to add one other obvious warning. The hypothesis does not imply that the only normal person is an analyst or someone who has been analyzed. The insight that successful analysis can yield is like infinity itself. It is an ideal which can be approached but never reached. Therefore the acquisition of insight, like education, is a process never finished. Insight is a point on a continuous, never-ending scale; it is relative and not absolute.

The struggle for insight goes on throughout life, demanding constant vigilance; and because it requires a continuous struggle, the possession of it never becomes an occasion for complacency. The man who knows himself in depth in doing so acknowledges with proper humility the impossibility of knowing himself fully, and the importance of striving constantly to maintain and deepen his insight. Concurrently, the more fully he approaches self-awareness, the more coherent and integrated become the various components of his personality. Insight therefore confers a modest right to trust impulses and intuitions. In this way, self-knowledge brings freedom and spontaneity to the human spirit, not obsessional preoccupations with oneself.

VI. Consideration of Various Objections and Criticisms

From many discussions of this hypothesis, I select for consideration the following doubts, criticisms, and objections.

A. Dr. Redlich, in personal communications and one published article (1952), has raised three important questions.

1. We have no methods for measuring quantitative differences in the relative roles of conscious, preconscious, and unconscious components in determining behavior. Is it not therefore premature or even unjustifiable to base our hypothesis on the assumption that such differences play a part in the process?

This is a useful question. I have pointed out elsewhere that in efforts to describe and explain complex phenomena quantitative concepts are often misused to oversimplify elusive problems (this volume, Chapter 1). This misuse does not, however, arise merely from a lack of measuring instruments, but rather from failure to characterize accurately the nature of the forces in which one assumes quantitative variations. Science has often moved forward by the help of quantitative assumptions long before those assumptions could be experimentally confirmed. In the mathematical approach to nuclear physics, for example, each advance began with the assumption that in a mixture of physical forces some one physical unit has increased or decreased with respect to some one specific physical characteristic. On the basis of such assumptions, it was possible to predict results before techniques had been devised to measure them. The assumption that, in an interplay of several forceful psychological processes, the dominant influence can shift back and forth among the conscious, preconscious, and unconscious systems is a similar working hypothesis, and as such is equally justified.

2. Dr. Redlich's next objection runs counter to basic psychoanalytic data. He writes (1952, p. 562) that "unconscious conflicts and their components, particularly ego defenses, are not necessarily pathological [pathogenic?], but in certain instances maximally adapted." The implications of this objection seem to challenge the cornerstone of psychoanalytic psychology, Freud's assumption that unconscious conflicts are the dynamic pathogenic force in neurosis. That some unconscious processes are not pathogenic is conceivable only if we make two further assumptions: that some processes owe their being unconscious to causes other than internal conflict, and that such processes can influence behavior without coming into conflict with conscious and preconscious processes. How this harmony is preordained is hard to conceive.

Dr. Redlich implicitly assumes more than this, however. He not only assumes the existence of unconscious *processes* that can influence behavior without coming into conflict with conscious and preconscious purposes; he also assumes that there may be unconscious *conflicts* that are not laden with conflict and hence are nonpathogenic. I cannot help feeling that this is a logical, psychological, and even semantic impossibility. If any psychological processes are at the same time unconscious and laden with conflict, they must have been the seat of a psychic struggle which has given rise to repression, dissociation, and the return of the repressed in symbolic form. This is the familiar sequence in the formation of neurotic symptoms. On the other hand, any unconscious conflicts that, in accordance with Redlich's assumption, were not pathogenic could not produce any symbolic manifestations. This being true, there could never be an opportunity to study them, whether analytically or otherwise, If they have produced no neurotic symptoms, personality disturbances, or other indirect symbolic manifestations, how could they make known their existence?

Actually I believe that this objection is a by-product of an *ad hoc* hypothesis, which was created for a quite different and worthy purpose, to bolster the argument that not all hidden depths of the personality are malevolent, and that they may even be artistically and culturally creative. I agree fully with this sound position, but, as Kris has indicated (1952, especially Chapter 14), it is more soundly and adequately supported simply by an adequate recognition of the role of preconscious processes in creative thinking. I believe that the hypothesis I am advocating provides a better framework for an understanding of the creative process than is implicit in Dr. Redlich's objection. We do not need the assumption that unconscious conflicts can be nonpathogenic to understand the creative role of the preconscious facets of the personality.

3. Dr. Redlich objects that my hypothesis implies a judgment of value. This is an error. The objection arises out of a misconception, shown in Redlich's misstatement that I maintain that only "rational conscious and deliberate acts" can be normal. Even in my earliest, faulty formulations I never made any such statement nor entertained such an idea. From the first, my hypothesis has been that acts are normal when their preponderant determining processes are not in the unconscious system. Normal acts may be impulsive, intuitive, trancelike, automatic, unreflective, or even dreamed. My point has always been that the critical difference lies not in the act, but in the nature of its origins. This is not a judgment of "value" of an act, but a pragmatic estimate of the implications and effects of the forces which produce it.

B. Dr. Margaret Brenman, in a personal communication (1952), raises three questions.

1. She asks whether the apparent "healthiness" of a group of underprivileged and undereducated young women, whom she had studied, would come under this definition. She has the impression that their "healthiness" is due not so much to the fact that they can "become aware of unconscious forces when

necessary" as to the fact that they possess "sufficient internal resilience so that they are able with a minimal expenditure of energy to make internal reorganizations as needed, so that the essential balance of the impulse-defense-adaptation functions is maintained. . . . In other words," she continues, "I have the impression that the defensive and synthetic functions of the ego may work very well while remaining largely unconscious. I am saying, therefore, that it seems to me that the criterion of *'accessibility to consciousness when necessary'* may not be the crucial variable in normality."

Her first objection stands or falls on her implied concept of "healthiness." If we were to accept freedom from symptoms and comfort under restricting conditions as adequate criteria of health, then these undereducated and underprivileged girls would pass as healthy. A more crucial test would be the extent to which their capacity to adapt to varying circumstances proved to be dependent on the relative roles of conscious, preconscious, and unconscious forces in their daily adaptation. This question would put my hypothesis to a crucial test.

2. Closely related to this is Dr. Brenman's next objection, that the "synthetic function" of the ego may operate unconsciously. To answer this, we must disentangle a verbal confusion. In the first place, as used here, "synthesis" is only a metaphor, a figure of speech to describe in approximate terms not one process but one outcome of many. In this sense, synthesis may more accurately be called a goal toward which the whole personality strives. It is not a distinct process operated by the ego or any other partial aspect of the personality. We cannot accurately talk of synthesis as being conscious or unconscious. We can talk of conscious and unconscious only with respect to the several processes that may or may not mediate synthesis. The ego (if indeed the ego is the culprit) is guilty of at least as many sick syntheses as healthy ones. All psychopathology is a synthesis. Whether any synthetic end product of psychological (i.e., ego?) functioning turns out to be sick or well depends predominantly on the relative roles of the preconscious-conscious as opposed to the unconscious systems in producing such a synthesis. Therefore I ask Dr. Brenman to go back to those same girls and to study the

processes that entered into whatever kinds and degree of so-called "syntheses" they attained, comparing them specifically with respect to the relative roles played by the three basic dynamic systems in producing these syntheses. If these girls are in reality as healthy as Dr. Brenman believes, I confidently expect her to find that they had dealt with their instinctual conflicts predominantly on a conscious-preconscious level, with minimal repression. If this is true, the method by which the "synthetic" results had been attained would go far to demonstrate the validity of my hypothesis.

3. Her third question concerns the "accessibility of normally unconscious functions in schizophrenia." She suggests that perhaps among some schizophrenics the accessibility of data that are "normally" (here she means not "normally" but "usually") unconscious is not limited to any such qualification as the "necessity" of such data, but may occur even when they are "unnecessary," and that in fact some other factor may render this insight nonfunctional in the total equilibrium of the personality. This question was raised by Dr. Hartmann also, in personal communications.

It is hard to answer this objection because the phenomenon to which Dr. Brenman refers has been too imperfectly observed and never fully recorded for adequate study (Schilder, 1942). My own unpublished data indicate that the apparent insight of some schizophrenic patients shows the same fragmented discontinuity as do the rest of their conceptual processes, with the result that it never succeeds in placing the conscious-preconscious systems in a dominant position among their psychological processes. If so, the core of my hypothesis remains unaffected.

There is, however, a more basic answer to Drs. Brenman and Hartmann. In the first place, my hypothesis does not stand or fall on the therapeutic efficacy of insight in influencing pathological dissociations. It stands, rather, on the differences observable between behavior the shaping of which is dominated by the conscious-preconscious system and behavior dominated by the unconscious system. The intricate problems centering on the question of the therapeutic efficacy of insight induced by therapy have only a derivative relationship to these differences. This is true whether we are considering the treatment of the neuroses or of the schizophrenias. Indeed, our knowledge of the processes by which the acquisition of insight during psychotherapy brings psychological processes under the domination of the conscious-preconscious system is still too incomplete for a full discussion of this issue. We know that neither in the neuroses nor in the psychoses does insight always or automatically produce control by the conscious-preconscious system. My hypothesis is that normality of behavior depends upon the control of behavior by the conscious-preconscious alliance. It does not necessarily follow that, once this control has been lost to the unconscious, the regaining of insight into these processes will always automatically shift the balance of control back to the conscious-preconscious alliance. This in fact is one of the unresolved problems of psychotherapy, and it is a problem in the psychotherapy of the neuroses quite as much as of schizophrenia.

C. Dr. David Rapaport, in a personal communication (1952), points out that consciousness is "a very important but very limited and specific characteristic of mental processes," and that there are, in normal persons, as many conscious processes that distort reality as there are unconscious and preconscious processes that represent reality correctly.

Here again we find an objection based on a recurrent misunderstanding which should by now have been clarified. A delusion or hallucination is conscious but distorts reality and is hardly normal. As I have repeatedly said, I am not concerned with the state or degree of consciousness of any mental act, but with the relative roles of the conscious-preconscious system as opposed to the unconscious system in its determination.

D. Dr. Molly R. Harrower raises no objections, but proposes to test the hypothesis by applying it to a single perceptual act. In a personal communication (1952) she writes: "I wonder whether it could be shown that a perception, which in itself is a psychological act, could ever be determined predominantly by unconscious forces, with the result that it would not be modifiable by forces which carried the suggestion to change. And as a consequence could such a perception deviate sufficiently from perceptual processes in similar previous experiences, so that it could be spoken of as bizarre or showing unrealistic forms?" Dr. Harrower then shows how this might be tested by giving three possible answers to one of the more familiar of the Rorschach ink blots. She also suggests ways in which the Szondi test can be used for experimentation along the same lines.

E. Dr. Heinz Hartmann raised several questions in a personal communication (1952).

1. Is it possible to classify an isolated action as healthy or unhealthy, or must this issue depend rather on its "functional position in the inner or outer environment"? Do we "have to add the genetic viewpoint to the cross-sectional approach in order to find an answer" to this?

I answer that this implied objection does not meet my hypothesis head on. As I have said, an individual act is neurotic when the processes which have converged to produce it predetermine its obligatory repetition, irrespective of need or function or environmental circumstances, or success or failure, reward or punishment, or other considerations of reality. This hardly leaves the psychogenetic point of view out of consideration, since every one of these converging processes has a relevant genetic prehistory. Genetic considerations are essential to understanding how these forces came into being and the forms they took. Genetic considerations do not, however, determine such distinctions, whether between good and bad or sick and well.

2. "What is the relationship between the accessibility of unconscious conflict and the integration of insight? Is consciousness the only integrative process? Is it even essential to the integrative process? What of the slow spontaneous evolution and disappearance of unconscious conflicts—e.g., the spontaneous resolution of the Oedipus complex?"

This is an interesting group of interrelated questions, but no matter how one answers them they leave my hypothesis unshaken. Freud assumed that if insight is to be effectively integrated during analytic therapy, it must become conscious. Whether this is always true is of course uncertain, and this is now a matter for basic research in the psychotherapeutic process. As I pointed out in answer to Dr. Brenman, this issue, important though it is, has no direct relevance to my hypothesis concerning the essential difference between human neurosis and normality; furthermore, the possibility that under certain circumstances unconscious conflicts may resolve spontaneously has nothing to do with their capacity to produce illness before such a resolution takes place.

3. Is it universally true, as I have claimed, that "we cannot have a neurosis unless some area of important function is controlled predominantly by unconscious conflicts"; or are there other conditions that must be brought into an inclusive definition of neurosis? In reality these are two separate questions. (a) Are there other causes of psychological illness than the predominant influence of unconscious conflict? (b) Are there other influences that help to give final shape to the illness? My answer to the first question is that psychological illness (other than organic psychoses and mental deficiency) arises when there is a preponderance of unconscious forces, which themselves arise out of unconscious conflicts. It is equally certain, however, that other conditions combine to shape the ultimate neurotic picture. My argument is not that the dominance of the unconscious system alone determines every aspect of the neurotic process, but that such dominance is the *sine qua non* of neurosis.

4. Dr. Hartmann makes a distinction between those components of the unconscious system that are instinctual in origin (derived from the id), and others which he calls "the unconscious defenses of the ego." He argues further that the existence of these unconscious ego defenses makes it necessary to recognize that there may be "normative" unconscious processes. Both logically and clinically this is a *non sequitur*. If a vertebral disc slips, the short muscles along the spinal column go into a compensatory, protective, immobilizing spasm. This limits further damage, but at the same time it locks everything out of place and produces acute pain and disabling immobility. In so far as it prevents something worse this is equivalent to the "normative" function of unconscious ego defenses. Yet a process that perpetuates the very lesion that it also restricts can hardly be called "normal," whether we deal with automatic muscular spasms or unconscious ego

defenses. In fact, our daily clinical work proves that unconscious ego defenses are not "normal," since they must always be altered during therapy if a patient's character neurosis is to be cured sufficiently to allow him to attain full normality. Unconscious ego defenses, therefore, are normative only in that they prevent something worse, and thereby make possible a working adjustment within neurotically (and unconsciously) determined limits. Such defenses against an unconscious conflict are always pathogenic, even when they protect the patient from more serious disintegration. But conscious and preconscious ego defenses against a conflict dealt with on a conscious-preconscious level are fully normative, for they make true normality possible. Any other assumption contravenes fundamental psychoanalytic data and would require extensive revision of basic concepts.

5. Dr. Hartmann is disturbed by the fact that my hypothesis does not make use of the metapsychological hypothesis. He wonders whether or not this constitutes an attack upon the metapsychological elements in psychoanalytic theory. This question must be given brief consideration here, although I will deal more fully with the metapsychological issue in another paper.

Freud characterized each of the "levels" of psychological activity as a system, the conscious system (Cs), the preconscious system (Pcs), and the unconscious system (Ucs). It may be asked, however, whether Freud ever exploited the full potentialities of his own conception of three systems of dynamic psychological processes, interacting at three levels of accessibility to conscious self-inspection. In fact, soon after he had made this formulation his interest turned away from it to his metapsychological picture of the personality as divided into its sources of energy (id), its implementing mechanisms (ego), and its self-criticizing functions (superego). This was an interesting descriptive step, but unfortunately analysts have ever since tended to reject fuller utilization of the rich dynamic possibilities latent in Freud's earlier topographical concept of interacting systems of conscious, preconscious, and unconscious processes.

Dr. Hartmann's concern makes clear that no reader will be

able to bring an open mind to my hypothesis if he looks upon it is a covert attack upon the metapsychological hypothesis merely because in explaining the distinction between neurosis and health I utilize only Freud's earlier conception. This attitude tacitly assumes that unless the metapsychological formula is included in my hypothesis, either the formula or the hypothesis must be faulty. This of course does not follow at all. A full application of Freud's earlier conception of dynamic systems may relieve metapsychology of the burden of attempting to explain phenomena better understood in other terms. We can clarify the values as well as the limitations of the later metapsychological conceptions by avoiding certain fallacious applications deplored by Freud himself on more than one occasion (personal communication from Drs. Felix and Helene Deutsch, 1952).

Even if we believed that we can understand the difference between health and illness without resort to metapsychology and solely in terms of the interaction of conscious, pre-conscious, and unconscious forces, no one should conclude that we are iconoclasts. Such a belief would not imply a denial that there is pragmatic value in the "elegant" structure of metapsychological theory. It would only force us to conclude that this distinction is one for the clarification of which metapsychological concepts are superfluous. If the concept of metapsychology is useful in other areas, the elimination of any misuse of it serves only to strengthen and clarify its proper uses. With this in mind, I answer Dr. Hartmann that we should consider the possible advantages of characterizing the quintessential difference between normality and neurosis from a purely dynamic viewpoint; and that only after we have done this should we consider whether the metapsychological formula adds anything that is necessary for an adequate differentiation of the two.

Let me also point out that my hypothesis does not exclude the mechanisms ascribed to the ego by Anna Freud (1936) and others, which certainly take part in the *secondary* shaping of the neurosis. Each of these ego defenses can occur on a conscious, preconscious, or unconscious level. For instance, conscious reversal occurs every day in all conscious and deliberate efforts at suppression. Conscious identification is what we ordinarily think of as imitation, taking someone else as a model. Similar examples can be given for every defensive maneuvering of the ego. Clinical experience demonstrates that where any one of these processes operates on a conscious or preconscious level, no pathological deformation of mental processes results. These defense mechanisms produce illness only when they operate under the concomitant influence of repression, that is, when as the result of conflict they operate on an unconscious level.

F. Dr. Bertram D. Lewin, in a personal communication (1952), takes up my argument point by point, dissecting the hypothesis into several propositions, each of which he declares to be true.

1. "Conscious processes are better for health than unconscious processes—an opinion which finds approximate or special confirmation in many clinical experiences, yet which alone is not enough for a definition."

2. "Health cannot be defined negatively in terms of the absence of overt symptoms."

3. "Repression is a necessary condition for a neurosis." (Or would it be more inclusive to say "for the neurotic potential," which is comparable to a subclinical infection or to some specific vulnerability?)

4. "The overt neurosis is a breakthrough, a return of the repressed in symptomatic form. Can we then say, 'without repression there is normality?' Certainly, because of the ubiquity of latent neurotic forces, we cannot say that 'without a breakthrough there is normality.' "

5. "What then of relatively accessible conflict material, which will not break through in symptomatic distortions but will come to consciousness with insight and dominantly in the molds of the secondary processes, i.e., tested for reality. . . . Certainly inaccessibility makes for neurosis, and accessibility for health. This is a sound pragmatic statement arising out of clinical experience and gives rise to a definition from method."

6. "The idea of areas controlled predominantly by conscious processes and undistorted by unconscious conflict seems valid

and approaches Hartmann's (1939) 'conflict-free sphere of the ego.' "

VIII. Summary of the Essential Thesis

1. The essential difference between what is neurotic and what is normal can be expressed only in relation to single behavioral events. Such expression makes possible the recognition of a basic distinction, which can then be extrapolated in successive steps to include general patterns and trends of behavior, then personalities as a whole, and finally cultural patterns.

2. In the determination of any individual moment of behavior many processes are always at work concurrently and at different levels of accessibility to conscious self-scrutiny.

3. Each unitary psychological process that contributes to a resultant behavioral event (whether by helping to initiate it, to energize it, to shape it, or to sustain it) must be either conscious, preconscious, or unconscious, or must result from various combinations or alliances among these levels. No other possibilities are known to us.

4. The processes that operate on a conscious level tend to function together as a system, as do also preconscious and unconscious processes.

5. Although we lack ways of measuring the relative roles played by conscious, preconscious, and unconscious systems in the determination of any single behavioral event, clinical evidence justifies a working hypothesis that there is a continuously varying and unstable equilibrium among them. It is reasonable to expect, therefore, that means will ultimately be devised for measuring with some degree of precision the relative role of each; for clear-cut differences in effects ultimately lead to devices for measuring differences in causes.

6. At any one moment, each of these three systems of levels has many ingredients. Within each individual system the varied ingredients may have both compatible and incompatible elements. Freud's concept of the conscious, preconscious, and unconscious as dynamic systems implies that where there

is harmony within any system, the various components reinforce one another and operate as a unit. Where there is
conflict among the component forces within any system, the
forces will neutralize one another's influence, either by compromise formations or by patterns of alternating behavior which express now the one group of forces and now the
other.

7. Furthermore, theoretically at least, there can be either
harmony or conflict between any pair among the three
different systems, that is, between conscious and unconscious,
conscious and preconscious, or preconscious and unconscious.
Thus there can be either harmony or conflict both *within* each
of the three basic systems or levels of psychological forces and
between the systems. The intermediate position of preconscious forces in relation to conscious forces at one pole and to
unconscious forces at the other has never been fully explored;
this is one reason why we still lack a full understanding of the
creative processes in science and the arts (Kris, 1952, especially Chapter 14).

8. This concept makes possible a number of combinations
of forces, our knowledge of which is still incomplete. Just as it
was not known for many years how many of the theoretically
possible elements in the periodic table actually existed in
nature, so too it has not been determined how many of the
theoretically possible combinations of conscious, preconscious, and unconscious forces actually exist in human
personality. We know merely that out of these undetermined
mixtures of forces, behavior arises as varied combinations of
purposes, actions, thoughts, and feelings. Such behavior must
be either a compromise which represents the algebraic sum of
all the active forces, or, if there is an alternating predomi-
nance now by one group and now by another, the resultant
behavior patterns must represent now one group of forces and
now the opposite group, each oscillation constituting an
attempt to negate, deny, and undo the other. This restate-
ment of familiar clinical data serves only to emphasize that it
is the balance among the various warring factions, both within
the systems and among them, that plays the dominant role in
shaping behavior.

9. Through all these generalizations runs one unifying thread, which provides us with the basic distinction between normality and neurosis. This distinction does not depend upon the detailed composition of any one of the systems, whether conscious, preconscious, or unconscious, nor upon their ultimate derivation from primary instinctual processes, interacting with the demanding standards of the world, represented in the superego. It depends, rather, on the fact that whenever the conscious-preconscious alliance is dominant among the operative forces the resultant patterns of behavior, no matter how varied they may be, will have one basic characteristic in common, namely that any repetitiveness which that behavior may exhibit with respect to impulse, thought, action, or feeling, or any combination of these, will be flexible, modifiable, satiable, and under voluntary control. A dominant unconscious alliance, on the other hand, whatever its detailed composition, produces behavior that in this specific respect will have precisely opposite characteristics; it will be repetitive, obligatory, insatiable, and stereotyped. Preponderance of the unconscious system predetermines the stereotyped and automatic repetitiveness that is the sign of the neurotic process. Herein lies the essential and pathognomonic difference between normality and neurosis.

6

A RECONSIDERATION OF
THINKING, THE DREAM PROCESS,
AND "THE DREAM"

INTRODUCTION

The purpose of this communication is to focus attention not on the form and content of the dream, but on dreaming as a process. Since we make use of the same apparatus whether we are awake or asleep, the dream process in sleep and the thought process when awake must be understood together, if we hope to understand the relationship between the two. It is my thesis that both awake and asleep, there is a constant asymbolic (imageless) preconscious stream of central activity and that this preconscious stream is sampled by means of conscious symbolic representatives, by a process which in turn is vulnerable to distortion under the influence of unconscious conflicts. In essence, this is what Freud called the "topological" aspects of mentation, and therefore of dreaming.

I will make no further use of this metaphor, however, nor of certain other metaphors which appear currently in psychoanalytic writings, and which are regularly miscalled "hypotheses." Nor will I debate them in this brief paper. I will only mention the fact that the term "topological" has never seemed to me a happy one because of its static connotations. Webster defines topology as "the description of a particular place; the

First published in *The Psychoanalytic Quarterly*, 35:191-198, 1966. Reprinted by permission of *The Psychoanalytic Quarterly*.

history of a region as indicated by its topography; the configuration of a surface."

For the sake of clarity I must register one other dissent. I believe that analysts of all schools are in agreement that the dynamic interplay among the systems Cs, Pcs, and Ucs implements all human psychological processes; that they have biogenetic roots in instincts and their derivatives (the id); and that they interact with the environment through the perceptual and effector apparatus (which is the essence of Freud's original concept of the ego). There is also general agreement that the interplay among these three systems in human mentation, as well as their interactions with the environment, are guided by a continuous feedback from the value judgments of conscience and self-critique (*ego ideals*), as these are developed and influenced by the expressed or unexpressed praise or criticism of others, and by the need either to conform to or rebel against the mores of the time and place. Moreover, it is generally agreed that these interactions occur on all three levels concurrently, to make up that mosaic of Cs, Pcs, and Ucs steering devices known as the superego. About this condensed statement of a vital aspect of psychoanalytic psychology I have no reservations. It is a later step that troubles me. At a certain point, perhaps out of his earlier interests in neuroanatomy, Freud called this the "structural" aspect of human mentation. This metaphor seems to me to have been even more unfortunate and misleading than the other, because it does not increase the precision of our descriptions of mental processes, but blurs them by an inexact analogy, and also because it has no explanatory value itself. Indeed, the effort to use his analogy as an explanatory hypothesis has led us into a morass of anthropomorphic pseudo explanations.

One of many examples of how far astray this structural metaphor can lead us is found in the strained and hairsplitting distinctions, devoid of realistic clinical or theoretical differences, in Arlow and Brenner's (1964) recent book. They allude in general terms to technical innovations which they attribute to the structural hypothesis, but they cite none. Nor, indeed, does anyone else who uses the structural metaphor. It was particularly unfortunate for the development of a truly dynamic psychoanalytic psychology that Freud's formulation of the structural metaphor coincided with his turning his attention away from the dynamic role of preconscious processing.

Since these are my strong convictions, any effort to force my formulations into the framework of either the topological or the structural metaphor would only introduce confusion into my hypothesis and would be personally dishonest as well. I will therefore present my thesis without further reference to them, returning instead to Freud's earlier dynamic concepts with some extrapolation from them.

Finally, let me state explicitly that this will be an exposition of my hypothesis, not its proof.

THE HYPOTHESIS

Evidence has long been accumulating that the brain is always active, even in deep sleep, and that this activity consists of a continuous preconscious (subliminal) processing of experience—what the Würzburg School called "imageless thought" (Humphrey, 1951). (In this connection, we must bear in mind the further fact that man is never completely asleep or completely awake, that the differences between the two states are relative and not absolute, and that these two states which seem so different when superficially regarded are in fact only widely spaced bands on a more or less continuous spectrum.)

All psychological processes have afferent roots, the nature of which will be discussed below with respect to their origins and levels. But whatever their sources, and whatever the levels on which they operate, each incoming "bit" or unit or gestalt stirs the residual imprints of prior psychological events. Consequently, the ensuing flow of processing always represents a condensation of the near and far, the past and present, plus their extrapolation into the future. These make up that continuous stream of inner psychological events which—both when we are, relatively speaking, awake and in the state of relative sleep—is carried forward in time preconsciously, implemented by what the engineers call "coded signals," which are the primitive forerunners of symbol formation. This preconscious processing of data goes on unceasingly throughout all life. A study of quantitative and qualitative variations in the preconscious stream awaits psychological and physiological investigation, by means of refinements and quantifications of our qualitative use of the techniques of free association, of dream analysis, of electroencephalography, and of other methods.

During sleep this flow of preconscious processing can best be called the *"preconscious dream stream"* (or, so as to avoid confusion by clang association with Lewin's "dream screen," it might be called the "preconscious dream flow"). What is customarily spoken of as "the dream" (both in popular and scientific parlance) is in reality only a fragmentary, weighted sample of this preconscious flow: a sample expressed for the most part in multivalent and therefore condensed visual symbols. This symbolic sample (i.e., "the dream") occurs primarily if not exclusively during transitions from sleeping to waking and from waking to sleeping, and also during those partial, abortive, incomplete transitions in either direction which occur many times during sleep (Fisher, 1956; Kubie, 1950a, 1961b). Clearly, then, "the dream" bears to the preconscious dream flow the same relation that the hypnagogic reverie bears to sleepy ruminations, or that our conscious processes in the fully waking state bear to the continuous waking stream of preconscious processing. In short, all conscious processes, whether awake or asleep, are weighted symbolic samples from a stream of continuous asymbolic or imageless preconscious processes. It follows that all creative learning and thinking (whether awake or asleep) is preconscious; our conscious symbolic processes serve primarily to sample, communicate, ruminate, and test.

Freud (1900b) long ago pointed out that the dream is fed and also modified by afterimages derived from the unfinished business both of the current day and of an entire lifespan. What I will emphasize here are certain additional facts. During both wakefulness and sleep, the preconscious stream is fed and also modified by a continuous afferent bombardment from the body and from the outside world by way of all afferent modalities. Like the central preconscious stream itself, a major share of this afferent input is preconscious, although it contains at the same time variable conscious symbolic components. During sleep the sources of the afferent input are predominantly enteroceptive, with secondary proprioceptive and minor exteroceptive contributions (Kubie, 1962). In the waking state the relative roles of these three basic sources of afferent supply are reversed: exteroceptive and proprioceptive predominate over enteroceptive components. This shift has relevance both to the preconscious dream flow and to those fragmentary samples of the process that are called "the dream." Hypnotism, drugs, and relative afferent isolation (erroneously called "sensory deprivation") (Kubie, 1945a, 1961a; Kubie and Margolin, 1944) have effects on the relative roles played by these three basic sources of input. These effects are similar to those which accompany sleep, in that there are parallel changes in states of psychological organization and disorganization, ranging from sleep to waking, from dream to hallucination, from neurosis to psychosis.

The changing tides of body needs and the incessant flux in the outside world send signals, both conscious and subliminal, to the central nervous system. In the body the messages arise from recurrent changes in tensions in muscles, joints, and tendons of the trunk and extremities, and from changes in the distribution of glandular, cellular, muscular, and vascular activities on the body surface, in the apertures, and in the internal organs. Recent work by seismologists has demonstrated the constant occurrence of "microseisms" (microquakes). It is said that awake and asleep we live on the "trembling, shuddering crust of the earth." These are transmitted as fine, subliminal vibrations to the bones, joints, muscles, and viscera, and thence to the central nervous system. Together all this constitutes the source of an incessant subliminal body-borne afferent input. Another input is exteroceptive in origin. For instance, Dr. John Bordley said recently (personal communication) that we live in a continuous subliminal sound stream. At the same time the eye, at least when it is open, sends a continuous bombardment of subliminal input from the perimacular retina. The contributions from subliminal olfactory and gustatory input await investigation. In any consideration of the mentational process, awake or asleep, we cannot continue to leave this imageless bombardment out of account; yet among analysts only Charles Fisher (1956) has investigated these phenomena.

Furthermore, the studies of Marsh and Worden (1956) and of others indicate that a direct overflow can occur from subliminal input and subliminal processing to autonomic responses. There may be individual differences in the ease with which, without the intervention of conscious processes, the subliminal input can influence the autonomic system and its output. If so, such differences might provide a clue to differences in thresholds of affective responses in general, including the affective color both of the preconscious dream flow and of the symbolic dream sample. Consequently, these investigations may add to our understanding of the contribution made by the preconscious afferent bombardment to the affective quality of the dream flow and of the dream, as well as to its content.

New techniques are needed by which to measure individual differences in rates and qualities of preconscious processing, differences in the threshold for autonomic responses to the preconscious input and to the ensuing preconscious stream, differences in the accessibility of the continuous preconscious stream to conscious symbolic sampling, and, finally, differences in the vulnerability of the process of symbolic sampling to the various kinds of dissociative distortion which lead to repressive inhibition. The qualitative and quantitative clarification of all such possible differences will be essential for the future development of a psychophysiology of psychoanalysis.

Clearly, future psychophysiological and psychoanalytic research in this area will be built around investigations of the preconscious stream both in the waking state and in sleep. This will be essential for our further study of dreaming, of creativity, and of symptom formation in the neuroses. Unhappily, we have as yet no precise methods by which to carry on such investigations. The development of appropriate tech-

niques will constitute a major methodological breakthrough
for all psychologies, but especially for psychoanalytic psychology.

Such methods will be important also for understanding the
nature of organic deficits in brain function. Here the
limitations of our knowledge are due to the fact that we do not
know what the aging processes (or brain damage of other
kinds) do to the preconscious stream. Up to the present time,
investigations of deficits in cerebral functions which are due to
processes of organic disease have been confined to studies of
disturbances in the conscious symbolic sampling of the
preconscious stream. Such studies have great importance, but
without more precise data on the influences of brain damage
on the preconscious stream itself, they provide us with only a
part of the story.

POSTSCRIPT

I do not relish my position about these matters, because few
who hear or read this will like or approve what I say. What
they do not realize, however (and by "they" I mean my many
psychoanalytic colleagues and friends, especially perhaps from
New York), is that they are in danger of becoming the
defenders of the most uncertain, the least necessary, and the
most easily challenged elements of psychoanalytic theory.
They are defenders of static elements in psychoanalytic thinking which they polish and refine but never clarify, never
re-examining their own premises. It is a strange experience to
travel over the face of America or Europe talking to colleagues
everywhere, as I have in recent years, only to hear the same
thing from the most erudite and diverse scholars in our field.
These scholars have several traits in common: for many years
they have contributed to psychoanalytic literature and have
taught and led psychoanalytic institutes. All are unassailably
Freudian. This adds to the significance of their uniform
plaint, which is: "I cannot read the literature in my own field
any more. It has become stereotyped repetitions of verbal
clichés." Some even called it "sophistry." All say that we must

break out of this rut and return to our fundamentals if we are to move forward again. They also bewail the way our younger colleagues repeat these standard formulae uncritically, almost as though they were afraid that they would be excommunicated if they had the temerity to do any independent thinking. They agree that it has become the major duty of senior and experienced theoreticians and clinicians in psychoanalysis to challenge this enforced stereotype.

This is what, in a small way, I have tried to do here. Whether my specific hypothesis is right or wrong is of less importance than the challenge which it brings to re-examine certain assumptions we have been taking for granted.

7

THE RELATION OF PSYCHOTIC
DISORGANIZATION TO THE
NEUROTIC PROCESS

I

This paper has several interrelated purposes:

1. To describe the nature of the neurotic process as a continuously evolving chain of reverberating relationships,
usually initiated by interactions among unconscious conflicts,
and further influenced by the impact of any central affective
potentials (X) which have been superimposed concurrently or
even earlier (Kubie, 1963a). Out of such processes come both
symbolic symptoms and symbolic distortions of ways of living,
which produce fresh distortions of further development, which
in turn give rise to new conflicts on all levels (conscious,
preconscious, and unconscious). These thereupon produce a
third order of symptomatic symbolic disturbances, out of
which a third order of distorting consequences arise, which
thereupon produce still another order of conflicts and symptoms, etc., etc.

All of this is mediated by a processing of inner experiences
which operates unceasingly throughout life, but on a preconscious level. This preconscious stream is under the concurrent
influence of mechanisms of selecting, ordering, steering, and
controlling which operate on conscious, preconscious, and
unconscious levels. Of special importance among these are the

First published in *Journal of the American Psychoanalytic Association,* 15:626-
640, 1967. Reprinted by permission of the Editor of *Journal of the American Psychoanalytic Association.*

processes by which the preconscious stream is sampled, the samples in turn represented by symbols. This process of sampling the preconscious stream by units which are then represented by conscious symbols constitutes, when disturbed, what is called "the consciousness process" (Kubie, 1954). When, however, both the sampling process and the processes of symbolic representation come under the influence of concomitant conflicts and affects, this vital relationship between symbols and their underlying referents becomes vulnerable both to distortion and to interruption (Kubie, 1958a; this volume, Chapter 6). Any disturbance in this essential relationship between a symbol and its roots disguises or obliterates the identity of the underlying referent. In psychoanalytic jargon this is called the "unconscious," and it has critical consequences. For example, if the underlying referent is an area of conflict, the rupture of the link between that conflict and its symbolic representatives renders the conflict inaccessible to conscious introspective evaluation, correction, or control. It can no longer be reached by logic, by emotional appeals, or by the experiences of rewards and punishments, success and failure. It is in this way that the rigidity, insatiability, and unchanging quality of the neurotic process becomes entrenched (Kubie, 1958b).

2. In no sense does this partial reformulation of Freud's original dynamic concept negate his hypothesis that unconscious conflicts are the major instigator of the neurosis. It merely suggests certain significant additions to it. However, it also deliberately discards his later structural metaphors. In their place it suggests that such conflicts arise not between organized anthropomorphic fragments of the personality, but directly between pairs or among groups of irreconcilable and often unattainable drives. In this connection it is essential to keep in mind the fact that conflicts among drives can take place concurrently on conscious, preconscious, and unconscious levels, but that the interplay among them is processed and sampled preconsciously, like everything else, and then represented by symbolic units. When such conflicts occur on any level they will cause confusion, indecision, and distress, but it is only when unconscious components play the dominant

role that they become neurotogenic. Linked to this is a tentative subsidiary suggestion that many drives, if not all, occur in pairs of opposite sign.

3. One further consideration must be added: namely, that similar conflicts can occur between pairs or among groups of irreconcilable symptoms (e.g., an agoraphobia and a claustrophobia in the same person). But since all symptomatic structures are themselves distorted symbols, conflicts among symptoms cause further distortion of symbolic functions. Here lies a clue to the special role of the disorganization of conceptual and symbolic processes in the psychosis.

This basic concept of the nature of the neurotic process as an endlessly evolving chain of progressive distortions with reverberating consequences makes it possible to formulate more clearly its relation to psychotic disorganization. The basic hypothesis is that a neurosis forms when someone has become trapped among irreconcilable, conflicting, and unattainable drives, one or more of which are unconscious. But it takes another step and points out that when, in addition, conflicting and irreconcilable *symptoms* are superimposed upon the irreconcilable conflicts among the underlying drives, the person becomes vulnerable to psychotic disorganization. It does not claim that this is the only way in which psychotic disorganization can evolve out of the neurotic process, but it does claim that it is one way. It has been so generally overlooked that it is not possible today to say how universal it may be.

Further observations by many clinical observers with different biases will be needed to demonstrate the general validity of these hypotheses. If valid, they will enable us to dispense with the current concept that neurotogenic conflicts occur between subunits of the personality (e.g., between id and ego, or id and superego). This will mean a gain in simplicity and clarity for psychoanalysis, if the descriptive "structural" metaphors can be dropped from our vocabulary, both because of their static implications and because of their vulnerability to anthropomorphic misuse as pseudoexplanatory principles.

Examples will be given of the neurotic process and of how psychotic explosions can arise out of such entrapments as these in the course of the evolution of the neurotic process.

II

I shall describe briefly a few examples of the evolution of the neurotic process as a reverberating chain reaction which reaches an impasse out of which psychotic disorganization precipitates. I will not make any generalizations about this, nor suggest any universal laws.

1. In early childhood a woman had been molded into fear and angry depression by a total rejection at the hands of her parents. (This fact about her childhood was dramatically confirmed from an outside source.) She developed a sense of sexual, physical, and gender inferiority to her big, blond, flagrantly preferred brother, for the possession of whom her parents had fought bitterly. The external circumstances of her life were privileged, but an insightful and sympathetic older family friend compared her early years to those of a neglected slum child. Her only tender attachments and protectors were strangers and servants. After struggling through a long succession of transitory compulsions and phobias in childhood and early adolescence, she emerged into later adolescence with some success, but also with difficulties and disappointments. In spite of high endowments, her compulsions and phobias blocked her full use of her many talents; i.e., in music, literature, writing, education, and sports. Many years later in her analysis it became clear that during those years she had been struggling with many conflicting unconscious drives to possess her brother, to kill him, to supplant him in her father's and mother's love by becoming a big blond boy like him. At the same time she never wholly abandoned feminine goals or identifications, but tried to hold or regain her father's love by remaining his little daughter. Consequently she struggled over whether to grow older or younger, and over whether to be a boy or a girl, or both. With each birthday this struggle became sharper, and with each she became more depressed.

In later adolescence, from a safe distance, she fixed her affections on a young man who was about ten years her senior. When he married someone else she solaced herself, without realizing what she was doing, by making a substitute marriage to a close friend of her secret idol. There were other determinants of this choice. Her husband's father was a friend of her own father, his mother a friend of her mother. The marriage was, therefore, an effort to win the love of her own parents. Furthermore, during the earlier phases of courtship she received more attentions from her future husband's parents than she had ever received from her own parents. Unhappily, immediately after the marriage, her "in-laws" turned away, making her realize that their many attentions to her during the courtship were in fact only an expression of their need to cling to their son. Thus the turning away repeated the childhood pain caused by the flagrant way in which her parents had favored her brother. In her unhappiness she began to become bewildered and impulsive. Not long after the marriage her husband went through an illness which seemed dangerous. Although she did not allow herself to realize it at the time, his illness seemed to promise a release from her prison. Consequently his complete recovery was a psychological catastrophe for her, trapping her again, reactivating her unconscious death wishes toward her brother and her need to replace him in her father's love, and adding new phobias to her earlier phobic trends. From having been freely active in every way she now became anxiety-ridden and agoraphobic. She could hardly bring herself to move more than a few blocks from her home. (In therapy many years later, latent prostitution fantasies became manifest.) In the next years, difficult experiences over becoming pregnant trapped her even more completely in a home that had become for her a prison. At the same time there was a further deterioration of the marriage, partly because of the husband's total withdrawal. Thereupon a previously latent or subclinical claustrophobia became manifest, and thus she was trapped not only between the older pairs of irreconcilable underlying drives, but also between two opposing symptomatic pressures, i.e., an agoraphobia and a claustrophobia. Sometimes she would stand on the threshold of her home literally for hours, equally terrified to go in or to go out, to be among people or to be alone; equally terrified of moving or of remaining motionless, of speaking or of remaining silent. There was nowhere to turn that would bring surcease from terror. This juxtaposition of the irreconcilable drives with the superimposed, conflicting symptomatic defenses brought on an imminent threat of a full-blown psychotic disorganization. Fortunately, at this point her behavior became so disorganized that it broke down the violent opposition of her medical advisor and of her own family to the psychiatric intervention for which she had been pleading. She entered intensive treatment just in time. The story of how this illness had arisen and of how it came so close to psychotic disorganization became clear only very slowly, out of several years of slow and painstaking analytic exploration, first by a woman analyst and then by a man.

2. Another example is a young engineer who spent his early childhood struggling to overcome multiple familial handicaps. First in the family was a sister who was beautiful, brilliant, and a magnificent athlete. An older brother was jealous of this older sister and took it out by bullying the patient, who was the youngest of the three. His father was weak, frightened, and unprotecting. His mother was a hostile, domineering, man-hating, pseudomaternal figure. In his early childhood the patient had lived in shame and terror. The conscious content of these fears was that he was too small and too young. Yet he also feared growing up, because of the new dangers to which this would expose him. Consequently he could barely function in sports, in studies, or socially, and this in spite of his native aptitudes in each of these directions. At a critical point, because of illness in the family he was sent away to school. This almost accidental good fortune saved him temporarily, because once he was out from under the destructive forces in his home he emerged as an outstanding student and athlete. Furthermore, he continued to excel throughout college and professional school, and during those years was free from manifest neurotic symptoms. Subsequent events demonstrated that he was not free from certain buried but highly charged residues of the earlier struggles. For

instance, psychosexual terrors were camouflaged as high principles. His ambivalent struggle between envy, hatred, and
erotic attachment to his sister persisted, but also wore
"healthy" disguises. She remained for him the ultimate
measure of desirability in women. Her smile or frown meant
success or failure to such an extent that for a long time he
dismissed all other girls, until finally he "fell in love" with and
married his sister's best friend, a piquant but masculinized
version of his sister. He was wholly unaware of the incestuous
ingredients in this choice, of the hidden identification with his
sister, and of the inverted gender role which this implied.
Nevertheless he seemed for a time to have found a workable
solution, until the sudden death of his sister brought on a
catastrophic chain of events. The unconscious purpose went
out of his relationship to his young wife, leaving him trapped
in a marriage to a masculinized substitute mate, trapped by
their two children to whom he had a complex and almost maternal relationship, trapped also by his professional activities
which had become interwoven with those of his father-in-law,
trapped in his own double gender identity. He was dimly
aware that he could no longer remain happily with his wife,
but he could not leave her. In this dilemma, he gradually re-
gressed into the anxious, depressive, self-doubting envies and
tension states of his early years. Then one evening on the ter-
race of the apartment of his wife's parents, he exploded quite
suddenly into a full-blown height phobia and fainted. This
phobia persisted for years, and it was one of the symptoms
whose destructive consequences brought him into analysis.
Much later in the course of his analytic work, he recalled that
in the instant before the terror of heights had assailed him he
had had a fleeting fantasy of throwing his wife over the para-
pet—this wife who no longer served his unconscious needs now
that his sister, her best friend, was dead. This lightninglike
fantasy, which he had buried immediately, had seemed for
that desperate instant to be the only way out of prison which
he could envisage. It had earlier roots in his childhood conflict
between hate, envy, and love of his deceased sister. This reactivated conflict infected his marriage more and more, trigger-
ing the related psychosexual fears of his adolescence, so that

he became impotent. This in turn precipitated him into an agitated depression of nearly psychotic intensity, with severe anxiety and a variety of psychosomatic disturbances.

The destructive evolution of the process did not stop at this point. Because of the height phobia, unless he knew the floor of the office or apartment which he would have to visit, it became difficult for him to make any appointments, whether with engineering firms or potential clients or even with friends. Because of the phobia, he had difficulty in driving over a high bridge to visit his family in the country or to take his children to the country for a weekend outing. Each day he awoke with a nameless dread. Later he could recognize the unspoken questions: "To what high place will I have to go today? To what humiliating terror will I be exposed?" He began to evade these challenges by developing somatic distress of various kinds, by making up excuses, sometimes by drinking in an effort to ease the tension. Both his career and his social life suffered. He became increasingly depressed and humiliated. He would erupt out of terror into rage, and he began to be haunted by suspicions that other people knew. His relationship to the world underwent a pseudoparanoid distortion. One nocturnal episode of acute panic with brief but full-blown delusional distortions finally brought him to treatment.

Seeing him in this phase of his illness any psychiatrist would have thought of him as a classical, acutely agitated, paranoid involutional depression, which for some reason was occurring atypically in the mid-thirties; and indeed he had been called that by several. It was only after long exploration and repeated reconstructions of his entire history that the story of the prepsychotic neurosis slowly evolving to the brink of this psychotic disorganization came to light.

This life history illustrates with the clarity of a laboratory demonstration the tragic chain reaction of conflicts among drives, the formation of primary symptomatic defenses, the secondary distortions of life which these produce, the further effects of the insoluble conflicts among drives, the new symptoms and new distortions which result, and then the even more destructive consequences of the insoluble conflicts among the symptoms themselves, and finally the disruption of symbolic functions which this produces. This is the neurotic process in action as it reaches the brink of psychotic disorganization.

3. Another young man, the oldest of four children, had lived an overprotected life with an oversolicitous mother. She oscillated between periods of retarded depression and anxiety and periods of open and imaginative warmth toward her children. During her "well" periods, her free and happy affection would lure him into closeness. Then when she swung off into her own black moods he would again be left alone for long periods of solitude and neglect. Her pattern had begun as a delayed post-partum disturbance during his first year, but it continued throughout his puberty and after. He emerged into adolescence shaken, uneasy, fearful, and depressive, scarcely able to use any of his many assets. His father's professional work moved the family around the country a great deal, so that the child had no sense of continuity and familiarity with either animate or inanimate objects. The familiar but fleeting presence of his busy father did not provide the inner security he needed if he were to withstand the recurring loss of his mother to illness. Shortly after a sister's birth the mother had to be hospitalized for a brief but stormy psychotic episode. During these months the anxious father tried to make it up to the child by mothering as well as fathering him. The child changed visibly, clinging fearfully to his father, yet angrily silent and aloof. With his siblings the rivalry for his father's attention increased, and since the father could hardly gratify this by killing them off, the child's frustrated ambivalent impulses spread to include his relationships not only to all girls and women but also to his father. Here he alternated between dependent adoration and silent, hostile, automatic rebellion, an attitude which colored his relationships with all men for years. Subsequently his mother's serious physical illness led to another long separation, whereupon his relationship to his home became even more ambivalent. He could neither remain at home nor leave it. It was a place to hide, but also a place of torment and frustration.

This unhappy story had also marred his career through school. Going to school had been difficult from the outset. The very first day in kindergarten had triggered in him what was essentially the prototype of a silent, retarded depression (Spitz and Wolf, 1946). This recurred each autumn as he started back to school. He was able to enter college only because of his very high native intellectual capacity (an I.Q. of around 160). Yet he barely survived there. His gender identification became more ambivalent, as he floundered back and forth between halfhearted heterosexual and homosexual involvements. At the threat of graduating into the world, i.e., into the maturity which he dreaded, he exploded into a state of acute disorganization with vivid hallucinatory and delusional distortions.

4. Finally I shall review the story of a youngster who was first seen at the age of five, and then for ten years was followed in treatment by a colleague (Ravich and Dunton, 1966). She was the younger of two children, the brother being several years her senior. The first steps in this story were described in an article entitled " 'Say You're Sorry' " (Kubie and Israel, 1955). In a few short weeks this child had slumped through the following steps: first, she would not respond to her name. Then she claimed as her own the name of a little girl up the street. Then she claimed the name of a neighboring boy. Then she stopped talking entirely. Then she stopped eating. Then she refused to stay in her bed or to wear a pretty new nightgown and bathrobe. Instead she rolled herself in a rug on the floor, pressing her face to the baseboard. She would lie there silent and motionless, wetting and soiling herself. The original article tells how this was resolved through the almost accidental use of a key phrase. By chance the child was once overheard whispering, "Say you're sorry." The examiner's solemn statement, "I am sorry. I am very, very sorry," initiated the swift resolution of the acute psychotic episode and led to the subsequent years of treatment of the prepsychotic neurosis (Ravich and Dunton, 1966). It was this treatment which made it possible to reconstruct the story of the development of this episode of psychotic disorganization out of the preceding

neurosis; a disorganization which seemed destined to become permanent if it had been allowed to go untreated. Out of this story I shall select those elements which are essential to illustrate my thesis further.

The later therapeutic work brought to light many preceding contamination phobias and protective avoidance rituals which had centered on the figure of the housekeeper. The child had been dependent almost exclusively upon her. She was her protector against an older brother and against the physical contacts which would trigger contamination terrors. The housekeeper was also enslaved by the child's phobic rituals.

Shortly before the acute regressive descent which I have described, an improvement in the family's economic position made it possible for her father to rent a larger apartment. They gave the child a room of her own which separated her from her enslaved protector. This precipitated night terrors which in turn led to explosive behavior, as a result of which her father spanked her for the first time in her life. (Hitherto the mother had been the sole source of punishment.) Presently the housekeeper left because she could stand neither the nocturnal separation from the child nor the general uproar. On a superficial level (i.e., conscious and preconscious) this trapped the child between her need for her family and her need for her departed companion. Other and deeper double binds were focused on dirt and cleanliness, boy or girl. Step by step she abandoned her own identity by changing her name. Then she abandoned her own gender for her brother's (as a reflection of a bitter conflict over this brother). Then came the effort to return to infancy by starting life all over again so that she could grow up different. She lost her ability to use speech as she became uncertain about who she was or with whom she wished to communicate or what she wanted to communicate. Then, as her old fears of contamination by contact and the old obsessional protective rituals for avoiding contacts were reactivated, she could no longer move, but curled up in an old rug and lay mute and motionless in her own excrement.

Again this illustrates my hypothesis.

III

It is not difficult to describe the varied sequences of events which are set in motion during the processes of psychotic disorganization, once these have been launched. It would, however, be fallacious to assume that these sequences necessarily have etiological significance. They make an etiological relationship possible, but the mere sequence of events does not prove it. The same caution must be used in interpreting the significance of the phenomena which can be recognized clinically in the psychotic picture. This caution applies particularly to all phenomena of regression, whether to earlier identifications, or to earlier periods of instinct-driven needs, or to earlier affective postures, or to earlier patterns of behavior. These are relatively constant ingredients in states of psychotic disorganization, and certainly such regressions activate complex chains of important secondary and tertiary consequences on all levels. Yet they are not invariably present, and there is no clear evidence that they initiate the psychosis. Therefore they constitute a relatively constant but *not* invariable link in the reverberating chain of psychopathological events.

Further, regression does not always involve the same consequences. It can lead to an abandonment of adult life itself, with the unconscious implication that if I go back to the beginning I can start over and then grow up all over again. Because this course can end in death, it is easy to misinterpret it as an expression of a drive to die. Indeed, Freud's concern with "death instincts" may well have been due to a failure to realize how often actions that end in dying or in the danger of dying express masked drives for resurrection: the *Tod und Verklärung* motif of Richard Strauss (Kubie, 1964a).

Regression can also express difficulties about gender identity which are involved in the desire to change sides so as to be the other sex, or to be both or neither. This is one of the more frequent unconscious conflicts out of which the psychotic process explodes and which it frequently expresses in varied and transparent forms.

Consequently, if we are to think clearly not only about regression but also about many other clinical ingredients in the psychotic process and state, we must keep in mind the differences between initiating, sustaining, and feedback mechanisms; i.e., between mechanisms which touch off the process of psychotic disorganization and those which are set in motion *during* this process once it is under way, and which both sustain it and complicate it through the complex secondary consequences which they feed back into the picture. Let me repeat that we have tended to make the logical error of assuming that the sequences which we find at work in the psychosis have initiated it. This assumption has led to many unwarranted hypotheses.

With these general principles in mind it will be important systematically to collect examples of these sequences, but this will take many observers many years. Furthermore, its correlation with the many different costumes worn by psychotic disorganization will take even more years, because psychological states, whether normal, neurotic, or psychotic, have as many variables as has the human face. Indeed, this is one reason why there is still no satisfactory system for the classification of psychological disorders. Where there are as many variables as this, either there is just one all-inclusive category (e.g., the "face" consisting of two eyes, one nose, one mouth, etc.), or else every individual face constitutes a separately recognizable entity. If we are to find out how consistently the psychotic disorganization erupts out of an insoluble impasse among irreconcilable and unattainable drives and symptoms, further data are needed on the nature of the noxious episodes which set off acute changes, and on the nature of those which lead more gradually to psychotic disorganization. Sometimes the impasse gathers slowly, as with the inescapable concomitants of aging. Sometimes the impasse confronts the patient suddenly, as with the threat of emerging from home, high school, college, professional school, hospital, or job; the threat of advancement as well as the threat of loss. Or the effects of the insoluble dilemma can be unmasked suddenly by the death of a spouse of a child or a parent, but also by the unanticipated survival of a spouse, child, or parent after serious illness. Pregnancies or the end of pregnancies may do the unmasking.

Furthermore, as one important part of this study the impact of such sequences will have to be correlated with the influence of drugs on the thresholds for the establishing of reverberating processes in the central nervous system, and for the organization and disorganization of symbolic processes both in the waking state and during sleep. In these connections the drugs we are testing today have puzzling and contradictory actions. Sometimes they seem to terminate the psychotic disorganization of symbolic processing and to re-establish the prepsychotic neurosis. In other patients the same drugs have an opposite action. Or again, after a patient has emerged from his psychosis on a certain drug level, lowering the dosage will sometimes, yet not always, re-establish the psychosis. During this transition some patients are able to describe their subjective impressions of these changes. One may describe it as resembling the shift from normal waking thought processes to the type of thought processes that occur during sleep. For instance, as it was taking place, one patient said, "I can see it coming on. I am beginning to think differently. I am awake, but I am thinking as though I were asleep." For the student of psychopharmacology, this is an important self-observation, both in itself and because of its paradoxical implications. Why can a drug, which under certain circumstances and at certain dosages may induce sleep, enable certain psychotic patients to shed the pattern of dreamlike thought processes and to think as a waking person thinks? Why does the withdrawal of that same drug, instead of "awakening" him still further and thus clearing his thinking processes, cause his thinking processes to become disorganized into sleeplike preconscious patterns during the transition toward the waking state? The study of many recorded samples of such transitions during minute-by-minute observations is vital for the illumination of these transitions.

About all of this I shall limit myself to making only one suggestion, namely, that these disorganizations in thinking and conceptualizing processes and in their symbolic representation have basically to do with changes in the re-

lationships among the three systems of symbolic processing
—conscious, preconscious, and unconscious. The exploration
of this will concern psychiatry for many years to come.

Summary

The neurotic process is a chain of distortions of
psychological development which have a dual origin in unconscious conflicts and in the early imposition of central affective
positions. The symptomatic expressions of these conflicts and
of the central affective potential produce secondary conflicts,
which in turn give rise to additional distortions and a secondary series of distorting consequences and then a third series of
conflicts, etc. These reverberating chains evolve as the neurotic process.

The underlying conflicts arise between pairs of irreconcilable and often unattainable drives. They operate on all levels
concurrently, and become pathogenic only when the unconscious components in this mixture of interacting processes are
dominant. When additional sets of pathogenic conflicts arise
between antagonistic symptoms, which occurs frequently yet
has been largely overlooked, the consequence of this superim-
position of irreconcilable conflicts among symptoms on the
underlying neurotogenic conflicts among drives leads directly
to psychotic disorganization. These facts make superfluous the
assumption that so-called "structural" conflicts arise among
subunits within the personality.

8

IMPAIRMENT OF THE FREEDOM TO CHANGE WITH THE ACQUISITION OF THE SYMBOLIC PROCESS

This paper is an attempt to make clear conceptually what one of the central goals of research in child development must be; and it does this by singling out for emphasis a neglected problem in the development of human thought processes, which from early childhood closely links the creative and the neurotic potential.

The symbolic process is the unique gift and attribute of human mentation, and its most valuable. At the same time that it is essential for all that is creative in human thinking, it is also most vulnerable to distortion. This is because it develops around a core of asymbolic or preconscious processing (what was called "imageless thought" by the Würzburg School). This preconscious processing begins in infancy to play an effective role through a process akin to conditioning (Kubie, 1959); but if it is to continue to play an effective role in our adult thought processes, weighted and fragmentary samples must be drawn from this preconscious stream and must then be represented by symbols which are used for

Presented at the Biennial Meeting of the Society for Research in Child Development in Philadelphia, Pa., March 30, 1973. First published (posthumously) in *The Psychoanalytic Study of the Child*, 29:257-262, 1974. New Haven: Yale University Press. Reprinted by permission of the Editors of *The Psychoanalytic Study of the Child*.

purposes of memory, rumination, coding and ordering, and communication. Thus the symbolic devices are linked to samples of the preconscious stream; but these links to the preconscious referents are also vulnerable to distortion, and when they become distorted they give rise to misrepresentation and obstruction, which in turn leads to the process known as "unconscious" processing. It is an effort at representation, but it leads to a misrepresentation or to no representation at all. This imprisons the preconscious stream between unconscious distortion on the one hand and pedestrian literal-mindedness on the other, and thereby limits its capacity to evolve, grow, and change. This may start in infancy, but it is a process which is sorted out and resolved only slowly with the years. Thus the impairment of freedom begins with learning, yet it is a problem which has not been solved by any method of education we have so far discovered.

The creative process depends for its freedom upon the play of preconscious functions which are balanced precariously between the rigidity of conscious processes at one end (with their anchorage in reality), and the rigidity of unconscious functions at the other end (with their anchorage in the stereotyped and repetitive symbolism of unconscious processes). It is a measure of the profound and tragic failure of our educational system that it does not accept the challenge of this problem, but tends if anything to reinforce the imprisonment of preconscious function by its dependence upon drill and grill.

Let me recapitulate briefly this essential element in my story. Conscious anchorage to reality is chronological and logical. It is rooted in conscious representations of perceptions which are built out of exteroceptive, proprioceptive, and enteroceptive units. Of these, the exteroceptive perceptions are readily checked and controlled because we can compare them and, when desirable, in some measure shut them out. The proprioceptive contributions come next. Internal perceptions are the most difficult modalities to control, compare, and interrupt. In turn, this is why the three perceptual modalities play different roles in fantasies, symptoms, and dreams (this volume, Chapter 6).

At the other pole (the "unconscious" end) the symbolic process never represents current perceptual processes, but only memory traces of a past to which it is unalterably and rigidly anchored. Specifically, this is because of the iron curtain which separates the "unconscious" symbol from what it both represents and disguises. As long as that iron curtain separates the two, their relationship to each other cannot be altered either by experience or by imagination. It is for this reason that the symbolic process at the "unconscious" end of the spectrum is sterile, repetitive, noncreative, and incapable of communicating even its limited store of meanings.

In between come the preconscious functions, with their automatic and subtle recordings of multiple perceptions, their automatic recall, their multiple analogic and overlapping linkages, and their direct connections to the autonomic processes which underlie affective states. The rich play of preconscious operations occurs freely in states of abstraction, in sleep, in dreams, and as we write, paint, or allow our thoughts to flow in the nonselected paths of free association. Yet preconscious processes are assailed from both sides. From one side they are nagged and prodded by rigid and distorted symbols of unconscious drives, which are oriented away from reality and which consist of rigid compromise formations, lacking in fluid inventiveness. From the other side they are driven by literal conscious purpose, checked and corrected by conscious retrospective critique. The uniqueness of creativity —i.e., its capacity to sort out bits of experience and put them together into new combinations—depends on the extent to which preconscious functions can operate freely between these two ubiquitous, concurrent, and oppressive prison wardens.

Here is where the neurotic imprisonment begins almost from infancy onward, not in strange and unusually traumatic circumstances but in the very process which we euphemistically call "education." Thereafter each neurotic symptom has its own distorting consequences, and each such consequence in turn tends to develop secondary symptoms, which in turn develop tertiary consequences, which lead to new symptoms. As this tendency multiplies, it forms the self-perpetuating, reverberating chain reaction which constitutes neurotic illness, or the neurotic process. This occurs no matter what the symptom may be—whether it is inherently simple and innocent, or whether it is deeply distorted. Actually, many symptoms are even socially rewarded, but that fact does not make their consequences any the less destructive to an individual life.

Once a reverberating chain reaction is built around the central stream of preconscious processing, only weighted samples are given symbolic representation, first by paralinguistic gestures and mimicry, then by preverbal sounds, and finally by verbal forms of symbolic representation. If the links between the symbolic representatives and their referents (whatever their nature) become strained, distorted, or disrupted, further distortions supervene; these then lead to the obligatory, unchanging, and unchangeable repetitive patterns which are the core of the neurotic process (Kubie, 1941b, 1958b, 1961c, 1963b). It is this which is at the heart of all neurotic processing. (Drugs such as alcohol, or alcohol and marijuana, or alcohol and barbiturates, and also brain damage may intensify this, sometimes to a parapsychotic or lethal degree.) This is the imprisonment of the freely creative preconscious stream of analogic processing, and it challenges us to revise our entire educational approach to child rearing.

Contrary to ordinary preconceptions and assumptions, we do *not* think consciously. All actual thinking is done without the magic of images. Thought is imageless, as the Würzburg School pointed out many years ago. It is fortunate that this is so, because it achieves an enormous saving of time. Furthermore, the freedom which can occur in imageless thought could not be achieved with thought processes which are anchored either to reality or to unreality.[1]

---

[1] The first two chapters of my book, *Neurotic Distortion of the Creative Process* (Kubie, 1958a), deal with this topic in great detail. See also my article entitled "Relation of the Conditioned Reflex to Psychoanalytic Technique" (Kubie, 1934b), in which I pointed out that time relations in chains of free associations are as important to the technique of free association as are time relations in the development of the conditioned reflex. Many years later (Kubie, 1959) I again wrote about the relation of the conditioned reflex to preconscious functions. That time I was dealing with the mechanism by which preconscious functions come to play such a major role in the development of the stream of thought.

Conscious thought carries on a pedestrian struggle to keep some measure of freedom, but it achieves very little. What we call conscious thought is really a slow and laborious weighted sampling of the continuous preconscious stream, which is thereby given conscious symbolic representation. This goes on day and night, asleep and awake, in dreaming as in waking fantasy and waking thought (this volume, Chapter 6). There is a rigid relationship between the preconscious stream and those weighted fragments of it which are represented by conscious symbols. Where, on the other hand, the relationship of these conscious symbols to what they are supposed to represent becomes distorted or severed, the thought process itself is subject to unconscious distortion — which is close to the roots of psychopathology. Instead of representing fragments of the preconscious stream accurately, it hides them. This is what is meant by unconscious processing. Note that I do not say "*the* unconscious." There is no "*the* unconscious." That is only an abstraction. But where the links between the symbol and what it is supposed to represent are distorted or severed, fragmentary samples of the preconscious stream which form the core of all human mentation are disguised and distorted or hidden (this volume, Chapter 6). But this comes at the end of the line. This is what happens, for example, to the adult use of language, as a paralinguistic or linguistic form of representation of the preconscious stream. And this is what happens when the preconscious stream, with its speed and extraordinary fluidity, its dependence upon analogic thinking, becomes trapped.

I have previously tried to show (Kubie, 1958a) how it happens that this imprisonment occurs between two jailors; i.e., between conscious roots on the one hand and unconscious distortions of the relation of the symbol to its referent on the other. This imprisonment of preconscious processing between pedestrian conscious sampling and its loss of linkages to the sampling process has many consequences. There is a loss of freedom of input, of intake, of representation, and of sampling. There is an impairment of freedom of expression. Most important of all is the impairment of the *freedom to change* and therefore to learn; because without change there can be no learning, and without learning there can be no therapy and of course no freedom to create (Kubie, 1972). This is the impairment of freedom which occurs whenever the preconscious stream becomes trapped between the conscious symbolic representation on one side and the encroaching neurotic process on the other side, with its distortions by the impairment of the linkages to the conscious sample.

In the early entrapment in neurotic illness there is also a carry-over of the affective imprisonment by a central affective potential. I dealt with this in a paper I wrote in honor of René Spitz (Kubie, 1963a), who was the first to describe this process (1945). (See also Bowlby et al., 1965.)

These are the challenges which child rearing and child education face. There are no greater challenges to us as educators of successive generations. Yet instead of facing them, the "educators" (so-called) continue to depend on drill and grill, which actually reinforce the obligatory repetition of the neurotic process and which are a confession of failure of education because they create an atmosphere in which a child cannot learn without reinforcing the neurotogenic processes. Obligatory repetition invades the picture as our educational hopes fail. What to do about it is another question. All I can plead for is that we face our failures and search for remedies.

9

THE DRIVE TO BECOME
BOTH SEXES

I. Prologue: The Beauty and Tragedy of *Orlando*

Over the years during which the material for this paper
has been accumulating, I have frequently thought back to
Virginia Woolf's (1928) *Orlando*—a book of moving beauty
and sadness, a book whose tragedy was underscored by the
ultimate suicide of one of the greatest and subtlest creative
writers of our day. It is a book in which the beauty of woman
and the strength of man are blended in courage and despair,
and in which the depths of lechery are interspersed with high
spiritual creativity. It is a story written by a woman about a
man who turns into a woman and then back and forth
between the two, but without ever losing completely his hold
on maleness. Implicit and almost explicit in this tale is much
that I will try to say in this paper.

In *Orlando*, as in life itself, the unresolved residues of each
day's unfinished business produce a fusion of reality and
dream, of incompatible, unattainable, and irreconcilable
goals. It transcends time and space, as adventures occur
almost simultaneously in England and in Turkey, and in the
sixteenth and twentieth centuries (1528 and 1928). And as it
fuses man and woman, so it fuses prose and verse. There are
passages which pass from verse to prose and from prose to

An expanded and revised version of a paper first presented before the Annual
Meeting of the American Psychoanalytic Association in St. Louis, May, 1954. First
published (posthumously) in *The Psychoanalytic Quarterly*, 43:349-426, 1974.
Reprinted by permission of *The Psychoanalytic Quarterly*.

verse without a break in the pattern of the lines. In her auto-biographical sketches (V. Woolf, 1926, 1929; also L. Woolf, 1953), the author repeatedly makes light of her verse and tends to regard the entire tale as a lark, a *jeu d'esprit*. This denigration of the legend is a measure of the strength of her tragic need to hide her eyes from its total personal impact. (See also Meaker, 1964; Pippett, 1953.)

In broad outlines, the tale begins in the England of the sixteenth century. Here the hero, in youthful pseudo masculinity, riots in a furor of fighting and of sexual encounters, culminating in a passionate involvement with a Muscovite princess about whom wild myths cluster. She is the embodiment of the strange and the different; half woman, half furry animal. There had been a devastating frost and a winter-long carnival on the frozen Thames. Then, "after one rain-drop," the "heavens open and a mud-yellow thaw" sets in. An ebb tide of deception and abandonment leads predictably through an explosion of jealousy into a deliberate, fury-laden, and vengeance-driven descent into a degradation of self and sex and woman. This is followed by depression and a trancelike stupor to the edge of death and rebirth, the first in a series of mystical experiences of *Tod und Verklärung*.

As a naïve writer, the hero wanders in the tombs of his ancestors, oscillating between the esthete and the hunter, a *male* Diana, as dual sexed as were the classical gods and goddesses of Greece. He turns toward poetry with a shyness of any adolescent, whether boy or girl. He becomes disillusioned about all writers and turns his back on them, saying, "I have done with men." Thereupon he is haunted by the dreamlike figure of a woman in a riding hood and mantle, taller and also older by many years, who later in the tale turns out to have been from the first a man in disguise. Here the change begins. Let us read it in Virginia Woolf's own words:

> Orlando stood stark naked. No human being, since the world began, has ever looked more ravishing. His form combined in one the strength of a man and a woman's grace.... We may take advantage of this pause in the narrative to make certain statements. Orlando has become a woman—there is no denying it. But in every other respect, Orlando remained precisely as he

had been. The change of sex, though it altered their future, did nothing whatever to alter their identity [1928, p. 90].

The setting is translocated to Turkey[1] where, as the Ambassador, Orlando nonetheless marries another ambisexual figure; this time a gypsy. Again he falls into a trance and is "reborn." "Orlando had . . . dressed herself in those Turkish coats and trousers which can be worn indifferently by either sex." In these sexually ambiguous vestments Orlando called up her hound, "then stuck a pair of pistols in her belt," and at the same time "wound about her person several strings of emeralds and pearls" (p. 91). Thereupon she goes out to fight and ride as she had before her transmutation, living thenceforth as both man and woman. Thus in this fantastic marriage to herself-himself, she achieves the transmutation so often sought with tragic futility in sex and marriage, and especially in neurosis and psychosis.

The shift to Constantinople and to Turkish garb made possible not only the sexual ambiguity of ambiguous clothes, but a continuous play of other ambiguities as well: Turk or Englishman; responsible ambassador or errant, runaway child; peasant or noble. A strange woman again is pursued. This time, however, she is a gypsy woman; and in the end it is not clear which of the two bore their children, Orlando or the gypsy "bride."

On the homeward voyage a scene occurs which has become famous.

Here [Orlando] tossed her foot impatiently, and showed an inch or two of calf. A sailor on the mast, who happened to look down at that moment, started so violently that he missed his footing and only saved himself by the skin of his teeth. "If the sight of my ankles means death to an honest fellow who, no doubt, has a wife and family to support, I must, in all humanity keep them covered." [And later:] "Heavens!" she thought, "what fools they make of us—what fools we are!" [thus] censuring both sexes equally, as if she belonged to neither; and indeed, for the time being she seemed to vacillate; she was man; she was woman; she knew secrets, shared the weaknesses of each [p. 102, 103].

[1] It is not irrelevant that the husband of Vita Sackville-West, Virginia Woolf's close friend, had in fact been in the diplomatic service in the Near East.

It was a bewildering state of mind, but it led slowly to a strange clarity.

> And as all of Orlando's loves had been women, now, through the culpable laggardry of the human frame to adapt itself to convention, though she herself was a woman, it was still a woman she loved; and if the consciousness of being of the same sex had any effect at all, it was to quicken and deepen those feelings which she had had as a man. For now a thousand hints and mysteries became plain to her that were then dark. Now, the obscurity, which divides the sexes and lets linger innumerable impurities in its gloom, was removed and if there is anything in what the poet says about truth and beauty, this affection gained in beauty what it lost in falsity [p. 105].

At this point I will turn from the poetry of *Orlando* to the clinic, but I will return to *Orlando* at the end of this essay.

II. INTRODUCTION AND HISTORICAL REVIEW

Freud was right, of course, in emphasizing the individual's struggle with his conscience, whether that conscience be conscious, preconscious, unconscious, or all three. He was right in recognizing the all-pervading role which this struggle plays in man's unhappiness and in his cultural development; and especially, when any elements in the struggle were unconscious, the role which this plays in the genesis of the neurotic process and in its ultimate psychotic disorganization. Yet he seemed to underestimate another source of conflict, namely, that which arose out of man's frequent struggles to achieve mutually irreconcilable and consequently unattainable identities. This study of the drive to become both sexes deals primarily with this second category of internal conflict and its destructive neurotogenic and psychotogenic influences on human development from infancy throughout life. (See Delay, 1963; Hart, 1941; James, 1933; Kubie, 1934a, 1941a.)

Out of early preconscious and guiltless identifications and misidentifications, rivalries, envies, hostilities, and loves grow many unconscious drives, among which the drive to become both sexes is one of the most self-destroying.

Since this paper was first presented before the American Psychoanalytic Association in 1954, parts of it have been read and discussed before various psychoanalytic societies on several occasions. Furthermore, it has been read privately, criticized, and sometimes praised by colleagues, several of whom have urged its immediate publication. I was tempted to do this, but held back because I felt that it needed additional data, and because I was never content with it as it was. In its original form it derived from twenty-five years of work with the neuroses. Through the subsequent years (and especially since my retirement from private practice in 1959) my increasing involvement in the problems of the psychoses at the Sheppard and Enoch Pratt Hospital and also at the Psychiatric Institute of the University of Maryland made me aware of the importance of the drive for the graver processes of psychotic disorganization. This has finally led me to decide to publish it without further delay.

To avoid any misunderstandings I will point out that this formulation of the conflict does not discard as incorrect Freud's concepts of phallic envy or castration fear, but attempts rather to supplement them in several directions. I had become aware that the original idea of penis envy focused solely on the genital differences between the sexes. Although demonstrably valid from earliest childhood (Kubie, 1934a, 1937), this concept was also incomplete both because it omitted other differences and because it overlooked the importance of the reverse and complementary envy of the male for the woman's breast, for nursing, as well as his envy of the woman's ability to conceive and to bring forth babies. Furthermore, as originally formulated, the concept of penis envy paid scant attention to many of its subtler psychological manifestations, or to its culmination in a frequently unrecognized and unconscious obsessional concern with gender transmutation (Kubie and Mackie, 1968). For all of these reasons, as I now look back over the years since 1954 it seems to me that it was fortunate that I held up publication until my own understanding of the drive to become both sexes had matured to the point which it has reached today.

In addition to what I have written here, much more could still be written about this drive, and surely will be in future years. Nevertheless, since I have now gestated this conceptual child as far as I am able to carry it myself, it is time to set it down on paper as a foundation for future building by others.[2]

This communication also has a personal prehistory which is relevant to its development. The first paper that I ever read at a meeting of the American Psychoanalytic Association was in Philadelphia in 1932. It was a report on a fifteen-year-old girl who was a transvestite by day, wearing only riding togs, and a woman by night, always in long, formal ball gowns. Because the patient's family forced a premature interruption of the analysis this report was never published, but on going back over my notes and the incomplete manuscript I find that much of the material is relevant to my present thesis (see also Baker, 1962; Follett, 1927).

That paper opened with the proposition that latent and unconscious transvestite tendencies may well be more widespread than is generally realized, and may be a manifestation of "more or less universal" impulses, which at the time I called "bisexual." It now seems to me that under the influence of this almost forgotten yet self-evident thesis I have been gathering clinical examples of its validity for many years. The mere enumeration of these clinical manifestations would be so lengthy that all I can hope to do here is to present them in a fairly systematic fashion and to suggest possible reasons for a few. I will content myself largely with illustrating my thesis, rather than proving it. Underlying all of them, of course, are many perplexing and unsolved questions.

1. Why have the ontogenetic repetitions of universal phylogenetic experience through generation after generation failed to resolve the problem through genetic changes? The human race has been divided into two sexes for quite a long time. If recurring racial and individual experiences imprint anything, one might assume that the acceptance of gender differences

---

[2] In recent years, under the misleading title of "transsexualism," this concern has been engulfed in a wave of ill-considered surgical and endocrinological efforts to implement the neurotic and even psychotic demands of some patients for gender transmutation.

would by now be deeply ingrained in every one of us from the beginning of life. Yet it is patent that this is not true. Anyone who has observed and listened to uninhibited children has heard them voice their perplexities over the anatomical differences between the sexes, and their rejection and denial of these differences.

2. How then, and when, do we establish such contradictory drives as those I am about to describe?

3. By what different sequences and with what different symptomatic manifestations do they subsequently develop in different individuals?

4. What role do cultural variables play in producing these mutually antithetical and unattainable drives, in determining the levels of consciousness on which they are experienced and expressed, in shaping their direct and indirect manifestations, and in determining the age at which they first begin to dominate the life of any particular individual? (See Mann, 1951; Mead, 1935.)

5. What is the role of culture in determining the differences between the manner in which the drive evolves in man and in woman?

6. What are its implications for some of the dynamic constructs of psychoanalytic theory?

7. What are its implications for the relative roles of identification and/or incorporation in the development of gender identity in general, in the development of the boundaries between the "I" and the "non-I" worlds, in the evolution of object relations, and in the development of compulsive and phobic overdrives or inhibitions in relation to all instinctual activities?

8. Finally, what special role, if any, does this dilemma play in the precipitation of psychotic disorganization out of a neurotogenic impasse? (See Follett, 1927; Kubie, 1966c, this volume, Chapter 7; McCurdy, 1966.) This is the question into which I had no insight when I first presented this paper in 1954, but about which I hope and believe I have learned a great deal since 1959 when I took over the training program at the Sheppard Pratt Hospital and immersed myself in the study of psychotic disorganization.

These and other unsolved problems challenge me as I re-study the file of clinical and theoretical notes accumulated on this topic over the years since 1932 when I read my brief note, "Transvestitism in a Teen-Age Girl." Although I will not even attempt to answer all of these questions, it is valuable to confront them.

As I have already pointed out, after its initial presentation in 1954, fragments of this paper have been read before many psychoanalytic societies and criticized constructively by many colleagues. It has been rewritten many times. Each time I considered that it might be ready for publication, some new observations came my way to lead me to postpone it. Now this process of postponement must come to an end: I must grapple with the process of putting it into final shape as best I can.

These new data have come from many sources: e.g., from the process of aging, which has sensitized me and made it possible for me to see more clearly the relationship of the drive to become both sexes to certain distortions which are introduced by the process of aging in myself, in friends, in relatives, and above all, in patients. Furthermore, there was a change in clinical material that came with my retirement from private office practice in 1959 and a deeper involvement in the clinical data of hospital psychiatry. Finally, there have been the profound changes in the mores in which we live: the "hippie" culture; the pseudofeministic "Woman's Lib," which represents itself as a fusion of man and woman; the feminization of men's clothes and hair style, and the mas-culinization of women's clothes. In all of these it has become increasingly evident that the unconscious drive is *not* to give up the gender to which one was born but to supplement or complement it by developing side by side with it the opposite gender, thereby ending up as both, as did Orlando. The physiological and endocrinological changes of aging accentu-ate this. We have seen swift changes in recent fashions from the compressed breasts, hips, and buttocks and the close-cropped boys' heads of the adolescent "flappers" of the "flaming youth" period to the cavalier haircuts of "hippie" youth; the shift in men to the florid colors and even cosmetics which only a few years ago were reserved for the so-called fairer sex, etc.

All of this has brought something else into sharper focus. A closer study of movies of intercourse (Réjaunier, 1969), and especially perhaps of intercourse among groups of men and women of mixed races (Maurois, 1953; Réjaunier, 1972; Scott-Maxwell, 1957), has made it clear that the goal of a great deal of these frantic struggles in sexual intercourse is neither orgasm nor the begetting of children, but rather a process of magical bodily change. The old Latin phrase *post coitum triste* (sadness after intercourse), even after an orgastically successful psychosexual performance, bears this out. These are frantic searches for something which is never achieved. One climbs a mountain successfully, but ends in depression and not in exultation. When driven by this need for a transmutation into both genders the goal of intercourse is unattainable, and no matter how orgastically satisfactory the experience may have been psychologically, it can only end in frustration, depression, and rage. This is what occurs all too often. In fact, the major, soul-searing penalty that is paid by the homosexual is not the degree of social disapprobation or persecution or legal unfairness and injustice to which he may be exposed by society; it is the inescapable injustice to which he exposes himself through the unattainability of his own unconscious goals. It is this which tumbles him into depression and rage (see Grebanier, 1970; Maurois, 1953).

Yet there are unattainable goals in heterosexual intercourse as well, which is one of the many reasons why the attainment of lasting peace and happiness through sexual fulfillment is not a problem that has been solved in any culture of which we have any knowledge in depth. It is childish naïveté to claim that the orgasm is the whole story (Kubie, 1948, 1955).

When the unconscious goal of sex is the unattainable one to change sides, intercourse ends in frustration. And if this unattainable goal also represents a drive to go in two divergent directions at the same time, it results in a deeper inner schism in the personality—a schism which can be represented by insatiable compulsions and obsessions and by the superimposed construction of opposing phobias. Everything becomes split, and it is on this splitting among conscious and unconscious purposes, and preconscious struggles to achieve these purposes, that psychotic disorganization is based (Kubie, 1964b, 1966b, 1966c, this volume, Chapter 7; Pippett, 1953). This implies not that the only focus of such schismatic processes is gender identity, but merely that this is one of the most devastating of such schisms. Indeed, it is the only schism which gives us any right to use the question-begging, misused, and extraordinarily inappropriate term, "schizophrenia." The schism is not between cognitive and affective processes. Far deeper is the schism between purposes, and in identity struggles to achieve divergent goals and divergent identities. This type of schismatic process, with counterschismatic attempts to achieve both yet to give up neither, can be found in hospitalized psychotic patients and in a great many prepsychotic neurotic patients as well.

Perhaps a further reason why I have found it so difficult to complete this paper and have postponed it repeatedly is that the more I worked over and contemplated the whole concept, and the more clinical examples I gathered, the more I came to realize that in subtle ways it radiated into almost every aspect of our culture and particularly throughout the creative arts. Gender identities are deeply ambivalent among many creative people (Kubie, 1973). Furthermore, the effects of these conflicts and their pathogenic influence are especially serious in the arts. The arts automatically provide individuals with ways of hiding their conflicts while at the same time giving them partial gratifications. In this sense they reward the neurosis in us until we become psychotically disorganized, or commit suicide (see Bell, 1972; Pippett, 1953; L. Woolf, 1963). In fact, this is one reason why creative people, no matter how deeply they suffer from their neuroses, are so loath to subject themselves to treatment. Another reason, of course, is that they fear that if they give up their neuroses their creative potential may "fly out the window" like Orlando's goose.

I realize that to emphasize this concept brings me into conflict with artists and indeed with almost all creative people in the world, although more in the arts and letters than in the sciences. Time and again it has blocked me from carrying this project through to completion, but now I feel that it can no longer be postponed. No matter how much it may expose me to misunderstanding and misinterpretation, I will have to carry it through to its own logical conclusion.

III. HEREDITY AND THE DRIVE TO BECOME BOTH SEXES

The fact that an unconscious drive to become both sexes exists at all is in itself perplexing. If the experience of the race, acting through the genes, exercises any influence on psychological patterns, why is its influence not manifested precisely here? We have been divided into two sexes for quite a long time. How does it happen that the human race has not long since accepted consciously, preconsciously, and unconsciously this universal fact of human life? How does it happen that we reject both the anatomical and functional differences between the sexes?

In every other aspect of human life, analysts accept the fact that man harbors opposed and irreconcilable goals, judgments, feelings, and thoughts in different "systems" or on different "levels" of consciousness. Indeed, it is usually assumed that such ambivalence is universal and ubiquitous. It is noteworthy, therefore, that with respect to gender we have tacitly tended to assume that the goal of a human being is to be either one sex or the other,[3] i.e., to be whatever he was born to be. Yet this is not the case.

The assumption, whether tacit or overt, that any human being can ever want to be only one sex to the exclusion of the other is psychoanalytically naïve and runs counter to all analytic experience. Unfortunately, analysts, like their lay brethren, can put their heads in the sand too. The abundant data from children as well as adults should long since have

---

[3] In the history of psychoanalysis one finds that analysts have lined up in opposing camps about various aspects of this problem, seemingly oblivious to the role which their own multilayered and conflict-laden gender identifications played in determining what side of these controversies they espoused. The consequence has been some of the most heated, least fruitful, and least scientific of all psychoanalytic controversies.

made it clear to us that from childhood, and throughout life, on *conscious, preconscious,* and *unconscious* levels, in varying proportions or emphases, the human goal seems almost invariably to be *both* sexes, with the inescapable consequence that we are always attempting in every moment and every act both to affirm and to deny our gender identities (Stein, 1950; Watson, 1964). These irreconcilable goals are represented by many complex constellations, with many direct and indirect consequences, to be illustrated below. The forms in which they express themselves are manifold. The problems they create are among the most difficult both in life and in psychoanalytic therapy. Perhaps the most puzzling of all are the rare apparent exceptions to this internally contradictory phenomenon (Kubie, 1934a, 1948, 1955, 1956; Kubie and Mackie, 1968).

In this connection it should be borne in mind that this is not the only recurrent, basic, experiential fact of life that we reject. We also deny such recurring and universal experiences as pain and the law of gravity and the ever-recurring experiences of differences in size and age which occur with the processes of growing and aging. If the hereditary imprints of racial experience had the capacity to shape, circumscribe, and guide human fantasies, feelings, and goals, each one of us should by now accept without question all of those universal experiences which have recurred throughout the ages. Infants would not then have to learn to avoid fire and pain and deep water and high ledges. Nor would each successive generation rebel with identical impatience against the seemingly endless years of childhood. Certainly if there were a hereditary acceptance of ever-recurring experiences, it would in countless ways have exercised a stabilizing psychological influence which would have made the business of being a human being far easier than in fact it is. Where and how, then, do the influences of the race's experience operate correctively in mental life? Or is this question itself based on a wish-fulfilling myth?

When we apply these ruminations specifically to the manifestation of the drive to become both sexes, we find ourselves beset with many clinical paradoxes. For instance, after a long and successful struggle with overt homosexual trends, a man was freed of the compulsive component in his homosexual impulses, made a happy marriage, and had several children. Yet this did not release him from his symbolic work block. To work was still to expose his body, which to him still seemed dangerously and humiliatingly and genitally incomplete. Not even the conscious and preconscious affirmation of his penis through intercourse and fatherhood was enough to dispel his feeling that his phallus was illusory. Indeed, nothing was enough, until finally he discovered in analysis that what he had always wanted unconsciously was to possess at the same time not only the phallus but also the woman's breasts as part of his own body, that he craved also the ability to inseminate himself, to gestate, to produce, and to nurse his own progeny, and also to castrate other men. Indeed, these were precisely what the unconscious goals of his entire artistic career had been for him. The inevitable result of his failure to attain these unconscious and impossible goals was that every artistic triumph left these deeply buried needs unfulfilled, thereby plunging him deeper into depression.

One day he stated the issue succinctly. He asked: "Why is it that when discussing any problem in social groups I am friendly, warm, using words to win friends, almost to make love; whereas when I am writing I am vicious, shooting through the slots in a concrete pillbox. I am the same man using the same tool [i.e., words] for totally different purposes. Why?"

Such clinical data return me to my question: How is it that the cumulative experience of the race can neither prevent nor modify such fantastic distortions of our expectations and drives?

IV. Use of the Term "Drive" in This Essay

Before going further I want to explain why I have deliberately chosen to use the term "drive," and what I mean and do not mean by it. In the first place, by drive I do not mean direct expressions of biological levels of the body's processes or those primitive activities which accomplish all interchanges with the outside world: i.e., of materials, energy, heat, and especially communicative signals, without which neither the individual nor the species nor any social organization can survive. Specifically, I do *not* mean a primary instinctual pattern—i.e., a basic activity such as eating, drinking, breathing, excreting— which mediates the organism's biochemical and biophysical interchanges with the environment. What I *do* mean are those urgencies that derive from the symbolic representatives of biogenetic needs which are experienced as *appetites* on all levels: conscious, preconscious, and unconscious (Kubie, this volume, Chapter 2, 1956). I mean those complex patterns of secondary and tertiary *symbolic* activities that derive from the primary patterns. And we must remind ourselves that whenever these symbolic derivative actions are dominated by psychological processes which are predominantly unconscious, they acquire that rigidity which is familiar to us in all phobic and obsessional-compulsive states, as well as in the psychoses. Symbolic processes in which the relations of the symbol to what it is supposed to represent are distorted or severed, become frozen into rigid, repetitive, unlearning, and insatiable patterns. This is the essence of all psychopathological mechanisms, whether obsessional, compulsive, phobic, or psychotic (see this volume, Chapter 7).

Used in this way, the multiple connotations of the term "drive" carry a breadth of implications sufficient to cover all of the relevant phenomena to be studied. Any drive may represent in part conscious and preconscious yet incompatible wishes, which may be dealt with by deliberate, conscious, and also preconscious compromises, as in sports, manners, posture, voice, clothes, art, etc. Concurrently, however, some of the determinants of the same drive may also be unconscious, as a consequence of which this aspect of the drive can be expressed only through the disguised symbols of dreams, neurotic and psychotic behavior, and symptoms. Thus the fate of any drive and its manifestations, as well as its resolution in analysis, depends on the relative roles of the three levels on which it may simultaneously be operative. When a drive does not operate predominantly on conscious or preconscious levels but operates rather on an unconscious level to determine such important matters as the choice of a mate or of an occupation, the consequences become important. While this may sound complicated when stated in general terms, when considered in terms of concrete examples it becomes transparently simple.

For instance, a well-known couturier was obviously effeminate in manner but highly endowed and artistic. He launched a successful career as a designer of clothes for the sex he envied and could not become. His choice of career drew from all levels: conscious, preconscious, and unconscious. All went well until the unconscious components took over, compelling him to violate his own essentially good taste by fantastic misuse of color and form, garish accentuation of apertures, burlesqued distortions of body form. His unconscious hate and envy of feminine apertures, breasts, and buttocks forced him to make monstrosities out of the styles he created for the women he scorned but longed to become.

In a previous work (Kubie, 1958a), I used diagrams to clarify this meaning of "drive," and several are reproduced below. Figures 1 and 3 are deliberately oversimplified, omitting preconscious processes in order to show the gradations between a wish, a trend (or drive), and a compulsion. They illustrate a single purpose operating under the simultaneous impulsion and guidance of both conscious and unconscious processes. Where conscious determinants are dominant, no symbols are required other than the usual conceptual tools and the verbal and visual symbols for their communication. Where unconscious determinants are dominant, they are represented by activities which constitute a pattern of disguised and distorted symbolic actions—the only way in which preponderantly unconscious processes can be expressed.

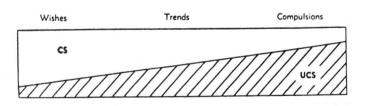

FIGURE 1

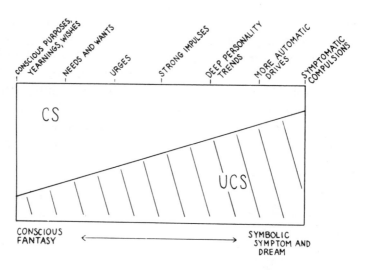

FIGURE 3

Therefore in Figure 4 these same relationships are represented in a more complicated way which comes closer to doing
justice to their full complexity by including the important role
of preconscious codeterminants. Thus it portrays areas in
which preconscious processes dominate either conscious or unconscious processes or both — areas in which preconscious and
conscious processes are oriented toward the same goal but are
distorted by the unconscious processes which aim at a similar
goal. Every human impulse, feeling, thought, act, or pattern
of living may fall somewhere along such a spectrum as this. It
will be noted that this diagram indicates that there are no
acts in which any one level of processing exercises its
influence alone. There are no unconscious processes devoid of
conscious and preconscious codeterminants, and no conscious
or preconscious processes devoid of unconscious codeterminants.

One of the most important unsolved technical problems
among those which challenge all students of human behavior
is to develop methods which will show with a fair degree of
precision where on such a spectrum any individual psychological action falls, by determining whether conscious, preconscious, or unconscious processes play dominant roles in its production, and to what degree. No attributes of human

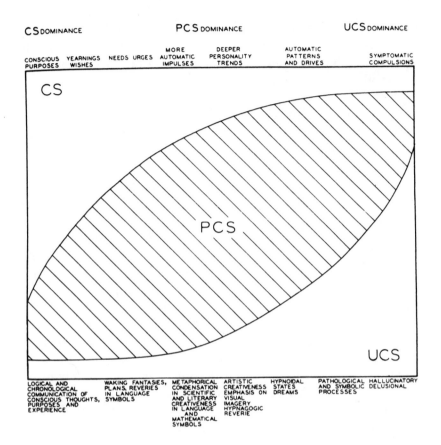

CS DOMINANCE PCS DOMINANCE UCS DOMINANCE

CONSCIOUS PURPOSES | YEARNINGS WISHES | NEEDS URGES | MORE AUTOMATIC IMPULSES | DEEPER PERSONALITY TRENDS | AUTOMATIC PATTERNS AND DRIVES | SYMPTOMATIC COMPULSIONS

CS

PCS

UCS

LOGICAL AND CHRONOLOGICAL COMMUNICATION OF CONSCIOUS THOUGHTS, PURPOSES AND EXPERIENCE | WAKING FANTASIES, PLANS, REVERIES IN LANGUAGE SYMBOLS | METAPHORICAL CONDENSATION IN SCIENTIFIC AND LITERARY CREATIVENESS IN LANGUAGE AND MATHEMATICAL SYMBOLS | ARTISTIC CREATIVENESS EMPHASIS ON VISUAL IMAGERY HYPNAGOGIC REVERIE | HYPNOIDAL STATES DREAMS | PATHOLOGICAL AND SYMBOLIC PROCESSES | HALLUCINATORY DELUSIONAL

FIGURE 4

personality and behavior are more important than these, and we lack the instruments of great precision which we need for the exact scientific analysis of the relative roles of these concurrent processes. Perhaps some day clinical psychology will provide them. At present our only methods are impressionistic and clinical, and derive from the fact that to the degree to which unconscious processes are dominant, behavior will be insatiable, unvarying, repetitive, and rigid, whereas a preponderance of conscious and preconscious determinants makes for flexibility and the free use of analogy, metaphor, allegory, similarities and dissimilarities. Conscious processes test these for degrees of identity with external data (the crux of reality testing) and also for degrees of flexibility and the capacity to change and to learn through experience. Conscious and preconscious preponderance ensures the freedom to learn from experience, to grow, and to change: this, in turn, means freedom from neurotic imprisonment (Kubie, 1973).

The last, more complex diagram (Figure 4) is reminiscent of the nomograms with which the late L. J. Henderson used to illustrate the interdependent relations among the chemical constituents of the blood stream, where no single element could vary without a shift and movement in the chemical and biophysical concentrations, states, and behavior of every other element. In psychological activity this may be equally true of the interplay among these three systems. If so, it is impossible to understand any basic conflict (such as the conflict over sexual goals and gender identities) unless the conflict is considered as the expression of a continuous interplay of concurrent conscious, preconscious, and unconscious processes. I regret the complexity of the diagram, but unfortunately one cannot use simplified diagrams to represent complex phenomena without doing them an injustice. Naturally, the diagrams must be regarded merely as visual, graphic descriptions of a hypothesis which is to be explored, and which ultimately must be subjected to quantitative studies when appropriate techniques have been developed. Such techniques will be devices for ascertaining the relative roles in any single moment of life of concurrent conscious, preconscious, and unconscious processes whose algebraic summation is expressed in everything we think, say, plan, shun, feel, desire, and do. Parenthetically, I will say that I anticipate that only through the development and application of entirely new clinical psychological tests, and through a fresh approach to the study of the processes of free association, will we develop the tools by which the relative roles of these three concurrent systems can be appraised.

V. MULTIPLE MANIFESTATIONS AND FORMS OF THE DRIVE

A man who now stands over six feet, three inches, and weighs about two hundred and fifteen pounds was a sick, weak, undersized infant and child who suffered from severe gastrointestinal disorders. As a result, until late adolescence he lagged behind his age mates in growth. He had one brother two years younger and another twelve years younger. The step-by-step loss of his mother to his siblings was completed after the birth of the third son when the mother developed an incurable illness. As the saddened family tried to make up for this to the last child by focusing all attention on him, the patient developed a double envy of him, for which he over-compensated by an erotized mothering of the little brother. Throughout his formative and growing years this pattern of behavior dominated his physical development and his behav-ior in studies, sports, voice, posture, gesture, in art interests, in choice of friends, and in his psychosexual relationships.

During his analysis it became clear that this was a dream-like, symbolic expression of multiple, irreconcilable, and un-attainable goals. He wanted to continue to be himself, but he also wanted to replace the mother he had lost by occupying her role both with his little brother and with his father. Yet at the same time he wanted to displace the youngest brother in the love of his parents by undergoing a process of physical transmutation in his fantasies of an imaginary, blue-eyed, blonde, curly-headed little sister, who had never existed except in his mother's joking yet outspoken fantasies and wishes. He manifested all of this by denying the differences between little girls and boys in many ways. Thus in his oc-casional explorations of the bodies of little girls he always blinded himself to his own discoveries, insisting that they were like him. At the same time his behavior revealed the fact that he really possessed full knowledge of the realities which he verbally rejected. Thus he would tuck his own penis between his thighs, holding it there as he walked clumsily around, in imitation of the bodies of the little girls he envied and whose bodily structure he denied. His unconscious goal was to win the love of both his father and his mother by a masculine-feminine fusion or compromise.

Later in the analysis, he evolved a fixed fantasy that his mother had a phallus and that he actually had seen it on one occasion. He recalled that, when he was about twelve years old, he passed on the street an unknown woman who was striding vigorously along. She wore a powder blue tweed jacket and skirt. He never forgot her; she became the living embodiment of his fantasy, the proof that there could be a woman with a penis, the phallic man-woman he had been seeking to become. She *was* both sexes, and from this came the unconscious deduction that if *she* could be both, so could *he*.

In adolescence the duality of his unconscious goal led to repeated embarrassments. For years he masked this gender duality in a troubled preoccupation with the Jewish-Christian problem. Which was he? Then came the pursuit of compromise figures as "love" objects—i.e., young boy-girls—and a consistent and repeated turning away from all feminine women. As a young adult he married a woman who fitted the mold of the unknown man-woman in his-her powder blue tweeds. The marriage was tragic and destructive. All relationships, whether with men or women, were transient, quickly explored and quickly abandoned for reasons he could never articulate. Furthermore, despite great native ability, before his analysis he had been unable to commit himself lastingly to any field of work. Such a commitment would have meant affirming and accepting his position as a man and abandoning his fantasy that he could be a woman at the same time. In this man's life the drive operated on preconscious as well as unconscious levels.

In the analysis the resolution of his struggle started as he began to glimpse the fact that he handled his entire social life as though he were an adolescent girl, side-stepping all direct competition with men. Then came the realization that he had also done this in his business relations and ventures. This led to a further realization that every element in his work and home life, in his sexual life, and in his relationship to his children (especially his sons), both expressed and masked his simultaneous identification with women. Through a dream and through the analysis of his masturbatory fantasies he discovered that his pipe and cane, from which he had been inseparable, quite directly represented to him both breast and phallus. Again, he could neither commit himself to either, nor give up either.

These insights came to him in moments of fantasy, in dreams, while dancing, sometimes in sudden momentary flashes of illumination in the midst of intercourse. With his growing understanding and insights, certain changes occurred in his posture, voice, and social attitudes. His sleep improved. Gastrointestinal symptoms (for which he had twice been hospitalized) disappeared. The hostile suspiciousness, which had frequently been mistaken for a true paranoia, dropped away. It was particularly significant that for the first time in his life he could accept deprivation and postponement, and could plan his days not in terms of moment-to-moment and day-to-day gratifications, but in terms of long-range purposes.

The study of this patient, and of several others of both sexes ranging in age from adolescence through the fifties, has led me to believe that the inability or reluctance to commit oneself to either gender can play a major role in producing the work blocks of childhood, adolescence, and maturity.

It is not yet possible to trace in a fully representative series of cases the developmental sequences by which this drive reaches its adult forms. In a few instances I have been able to trace it almost step by step, but it is impossible to say that these represent statistically adequate or broadly representative samples of something which seems to be so widely diffused in our culture that it would be quite unrealistic to expect to find it growing in any one psychopathological soil. At most, a few broad principles may be tentatively proposed.

Anything which is found almost universally in human culture must have universal roots. This forces us to conclude that both for the little boy and the little girl one of the deepest tendencies in human nature is to attempt to identify with and to become both parents: with the stronger parent so as to acquire his strength, with the weaker out of sympathy and to seek and provide consolation. It would be strange if the drive to become both sexes did not arise. The questions to ask are: How and why does it vary in its development, in its expression, in the toll it takes? And how is it resolved, if it is resolved? And what are its residual consequences in adult life? How do its consequences differ when it is lived out on predominantly con-

scious, preconscious, and/or unconscious levels? What determines whether or not it will have a specific and distorting
influence on genital sexual life?

The drive can be recognized concurrently from early childhood to old age. The level of consciousness on which it is
experienced and expressed, and the extent to which it becomes
a focus of repressed conflict, seem to depend in part on variables in the family mores: what the family talked and joked
about, how they dressed, etc. Furthermore, it is shaped and
influenced by such events as (a) the birth of a new baby, and
whether this baby is of the same or the opposite sex; (b) the
age difference between the child and his newly born sibling;
(c) illnesses, accidents, deaths, and disappearances from the
home group of emotionally important individuals; (d) triumphs, failures, and emotional attitudes in the immediate
family; (e) the phase of instinctual emphasis through which
the child is passing at the time when such events occur—
especially true in twins and siblings, or stepsiblings, of opposite gender.

A boy of ten and his eight-year-old sister were left mother-
less by the sudden death of their lawyer mother. The father, a
man of unusual "sweetness" and gentleness (almost to the
point of effeminacy), played the roles of both parents to his
two children, mothering them as well as fathering them. One
could sense the hold on the daughter of her identification with
the father as a man, and the influence on the son of his identification with his mother as a woman. When the father remar-
ried, it was again to a professional woman. She was warm,
intense, and stimulating, but gaunt. Presently they had
nonidentical twins, a son and a daughter. The half brother
became the twins' nurse, obsessively and jealously guarding his
right to feed, bathe, and carry them, change their diapers,
push them in the baby carriage, and play with them. His sister
took over none of these mothering roles, but turned instead
toward a male role and shared her father's interests. Ultimately the son became a lawyer like his mother, but like his
stepmother he did not marry until relatively late in life.
Through the years he lost the faint hint of precious femininity

of manner so marked in his early years, but his dual identification and dual goal determined his choice of a mate and his relation to his three sons, as well as many of the vicissitudes of his brilliant career.

The relative positions of the two parents of older siblings of each sex influence the subtle processes of preconscious identification. One or both parents may have caused the patient disappointment by "failing" in a major role as an adult, or perhaps by dying or disappearing. I have encountered this constellation repeatedly, and equally in men and women. For example, in the son of a weak, ineffectual father and a sick mother; in the son of a man always away on business and a strident, harsh, and at the same time anxious and exhibitionistic mother; and in the son of a remote, scholarly father and a young, seductive mother; in the daughter of a beaten, defeated man who was a sensitive but thwarted artist and a woman who was illegitimate; in the daughter of an arrogant, tyrannical father and an abject, whimpering mother. In the group as a whole a high percentage have been oldest children, but the total number is not large enough for this observation to have more than a suggestion of statistical validity.

In the life stories of the patients in whom these irreconcilable and antithetical drives seem to have played both a dominant and a destructive role, there were an almost infinite number of concatenations of circumstances which discolored their early identifications with envy, emulation, and abasement. Among these parental figures who should have been objects of confident support and of wholehearted emulation, one died early, another was a cripple, a third a drunkard, a fourth a spiritual weakling, a fifth a seductive sadist. In every instance there was a common feature: a combination of envy, helpless fear, identification with the aggressor, plus hate and scorn.

At some point in the life story of each of these patients envy of some contemporary of the opposite sex crystallized, usually another sibling or cousin. With this, there was a simultaneous debasement of the envied figure, so that the identification included hostile and contemptuous reservations. Frequently the dreams in which this is expressed both incorporate and regurgitate. In one clear example, the male patient suffered a dreamed sensation of "indigestion" which he called "morning nausea." This physical sensation also occurred in hypnagogic reveries as he drifted off to sleep. In his childhood the two major objects of identification, emulation, and incorporation had been, first, a vigorous maternal grandfather who had lived in the home until his death when the patient was nine, and second, his mother, who was hostile, possessive, and castrative, and who dressed his younger brother (his only sibling) in curls and frills for years. The father, a cripple, was an eclipsed figure.

In general, therefore, it seems to be true that when a child is unable to emulate either parent wholeheartedly, his preconscious and unconscious identifications will be negative toward both; each tends to be an object of envy and scorn rather than of positive wholehearted identification. This seems to be one of the forces which may obstruct the formation of unifying identifications.

As the child develops further, the focus of his attention shifts back and forth between the body as a whole and its various parts — part functions, apertures, and products. These include the breasts, genitals, hips, hair, eyes, mouth, facial expression, posture, gesture, intonation, voice, body smells, body tastes, and body products. Thus auditory, tactile, olfactory, and gustatory as well as visual components of experience play roles in orienting the developing child toward those with whom he strives to identify, but from whom he must at the same time differentiate himself. In general, these perceptual residues are so buried that it is difficult to recapture them except through techniques which employ hypnagogic reveries or other devices for inducing controlled states of dissociation with maintained communication (Kubie, 1943, 1945b; Kubie and Margolin, 1945). Consequently, analysis can rarely secure the essential memories of early perceptual data of this order through their verbal representations alone. This limitation afflicts all verbal techniques, whether psychoanalytic or other, because of the tendency inherent in words to screen perceptual data and the "gut" components of memory (Kubie, 1941b, 1948, 1950c, 1952a, this volume, Chapter 4, 1955, 1956). The relative lack of such data as these limits our ability to trace with precision the earliest stages of the development of such identifications.

This lack is of more than passing importance. The terms "activity" and "passivity" are value judgments. They are not the stuff out of which a child's concepts of man and woman, of boy and girl, evolve. The child builds these entities out of his sensory experiences of specific individuals; i.e., body warmth and smell and taste, the texture and rustle and color of skin and hair and clothes, the imprints of posture and movement and gesture, facial expressions of anger, rage, and love, the timbre and pitch and volume of voice. These are the stuff out of which bodily identifications are made. Victory and defeat, power and weakness, status, activity and passivity, dependence and independence, are adult abstractions which evolve slowly and late out of the raw material of primary experiences, and under the conventionalizing pressures of social forces. As this occurs the primary sensory data become obscured by a screen of reified conceptual abstraction. The difficulty of recapturing such early sensory components of early identifications poses a serious obstacle to exploratory and therapeutic research.

Nevertheless, I have a few clear samples of sensory data derived from early oral drives, expressive of a man's envy of and desire for breasts, as a step toward becoming, possessing, and containing his mother, while at the same time maintaining his own phallic integrity. In another instance, a woman's older sister had been physically cruel and oppressive to her all through her childhood, yet was her only symbol of strength and fancied security. This sister therefore became the main focus of need and attachment, but at the same time of envy as a phallic woman. The younger woman dreamed that she saw her sister naked, with full breasts and a banana in her hand; then, as she watched, the banana became a phallus. At first the patient was horrified at this. Then she suddenly thought, "That's all right; it means that I am soon going to have one of my own."

Contradictory manifestations can coexist with bewildering variety, e.g., the swaggering and aggressive man who out of sudden shyness cannot go into a store to buy a tie but must ask friends or his wife to do it for him; the young prize fighter who knowingly marries a lesbian; the woman who drinks like a man, swaggers like a man, swears like a man, fights like a man, and whose voice breaks at times to resemble that of a man, yet who demands to be made love to as a woman; the many men who are aggressively male in all their external relationships but who are feminine in bed; and, conversely, men who are feminine in their orientation toward the world yet who are compulsively and insatiably masculine in bed. Contradictory manifestations can also follow each other in successive stages of development. Some of these are familiar; e.g., the transmutation of tomboy into female adolescent, or the rough-and-tumble lad who asks for a doll for Christmas.

Such agglomerations of contradictions express crisscrossing identifications, while at the same time giving rise to a multiplicity of incompatible goals. I have cited the man who needed to become his father's daughter without relinquishing his identity as his mother's son. (This can occur even when there are no actual daughters in the family.) He is matched by his opposite number—the woman who wants to be the son her father never had without relinquishing her status as a woman.

Out of these contradictions arises a special form of insatiability, because whenever we attempt to gratify mutually irreconcilable drives the gratification of either component automatically frustrates its opposite. Inevitably such insatiability has oral components, yet it need not arise out of an overaccentuation of primary orality, with which it can be fused or merely confused. Rather, the oral ingredient may be the instrument by which the unconscious drive to become both sexes is to be achieved, through incorporation of breasts or penis or both, or of the body as a whole. This plays a role in sudden, explosive episodes of heterosexual or homosexual fellatio. The dream of the envied older sister with exaggerated breasts and holding a banana which becomes a phallus is another self-translating example of this. In short, merely because orality may be expressed in insatiability does not warrant an assumption that insatiability arises always and solely out of orality.

Similarly, the material derived from this drive is frequently mistaken for primary Oedipal derivatives. For instance, in one dream and also in one waking fantasy, the image of a father violating his daughter represented not an act of love-making, or of "making a baby," but a demand that he plant his phallus in her so as to turn her into a boy-girl. Similarly, a man whose dreams and fantasies seemed to demand intimacy with his mother's body was trying instead to incorporate the mother's breast and vagina so as to achieve his secret aim to become both sexes without relinquishing either. In such instances it is not easy to disentangle true Oedipal drives from those which make use of Oedipal acts for purposes of magical bodily transformations. The fact that both sets of unconscious implications may frequently coexist, side by side, in the same individual makes the distinction especially difficult.

If I were asked for my clinical impression of the nature of the most universal, the most highly charged, and the most characteristic manifestations of the drive to become both sexes, I would say that they are: (1) An angry and perpetual search for a parental figure who is an idealized father and mother combined, to replace one who has "failed." (2) Insatiability—i.e., the demand to remain forever a bisexual infant who will be suckled, supported, and made love to by the same parental figure over whom there is also a necessity to triumph (all of this to be represented by the analyst). (3) The demand actually to become and thus to displace both parental figures. (4) The demand to replace a younger sibling of the opposite sex while remaining the same sex oneself.

Finally, there is a special relationship of the drive to become both sexes to both the verbal and the graphic presentation of "pornography." What any word means depends in part on its past history, but what a word comes to mean through usage may be quite different. A word may be worn by usage as a coin may be worn away until almost none of the original marking remains. This is what has happened to the term and concept of pornography. The Greek root tells us little of its present implications. From history and from usage comes only one significant implication, namely, a desperate struggle toward an insatiable, conflicting, and therefore unfulfillable goal.

This is where the term comes closest to the implied consequences of the drive to become both sexes.

Whether it is a description in vivid words by Jeanne Réjaunier (1969, 1972), or Mickey Spillane, or Henry Miller, pornographic literature represents the endless, sad search for something unattainable, often repellent. It also carries the implication of a frustrated orgy, of a whole group of men and women struggling nakedly together in a frenzy of futility as they attempt to achieve an impossible alchemy of change in which all differences will be transmuted into one likeness, multiple sexes into one sex. No matter what kind of physiological ecstasy is achieved, the end is spiritual disaster. These concepts underlie what is pornographic in today's art and literature: the desperate search for unconscious goals which are opposites, irreconcilable, and therefore forever unattainable and insatiable. Furthermore, because of the frustrations involved, what may have started as attraction or even as some form of love becomes hate, destruction, violence, and gore, while what started as a mutual act becomes purely onanistic, no matter how many other people are involved. All of this is the expression of the drive to become both sexes, its futility, its misery, and its desperation, as we see in the frustrated pseudo-erotic frenzies of encounter groups.

VI. Relation of the Neurotic Drive to Become Both Sexes to Psychotic Disorganization

When we study the psychoses closely on the basis of a searching anamnestic survey of the prepsychotic neurotic process, we find in the life histories of psychotics every symptom and every problem with which we become familiar when we study the neuroses. But we also see that certain crises occur on the path from neurosis to psychosis. For any of many reasons the price the patient has to pay for his unsolved neurotic problems may increase, sometimes suddenly and sometimes insidiously. Or his methods of evasion may lose their efficacy. Sometimes he reaches an impasse from which there is no escape except the psychotic explosion. The simplest paradigm is the individual who after many years of struggling with a claustrophobia develops a superimposed agoraphobia. Thereupon, as he becomes trapped between them, he ends literally standing on his doorstep, unable to move in or out. Then comes the explosion. Although this may sound oversimplified, it actually occurs even in as simple a form as this, and I could point out innumerable subtler and more complex examples of precisely such entrapments between polar neurotic binds which produce that tragic transition from the neurotic process into disorganized psychotic episodes.

In recent years much has been written about the operation of a process called the "double bind," a term which has been used in various ways. By some it has been applied to the earliest steps in the development of the child's personality, with a concurrent premise that something in the attitude of the family (and more particularly of the mother) traps the child in a situation in which it becomes impossible for him to move either to left or to right. Others have found evidence that this type of dilemma can also crystallize much later. It is my impression that the double bind can exercise its destructive influence both early and late, and that, although they are important, the parental attitudes toward the young child play a less unique role in determining this than has been assumed. For instance, conflicting unconscious and/or preconscious identifications may form more often than was realized, and whenever this occurs it results in an insoluble dilemma and entrapment. It arises with catastrophic effects out of the drive to become both sexes when the patient cannot reconcile himself to being either a boy or a girl, either a man or a woman, either his father or his mother, but wants to be both and/or neither.

As was pointed out some years ago, there is no psychopathology which does not involve dissociative processes: that is to say, dissociations among components of psychological processes which should normally operate together (Kubie and Margolin, 1945). These dissociations can be simple dissociations in time and place—things which occurred together are recalled and responded to as though they had occurred quite separately. Alternatively, the memories of bits of experience which occurred separately may be recalled and responded to as though they had occurred concurrently. This leads to dissociations between the symbols which are used to represent these bits of experience, the items of experience with which they were originally linked, and the affects which should have accompanied, preceded, or followed them. Thus these dislocations in time and space can also dislocate their affective colorings. There can also be dissociations between effects and the initiating precipitants of the neurotic impasse, or between effects and the sustaining causes of these head-on collisions or their consequences. Furthermore, bits of processes that become dissociated from one another can be reconnected, either with their original roots and links, or to form new combinations and new patterns. Moreover, all such dissociations and their reorganization into new combinations have their own secondary and tertiary consequences. Such alternatives give us hints of the enormous complexity and variety of the changing, kaleidoscopic mosaics of experience which enter into all neurotic processing. This is part of the secondary inescapable buildup of the neurotic process which gives rise to new formations of the consequences of human experience.

Yet none of this is a primary, initiating, or instigating element in the neurotic process. These are its symptomatic products. They resemble a fever in that they are the products of a disease process, while at the same time they have their own secondary consequences which lead to further steps in the process of illness.

Furthermore, there are other important kinds of dissociative processes: dissociations involving personal identity and dissociations which produce confusion and inner conflicts over gender identity and gender purposes. Here the basic issues are: What do I want to be? Do I have to choose? Do I have it in my power to choose? Can I be both? Can I alternate? This in turn is linked to complex problems which involve conscious, preconscious, and deeply buried unconscious ingredients of our secret body images.[4]

---

[4] If one thinks of the schism in what is miscalled "schizophrenia" as being not a secondary schism in the relationship of cognitive, ideational, and affective processes but as primary schisms in identity such as these, the term itself may begin to have some valid meaning and significance.

As I write this, many images and memories of patients come to mind. What was the concealed fantasy about himself in the man with the inturned, unsmiling smile, a small, weak, and motionless mouth, frightened eyes, and sudden explosions of apparently unmotivated rage? Then it came out that his rage was not unmotivated at all. Some subtle clue had made him feel not only that this was the way he saw himself but that it was the way others (including the therapist) saw him too. Furthermore, without knowing it he had been trying to be not one person but two because of his hostile, conflicting, and unconscious identifications with a tempestuous father on the one hand and a weak, frightened, placating mother on the other.

Another memory is of the man whose face was also masked in shyness, whose way of using his head and neck, his evasive postures, all finally came to expression in a dream of being someone whose eyes and nose were masks and substitutes for another triad (i.e., for his phallus and testicles) and his mouth a surrogate vulva, as though he wore genitalia on his face. He lived in constant terror that his face was betraying and unmasking him. These were not delusions; they were his inarticulate feelings about his own image, feelings whose content was unconscious but which caused him intense pain. Interestingly enough, drugs came into this picture too, because as one explored further one discovered that, for him, the purpose of drugs was to fulfill his need to change genders. I have reason to believe that this is not infrequently true among adolescents and may in turn be related to the desperate terror so many gifted young people have of committing themselves to any one gender—the terror of success in studies, in sports, in careers, in social groups, and even the terror of sexual success in bed. Success itself carries for them the threat and terror of committing oneself to being one or the other, and the terror of relinquishing the opposite goal.

Obviously such considerations raise other questions. What happens to the secret self-image of a man or a woman after a so-called "transsexual" operation for gender transmutation? No one can answer this question as yet for the simple and self-evident reason that those who have been involved in experiments with gender transmutations (miscalled "transsexualism") have never made specific before-and-after studies of the psychological changes such manipulations produce in self-imagery. These subtle, elusive, and concealed elements in the human psyche are difficult to study, but that they must be studied is evident.

Related to all of these issues are identifications with the parent of the same sex and/or of the opposite sex, cross- and mixed identifications with parents of both sexes, and also with older or younger siblings of the same or opposite sex. Obviously these too must be influenced by operations for gender transmutation, yet they have not been studied from this point of view in spite of their profound, transparent, and potentially blighting influence on human development and on the utilization of human potentials. I think of a vigorously masculine and hirsute older brother of four male siblings, a man of extraordinary ability, but so paralyzed by his hopeless yearning to replace a blue-eyed, pink-cheeked sister that he could never allow himself to achieve anything which would have meant turning his back on the feminine identity for which he was secretly and unconsciously yearning. He wanted to be both.

This brings up what is perhaps the most destructive element of all: i.e., the fact that these internally conflicting, contradictory, and unattainable goals can so dominate a life as to cause dissociations among purposes and activities on all levels —conscious, preconscious, and unconscious. It is out of such soil as this that multiple dissociations and depersonalizations can lead to psychotic schisms and disorganizations.

This endless fluctuation between satisfaction and dissatisfaction with the body has manifested itself for centuries in both sexes. It is nothing new. Since the Second World War we have seen it accentuated in the "hippie" culture, with its sharp swing from the woman turned male to the male turned woman. What has been most striking about this latest swing has been its ambiguity, so that one often has to ask oneself, "Am I looking at a man or a woman or at both together?" The same ambivalence has been manifested in erotic practices which have become equally ambiguous, in so far as what the male or female did in bed together became less and less distinguishable. To implement these unattainable fantasies has required the use not merely of plastic surgery and prostheses but also of drugs.[5] Why this has been intensified in recent years and why it has been linked by steps of inherent frustrations to carnage and bloodletting and the cult of violence in today's movies and TV is again an extraordinarily important problem. But it is not a problem on which anyone has the right to be dogmatic or to pretend to have answers. For the most part, these are questions which no one has asked. Therefore it would hardly be reasonable to expect that someone would have found answers to unasked questions about unsolved problems, the very existence of which has not even been acknowledged.

As for myself, I must make it clear that the most I can hope to do here is to call attention to and illustrate some of these many unsolved but deeply important problems of human culture.

VII. The Interplay between the Drives to Be Both Big and Little, Both Adult and Child, and Both Sexes or Neither

Anyone who has lived close to and observed children objectively is aware that the human child is not reconciled to being a child. One sees the manifestations of this every day. But why do the smoldering rages over being a child, over being "smaller" than others, sometimes last throughout life, producing irrational competition for size in buildings, cars, etc.? And if sometimes, why not always? Equally perplexing is the observed fact that there may be at the same time an equally violent rebellion against becoming "grown up." Here again we encounter an entrapment in an inability to accept

---

[5] This passing fad for what is miscalled "transsexualism" has led to the most tragic betrayal of human expectation in which medicine and modern endocrinology and surgery have ever engaged. In the name of gender transmutation they have led people to believe that alchemy is possible, thus fostering in individuals and our whole culture conscious and unconscious neurotogenic fantasies whose only possible outcome is an intensification of the neurotic fantasies which underlie their expectation and ultimate psychosis.

either of two irreconcilable and therefore unattainable states and goals—that of remaining a child and that of becoming an adult. Furthermore, the drive to remain a child may be merely a path to still another unconscious goal: namely, to go back to the brink of the beginning in order to start over again and grow up as a member of the opposite gender. This is a special and important form of "brinksmanship," a perplexing and tragic source of youthful suicide attempts. Consequently, the human being, child and man, who is not reconciled either to the fact that mankind is divided into children and adults, or to the fact that it is divided into two sexes, may find that he also may reject his own growth toward maturity. In this way, these two basic rejections of reality become interwoven, and by this tortured path an individual may harbor concurrent drives to be an adult-man and a child-woman, or to be an adult-woman and a child-male, or even to be a child of both genders. I must repeat here that, in the imprinting of these crisscrossing roles, confused early identifications play dominant roles and produce individuals who cannot commit themselves in life to any enduring role, whether in study, work, or play.

Clearly, when one wants at one and the same instant to be both a daughter and a son, whether of a father or of a mother, or if one wants to be both a wife and a daughter, or both a husband and a son, or alternatively a husband and daughter, it is difficult to commit oneself to anything and yet remain at peace with oneself. Out of such irreconcilable demands it is inevitable that frustration and hostility will arise, with an involuntary and savage turning against the sexual partner. Such concealed but irreconcilable identifications lead to many rationalized dissatisfactions in marriage, some of which will be discussed below. These conflicts and their consequences can be recognized throughout the history of human culture. Why they are playing such a devastating role in the "hippie" culture of today is less clear.

There can also be a concurrent, alternative, and often tragic drive to be *neither* sex, a complication that often leads to depression and terror, to unreality feelings and depersonalization. The individual fluctuates between the need to be both and to be neither, challenging life insatiably and even viciously with the demand: "Give me all or nothing. Let me be both or neither." I have seen this precipitate psychosis after relatively "successful" plastic operations, whether on the face or on the genitals, and after medication for gender transmutation.

Furthermore, in my experience this gives rise to some of the most intractable difficulties we encounter in all forms of psychiatric therapy, whether with electroshock, chemotherapy, psychotherapy, or psychoanalysis. Frequently it is the hidden source of what is defensively and confusingly misnamed "the negative therapeutic reaction." Just as political freedom is a mockery to someone who is dying of starvation or disease, so "getting well" is a cruel joke to someone whose unconscious and intransigent demand is inherently unattainable—to become both sexes and/or neither. This is well illustrated in my review of *I Never Promised You a Rose Garden* (Kubie, 1966a).

VIII. Relation of the Drive to Marriage, Sex, and Aging

Another manifestation of this perplexity influences the phenomena of courtship, and the shift from courtship into marriage.

A. COURTSHIP

Superimposed upon his conscious yet largely inarticulate hopes, the human being brings into courtship a wide constellation of unconscious expectations. He hopes that the new relationship and the new affirmations which he seeks through this relationship are going to solve all of his problems, both internal and external; and that those which are not solved are no longer going to hurt, so that they will no longer worry, perplex, depress, frighten, or anger him. As after a lobotomy, the words may be unchanged but the tune will be different; and where they cannot cure they are at least going to make life relatively painless as they resolve and smooth out the wrinkles left on the human spirit by conflict. In the words of the old song, there will be "no more sorrow, no more trouble, no more pain" (James, 1933). Furthermore, the magic of the new relationship is going to make the individual permanently into the kind of man or woman that he can temporarily pretend to be during the process of courtship. This engaging, delightful, humorous, witty, winning, attractive, enduring, generous, adaptable human being that he has suddenly become will be "me forever." And effortlessly, mind you. All of this is part of the magic that is sought during courtship.

But a deeper concomitant is also longed for, namely, a magical change in the body. The new relationship will eliminate everything about the body which has been secretly, dimly, and barely consciously found dismaying. And most important of all, the courtship is going to work magic on sexual differences. The ancient magic of laying on of hands, "the king's touch," will either change one into the opposite sex, or — and far more frequently — it will make it possible to become *both* sexes. This is the hidden meaning of the old dream of a mystical union. The mystical union of the spirit is easily acceptable as a romantic goal, but far more significant is the mystical union of two bodies which will transmute the differences between the two sexes, so that they become one, as happened to Orlando.

Unhappily and tragically, as we all know, this magic cannot work, and it is this which precipitates bitterness and resentment and a sense of betrayal in the budding love relationship. Actually, of course, once these magical expectations are stripped away, it becomes possible for the first time at least to seek a realistic and attainable relationship. For the first time the individual can start to consider not what kind of a person he marries and whether he can love that person, but what kind of being he can or cannot become, and therefore what kind of a life can anyone live with him. Can he not only love the so-called "love object," but can he do this while remaining reconciled nonetheless to being himself? Because if this is not possible, then the more he loves this "love object" the more he is forced to hate himself. This is perceived now through a haze of disappointment, dismay, and pain, a sense of betrayal and bitterness, and the tendency to say, "Anyhow, it is all your fault. I wanted to end up both, and you cheated me into thinking I could; but I cannot, at least not with you."

This sad and nearly universal human experience occurs daily on every level, conscious, preconscious, and unconscious. What is more, it also occurs at different intervals. Time relationships are of particular importance here. In one case it happens an hour or so after the young woman first meets her man, because her unconscious expectation has been that the magic would take place at once. She is to be magically changed in the first hour, and when this does not happen she turns with savage and bitter jibes and taunts, driving her young beau away, and then mourning her loss and her loneliness with a renewed sense of desperation and defeat. With another it happens in a matter of days or weeks. For business or professional reasons, her beau frequently may have to be away. Each separation is greeted with a secret initial sense of relief. Then, however, comes a painful longing, a sense of nothingness. "When he is not around I am neither a man nor a woman" is the way she puts it. Then comes the return, an exultant, happy reunion, and a joyful erotic affirmation of her womanhood, only to be followed by a period of hovering uncertainty, a slump into depression, a growing sense of tension, a claustrophobic feeling of having been trapped by loving this man or any man. This brings on a gradual and insidious anger, and with the anger this hitherto quite feminine woman becomes harsh and bitter. The kind of clothes and the colors she wears change; the actual timbre of her voice alters; she swears and drinks. A solid core of masculine rage begins to show itself as she turns her resentment onto this man who has done her the great injury of proving to her that she is a woman and not a man, proving the very thing she had thought she wanted but that unhappily she also did not want unless she could end up as both. Other alternative consequences may occur swiftly or slowly. For instance, instead of a turn from joy to rage there can be a precipitous drop into violent alcoholism.

B. MARRIAGE CHOICES

The influence of the drive to become both sexes may also be manifested in the choice of a sexual and marriage partner.

Many fine gradations of sensory experience, such as perception of height, shape, eye or hair coloring, voice, manner, combine to form subtle pathways of preconscious or unconscious identification. Sometimes buried patterns of preverbal sensory memories, formerly too elusive to bring into full consciousness, come to clear expression.

The effects of the drive to become both sexes on such object choices can be illustrated in many ways. Most familiar is the tendency to choose a heterosexual equivalent of the self; e.g., the cadaverous man who repeatedly marries cadaverous women, or vice versa; or the opposite tendency to marry one's physical opposite in size, weight, coloring. There is the familiar story of the vigorously aggressive man who chooses the weakly clinging woman, and of the effiminate man who chooses a notably aggressive woman. Out of this subsequently comes the depreciation of the chosen object, again with a sense of having been cheated and outraged. Then follows a familiar sequence: the depreciation of the partner, interpreting all difficulties as being the fault of the other, only to repeat the identical pattern in another union. In such marriages the unconscious goal of contrasexual equivalents is to neutralize and eliminate all gender differences, both genital and secondary, while at the same time acquiring both. These irreconcilable goals may coexist side by side, and can be expressed in the same dream. It is of further interest that the differences between identification (i.e., becoming) and incorporation or introjection (i.e., possessing) are paralleled by the content of such dreams.

This is illustrated in the unpublished recent work of the late Arthur Sutherland and his associates on the tendency of some women after mastectomies to develop "phantom" breasts; it is paralleled by dream material in which men with strong identifications with their mothers dream of phantom breasts comparable to the phantom penis described by Rado (1933). Another example is the dream of a woman patient, in which she became "as smooth as a china doll"; i.e., without apertures, folds, pigment, hair, body or genital odors, and also without appendages of any kind. Thus she simultaneously eliminated the genital and secondary attributes of both genders and became neither. The outcome was panic. Still another example is the almost somnambulistic and paradoxical behavior of a model who was thrown into a rage every time anyone expressed enthusiasm over her appearance, especially if she had made an effort to appear at her best. She wanted her appearance to be something that happened inadvertently, without thought, effort, or attention. If she dallied for a moment over her appearance, any subsequent favorable comments triggered an angry impulse to hurry home to destroy her own attractiveness before anyone else could comment on it. At the same time the least criticism of her looks was resented with equal violence.

C. PARADOXICAL REJECTION OF THE FULFILLING LOVER

In intercourse itself the drive to become both sexes often results in one of the most distressing paradoxes which can occur in the whole range of genital and marital relations. Under its influence, the more successful the love relationship the more inescapably is it doomed. The man (or woman) cannot do without a mate, yet also cannot do with the mate. Without the mate the individual describes himself variously as being "incomplete," "unsure," "unloved," "a monster," "nothing," and obsessed with angry, yearning thoughts. Even though the moment of sexual union may be ecstatically intense and the physical relationship complete and fulfilling, it is followed by a gradual upsurge of tension and restlessness, a sense of having been trapped and then abandoned, an increasing irritability over trifles, and then angry rejection of the partner. On analysis this turns out to be a direct expression of at least two unconscious feelings. One is, "You fooled me. You did not change me. I am just the same as before." The other is, "As long as you are around, I cannot be both." These in turn lead to a vengeance-driven, destructive sequence: e.g., "If I cannot *be* the other, I can at least conquer." In both men and women this unconscious formula frequently leads to equally frustrating promiscuity, and sometimes even to murder. It led one woman to bite halfway through the man's phallus.

It is only toward the end of the most successful and complete analyses that an understanding of this unconscious feeling is attained with fully emotionalized insights. The emergence of such deep insights is usually signaled by the occurrence of emancipating floods of transparent dreams of being both sexes. The tendency to reject the loved object is so general a manifestation of this drive that I will re-emphasize it. The lover feels, "I cannot do without you. Without you I feel miserable, unhappy, deprived, lost, and incomplete." Yet after the union comes the feeling that the expected magic has not occurred, that the presence of the loving partner is confining, restricting, and depriving. The unconscious substrate of this reaction is the feeling that the presence of the man prevents the woman from being a man as well; or that the presence of the woman makes it impossible for the man to be a woman at the same time. Therefore the full formula is: "I cannot do without you. Yet I cannot do with you because your presence confines and restricts me to being only myself." Alternatively, this may be expressed with the accusation: "Your presence keeps me from being myself," which in turn leads to a blindly driven need to be alone.

This impasse may arise at various points in the development of a relationship. An extremely attractive but virginal "bachelor girl" could not bring herself to think of marriage because every time a man started to pay attention to her she had to reject him at once. She wanted his attention, and without it she felt "monstrous." But with it she was precipitated into rage and mockery, because his attentions were paid to her as a woman and blocked and dissolved her unconscious fantasy of herself as being a man as well. In another case, the block became a dominant force only later, in fact during the very act of intercourse. Before intercourse the woman was free and responsive up to the point of orgasm. During intercourse a moment of frigidity would occur, an orgastic arrest at the very height of intercourse. In this instance orgasm itself had come to symbolize the giving up of the unconscious dual goal, and it was this which suddenly throttled any response but rage. Or the block may arise immediately postcoitally, or more gradually over the course of the succeeding hours. In two instances the woman had passed through successive phases during successive periods of life: in the first, the block became dominant during a celibate courtship; in the second phase it arose during intercourse.

An actress of great beauty was struggling with this problem near the culmination of her analysis. She dreamed of being on a train "going someplace"; but she could not find her "pants" —by which she meant her slacks. Everything was strewn around. She was "menstruating furiously." There was a "mixed chorus line," i.e., made up of both men and women, which she had been "trying desperately" to join, but she could not find where she fitted in. Still another woman, who was working through this problem in her analysis, dreamed of being seated on a man's lap with her back to him, gradually feeling that the man's phallus had become part of her, until she ended up at the "front" for both his body and her own, bearing both breasts and phallus. A third woman wakened from a deep sleep which had followed a particularly happy and successful intercourse. She looked over at the figure of her sleeping lover and realized suddenly, vividly, and quite overwhelmingly that he was the young man she wanted to be and that in fact there was a striking physical resemblance between them.

These crisscrossing relationships often express themselves in a significant interplay of accusation and counteraccusation. Frequently and with some truth the woman complains to her mate that he wants her to be the man; while the man in the same partnership complains that she wants him to be the woman. This was expressed quite directly in the dream of a woman patient that her husband was Lady Macbeth. It was expressed equally clearly in the life of a man who was obsessed by breasts, yet married a woman without any. Another man turned on his wife as she raced through the rain to capture a taxi for them, and said, "Jane has to be her own husband," a fact that Jane had in truth just been discovering in her analysis.

D. HOMOSEXUALITY AND MASTURBATION

As an expression of the rejection of sexual differences we encounter a wide variety of seemingly universal attempts to span the sexes; i.e., to be not one but both. We find the manifestations of this drive in the neuroses and in neurotic character disturbances, in occupational choices, in psychoses, in the content and form of art products, in marriage choices, and inevitably in all forms of sexual activity. In this connection, however, it is important to recognize that this drive is not identical with genital homosexuality, that it may conceivably offer a patient alternative goals, and that the interrelationship of the two confronts us with many difficult questions concerning the nature of those forces that determine the target on which the compulsive components of genital drives are focused, the bodily implements they use, and the activities in which they engage. A full discussion of them is beyond the scope of this communication. This much may be said, however. In the overt male homosexual, the goal of attaining an enhancement of one's own gender by the magic of contact with another man's genitals is usually repressed, whereas in the heterosexual male the goal of becoming the opposite gender by contact with the female breasts and genitals is repressed. Frequently, in both man and woman, the hidden conflict may be revealed only under alcohol or other drugs. Only rarely is the overt invert an alcoholic. Yet there are some men and women who must drink to permit the balance to shift from overt heterosexuality to overt homosexuality, and others in whom alcohol is needed to facilitate a shift of identification in the opposite direction.

Analytic material suggests that among male homosexuals some build up an unconscious, almost delusional, conviction that the body is not the body of a man, no matter how male it is in reality. He may awaken every morning with a panicky conviction that his penis is gone, or was always an illusion. Thus his homosexual genital activities have as their unconscious and paradoxical goal the attainment of triumphant heterosexuality by working a magical transformation on his own supposedly defective body through bodily contacts with another man.

On the other hand, in a woman the presence of the drive to become both sexes carries the unconscious assumption that despite all appearances to the contrary the body is really male, and the unconscious goal of all of her heterosexual genital activity is to add to herself all of the sexual attributes of the opposite sex by the magic of the sexual act, without relinquishing her own sexual identity. We meet this fantasy repeatedly in *Orlando*.

As I have already said, masturbation often embodies the quintessence of the fantasy of serving oneself in the capacity of being both sexes for oneself, which probably explains in part the tenacity both of the compulsive, insatiable component in masturbation and of the guilt that attaches to it.

E. THE RELATIONSHIP BETWEEN THE DRIVE TO BECOME BOTH SEXES AND THE DISAPPEARANCE OF A PARENT

The death or disappearance of the parent of the opposite sex is often the experience which precipitates a patient into confusion and ambivalence over gender identity, and sometimes leads to the first overt homosexual experiences. It is as though the patient were saying, "Now my father (or mother) has gone and can no longer make me whole, can no longer give me the missing bodily attributes; therefore I will seek to achieve my wholeness elsewhere." Then comes a desperate storm of homosexual activities with an unconscious reparative goal: i.e., "By bodily contact with a male I will become a real male," or else "By bodily contact with a female I will become a real female." Both end in frustration and despair.

A few other manifestations of the problem which are of special interest are related to self-evaluation, and especially to the under- or overestimation of one's appearance—the pitch of the voice, clothing, gait, posture, etc. A beautiful woman could not look at herself in the mirror without a feeling of revulsion. She had grown up with a deep hatred of a younger brother which turned to shame and envy as he outgrew her. This was always masked, however. She thought of her envy as an unrequited "love," which ultimately turned into an obsessive preoccupation with large men. She dreamed of them, yet ran from them. Her unconscious goal was that they should either change her into her brother, or else destroy him. As an extension of her reaction to her father's death she felt irrational anger at being left by a man; yet she had equally irrational flares of anger at a man's return. In no aspect of her life could she ever commit herself wholeheartedly, either to a woman's life or to a man's life. Yet without a man, she said, "I wither away."

In a comparable situation a boy with an intense love of and identification with his father, plus an intense rivalry toward a younger sister, had been hurt deeply when his mother abandoned the family. He spent the first years of his life attempting to be both his father's son and his father's daughter.

F. THE INFLUENCE OF AGING

Both for the added understanding which it can provide of the dynamics of this complex drive, and because of the current trend toward longevity, it is relevant to speculate on the fate of this drive in the older age group. In practice we see more and more older patients who are not mentally impaired in the formal sense. The sensorium shows little or no deficit of the kind that we have been accustomed to look for in the arteriosclerotic and parenchymatous deteriorations of *senium*. Nor are they caught in the old-age depressions. It is, rather, that their so-called "healthy" defenses against unconscious conflicts as well as their neurotic or symptomatic defenses are down.

This exposes the fate of the drive. Sometimes it seems to have been abandoned unconsciously. Sometimes one gets the impression that the drive has been unconsciously achieved, and that the aging patient lives in an innocent dream of bisexual omnipotence. Whether the drive is unconsciously abandoned or retained in unconscious fantasies, aging brings significant changes in body form, facial conformation, skin, voice, distribution of hair. Thus aging brings facial hirsutism in women, but also a thinning of hair of the scalp, more wrinkles, changing voices, changing distributions of body weight and skeleton, all tending to mask secondary sexual differences. All of these changes tend to lessen those secondary characteristics which differentiate the sexes in earlier years. In part these changes may also be due to glandular shifts which can both alter the emotional states and the neurotic pictures of age. Longevity itself thus creates problems which are not new to mankind but whose frequency has increased. This accounts for two opposite phenomena: one, the "heavy sugar daddy" with the chorus girl, and obversely, the bitter "love" affairs between aging women and young gigolos. It also plays a role in the eruption of homosexuality in aging men and women who had previously shown overtly only heterosexual tendencies.

We face here a profoundly difficult and intricate human problem which is being forced upon our attention by the triumphant progress of modern medicine toward longer life expectancy for more and more people without providing them with the defenses of a true psychological maturity.

IX. Relation of the Drive to the Diurnal Rhythm of Drinking, Sleeping, and Waking

The drive and its veiled and disguised fantasies are often expressed in alternating diurnal rhythms, one part of the day devoted predominantly to one role, other parts to another. A man or woman may live out the male component in the daylight hours, and the feminine at night. We are all familiar with the woman who dresses in harshly tailored clothes by day and in the most feminine and revealing of formal clothes at night. An example is the fifteen-year-old transvestite mentioned above, who in the daytime was comfortable only in riding breeches and boots, and at night only in the most adult, formal gowns.

Frequently this conflict in roles reaches its highest intensity toward the end of the afternoon and the two roles converge. It is no accident that this is the time of day when drinking often gets out of hand—the drinking of the woman who is in her home awaiting the return of her husband and the drinking of the man who is on his way home. One husband's occupation took him away repeatedly. His wife always yearned desperately for his return, feeling as though every absence proved afresh that she was not a woman but a monstrosity. At first his returns assuaged this feeling, but gradually his presence undermined her hidden fantasy that in his absence she had really become a man while seeming to remain a woman, and her tension mounted. The drinking came as this tension began to stir in anticipation of his return. For the man, the same hour of the day often marked a transition in the other direction, to a partial feminine identification.

To another woman the afternoon hours meant turning toward the time of day which throughout her childhood had been dominated by her bitter fear of and love for her father. This was coupled with intense rivalry with him and with her brother: she was both her brother's rival for her father's love and her father's rival for her brother's love. All of this she transplanted into her marriage, and in her episodic alcoholism she lived through a complete identification with her hated, admired, and feared father and brother, and simultaneously with a despised but consoling mother. Her voice, manner, choice of words, all oscillated between facsimiles first of the one and then of the other.

This diurnal rhythm also has something to do with the wholly artificial but culturally entrenched contrast between work and play, between the working week and the weekend's "play," between the week's activity and the exaggerated Sunday sleep in which the fantasy of the dual sexual role can be realized in dreams.

As already indicated, the transitional hours between the "male" and "female" parts of the day color the end of the afternoon, the "cocktail" hour, converting them into hours of mounting tension which sometimes accounts for precipitate bouts of alcoholism in both men and women. This is a black alchemy which supercharges the marital martini. Before marriage it may have meant release, warmth, gaiety, generosity; after marriage it often releases the most violent distillate of hate and jealousy.

This transition can also occur at the moment of awakening with a sudden plunge into panic each morning. I have in mind a man who in his sleep and in the symbolic language of the dream acquired breasts, thus becoming both sexes. From this he wakened, feeling comfortable, intact, and above all "whole," but only for a fleeting moment. Once fully awake he lost both his phantom breasts and his confidence in the reality of his phallus, thus becoming neither sex, i.e., "nothing." Therefore within a few moments after waking he was plunged into panic, with a feeling of having lost reality, of having lost himself, of "nothingness." It was not until well on toward the termination of a long and difficult but ultimately successful analysis that he discovered the reasons why he regularly wakened to terror and to feelings of unreality and depersonalization.

X. Influence of the Drive on Work and Play

As the objects for which a patient has been struggling lose their unrecognized symbolic magical values, the whole pattern of living may change. This sometimes accounts for change in a field of study or of work. In the case of one young man, his absorption in philosophy had as its goal not merely to know everything but to be everything. In psychoanalytic therapy, with the growth of insight this interest shifted to concrete science. I have seen similar changes from a preoccupation with esthetics to a preoccupation with engineering, in the shift from medicine to law, and in the shift of an already successful young lawyer from law to medicine. I have seen it in a compulsive and diffusely overactive woman who became quietly and steadfastly devoted to a single goal. Several women (and some men) who had been passionate devotees of riding turned completely away from this sport once it lost for them its bisexual significance.

Of special interest are the voice changes that can occur. For instance, after the resolution of this unconscious conflict, the high-pitched voice of a young man dropped into a normally deep male register that had remained unused, although obviously available for many years. I have known two women whose voices, whenever the struggle was heightened by bitter marital disputes, acquired a harsh, male quality during periods of stormy struggle over this bisexual goal.

As already pointed out, the drive to be both sexes may alternate with the drive to be either the one sex or the other. This frequently becomes a fear of ending up being neither—nothing, gone, or as one woman put it, "withered." This in turn may lead to feelings of depersonalization and to terrors of death and disintegration in a setting of malignant depression. In moments of transition among these varied manifestations of the drive to be both or neither, there may be stormy rages and acute fears during the diurnal cycle, as well as in dreams and in symptoms over longer life cycles. Sometimes the fear is represented quite literally as a fear of falling between two objects. Or there may be a dream of standing motionless, open-mouthed, with nothing coming in and nothing going out. One man dreamed that he was on his way to a Naval Training Station, not sure whether he was to be the gun, the gunner, the missile, or the target. The dream ended in panic.

As the drive takes shape and becomes more consistently organized, one can recognize a large number of secondary derivative mechanisms, reaction formations, and defenses. In this way it becomes one of the sources of the many fantasy-laden, paradoxical, and stubbornly rationalized compromises and inconsistencies which one encounters in life. These oscillations among the various methods of handling the drive give rise to characteristic changes in ways of living. Compulsive furors of work may be followed by inertia and apathy, then by alcoholism, promiscuity, or asceticism. Compulsive sexual furors may be followed by impotence and abstinence, elation by depression.

The inability to accept a commitment to any task, so prevalent among adolescents today, often represents unconsciously the refusal of a commitment to being just one sex. This may lead to an insoluble indecision or to self-defeating compromises among various roles—e.g., whether to be an actor, playwright, or director, whether to be a practitioner or a medical scientist, whether to be a housewife and a mother or a writer.

A woman of extraordinary grace and beauty competed with an older sister whose identification was with a weak but seductive father. The patient spent her whole life rejecting first a husband and then a lover for a bisexual career in journalism and international law. The inability to commit oneself completely to any work or to any relationship because such a commitment represents an acceptance of either the male or the female role to the exclusion of the other may become evident in school children of both sexes even at an early age. I have seen it take many forms in the armed services. And we see it every day in the housewife who may be an excellent crafts-woman in her home but can use her domestic skills only among women; if her husband is around to remind her by his mere presence that she is a woman, she cannot use her skills.

From early childhood one patient played obsessively with a cousin. The games were about fish, magic, model railroads, and a game of cowboys and Indians in which the cousins alter-nated between playing the role of the one who had to be nursed through the injuries inflicted by the Indians and the role of the one who did the nursing. This game was played for hours on end every Saturday afternoon through an entire winter. The patient was the younger of two brothers, and of the two he was the closer to his parents. Even in adult years there was a close identification with his mother in the love of his father. He was unable to commit himself to anything which would take him from his parents' sides. Although he had high intellectual and physical abilities, he could not use them in sports, studies, or any area of work. He had only one outlet — the simple tasks of a handyman in which he could be essentially a houseman (or a housewife), but even these tasks he could perform only around his own home and only if both parents were at home.

This same drive may make it impossible to accept either winning or losing. Paradoxically, of course, winning can be just as unacceptable as losing, and for the same reason; i.e., where to win is to be the man and to lose is to be the woman, and where neither can be accepted because it means the exclusion of the other role. This sometimes plays an important contributory role in the depressive reactions to successful careers.

Among scientists this sometimes influences the choice among the physical-mathematical sciences, or between the biological and the cultural-psychological sciences. In one in-stance the frantic and unrealizable drive of a young scientist to supplement his own body through his experiments in morpho-genesis led directly to the development of a period of psychotic decompensation. I have also seen it operating in the lives of a newspaperwoman, a painter, a woman physician, and a singer. Each achieved success in her respective field only to turn in rage from her career to a good marriage, then from the marriage in a rage against the man she loved for making her feel like a woman, and finally to drink. In other words, these men and women could not accept success either in their professional lives or in their love lives because to them success meant either, "Now you are a man and cannot be a woman" or "Now you are a woman and can never be a man." Each step in the process was punctuated by rage, panic, and depression. There can be essentially parallel developments in the lives of both genders.

The work patterns may interweave with the pattern of marriage. One instance was of particular interest because of the family background of the woman, who was a geneticist. After marrying a weak but affectionate husband, she had a long struggle with a serious chronic illness. She said to me in distress and with accurate insight: "I will lose him now, because now I am weaker than he is; and he married me for my strength." Then she told me how her great-grandmother had been a successful professional evangelist, her grandmother a successful professional woman, and her mother and two aunts successful businesswomen. Through successive generations it had been a proud family tradition for the women to marry men who were weaker, who were less capable both economically and in their respective careers, but who had the one virtue that they could give their wives sustained and sustaining affection. On this foundation the family had been built, but the keystone of the arch was always the woman's strength and the husband's weakness. Now, however, my patient's illness was cutting her off from this. She foresaw accurately and clearly the inevitable breakup of her home. This led her to explore deeply buried material having to do with her physical image of herself and indeed of all women. The focus of this image was the hair under the chin of her grandmother, how she had loathed this, and how she felt when she first detected hair on her own chin. Around this she wove an intricate network of secret fantasies that the women of her family somehow embodied both sexes. This unconscious fantasy, built as it was around her own unconscious drive to become both sexes, had played the dominant role in her choice both of her field of scientific work and of her mate. Indeed, many instances of successful women who choose ineffectual mates seem to bear the imprint of this concealed drive.

XI. The Influence of the Drive on Terminal Phases of Analysis, and on Its Success or Failure

This two-headed drive creates one of the most difficult obstacles that psychoanalytic therapy attempts to overcome. Indeed, it sometimes seems to be the rock on which we founder most frequently. Certainly it often plays a major role in what is inaccurately called the "negative therapeutic reaction."

Many of us have met the problem toward the end of an analysis which has been gathering momentum, an analysis which has seemed to be moving with increasing vigor and impetus toward what promised to be full therapeutic resolution. Symptoms may have disappeared. Patients may have acquired freedom from many other previously unconscious conflicts and may be producing material freely. They may be clear in their analytic understanding and cooperation, quick in their perceptions of meanings, free in their emotional responses to interpretations (whether these are the interpretations which they themselves make or interpretations suggested by the therapist), responding to them with feeling and with additional confirmatory data. It has begun to look as though the end of the analysis is in sight.

Then things begin to bog down, and the analyst finds himself up against a seemingly contentless, sullen impasse: a state of dulled indifference. He explores transference material, looks for deeper and earlier signs of conflict, for the reaction to the threat of separation, for unexplored areas of unconscious anxiety and resentment. Then comes a flood of dreams with multiple meanings. Among them, however, will be an insistently recurrent theme: "I came to you for something. I have been a good child. I have done as I was told. I have told all. I have even become symptom-free. Now I want my re-

ward, but you are not giving it to me. No magic has happened. I have not been given what I was waiting for. I have
not been given the ultimate reward. I am still only what I
was." What is left unspoken in the final complaint is: "I have
not become both sexes."

I can illustrate this with dreams from many patients, both
men and women. Before turning to these examples, however,
let me re-emphasize the fact that whenever a patient's unconscious goal in analysis has not been to "get well" but rather to
gratify some unconscious and inherently unattainable ambition—in this instance to achieve a transmutation not into one
sex alone but into both—this ambition will be for him the only
fully acceptable reward for "good behavior." Under these circumstances symptomatic improvement will bring no happiness, but rather a sense of embittered defeat and of having
been cheated. If left unanalyzed, this sense of having been
misled and cheated may flare up in later phases of analysis, or
after the analysis has been discontinued, and undermine all
that had been achieved. Furthermore, it occurs with equal
tenacity in men and women, although it may be more subtly
disguised in men because social taboos lead men to a deeper
repression of the goal to be a girl, to be the mother's or the
father's daughter, to be a man with breasts. In our culture the
woman who harbors unconscious goals to be both the daughter
and the son (i.e., to be a woman with breasts and vagina but
also with a penis) is not under as many taboos as is the man's
need for female bodily transmutation.

The dreams that represent this upsurge of resentment, this
defiant protest against remaining what one was when one first
came into analysis, take many forms. Some of these dreams
are quite literal and undisguised. Thus a woman dreamed
that she was chained to another woman, and that she stood
with her mouth open to the analyst to receive something
through her mouth, but nothing came in and nothing came
out. The associations led not to Oedipal material but to a
planting ceremony, the planting of the phallus so that it could
grow in her.

Another woman's dreams paralleled almost precisely her
conscious masturbatory fantasies as an adolescent girl. In this

case the dream was of the vague figure of a father who was violating his daughter in the presence of his sons. Here again the associations indicated that this expressed a resolute determination to have the penis planted in her permanently, so that she would end up possessed of all. She would show her brothers who it was who was ahead, who possessed everything. Her reward was to be that she would be allowed to become what she had always wanted, namely, *both*.

In these terminal battles we may discover belatedly that the sex of the analyst has played a heretofore unrecognized and unexpectedly important role, depending upon which parent had occupied the role of the healing magician in the long-buried fantasies of the patient during childhood. For instance, where the father was the miracle worker, a woman analyst may from the first be doomed to fail, although this may not become apparent until the terminal phase is approaching. In the obverse of this situation, a male analyst who does not accomplish the goal of miraculous healing by miraculous change may in the end be regarded by the patient as having deliberately withheld the miracle in a niggardly spirit. This ultimate struggle has to be worked through not once but repeatedly, but if it is successfully worked through the changes in the end may be striking.

A man said, "There is a part of me that has at last become a man and only a man. And there is a part of me, a lot of me, that is content to have it so. I don't know this part of me too well yet. Maybe I don't even know his first name. But it is the most relaxing thing that has ever happened to me."

A woman said, "When it finally began to dawn on me that this was not up to *me* to decide, that I couldn't be anything but just what I am and that I could give up this frantic effort that I have been making all my life, then a load rolled away. It is funny. As I walked out of this office even that dull ache and pressure on my back began to relax and disappear. I am fine."

Another man said, "And then as I walked down the street somehow I felt different. I stood erect, whereas I had always been leaning forward a little bit, folding my arms around my chest the way my mother used to do to hide *her* breasts—no, *my* breasts. Now I stood erect and I seemed to fill out my skin.

My bones and my muscles seemed to be firmer and more knit together, and I walked differently and felt differently." It was in fact true that his gait and his posture had changed.

One patient who had been struggling desperately with this problem spent a period in her own home during the prolonged absence of her husband. Before his absence the relationship with her husband had been improving steadily. Again, while they had been away together it had been particularly good. This time, however, on the way to her temporarily empty house, she had begun to feel tense and anxious. She toyed with the idea of having an affair, not an affair she wanted, but one for which she felt a desperate, blind, and angry hunger. A similar anxious tension and need had often beset her in the late afternoon. She felt it in her hands to such an extent that even as she talked about it she gripped her hands almost convulsively. There were no consciously felt erotic needs, but in bed at night she would be assailed by a flood of angry fantasies of an endless series of promiscuous relationships, one after another. For the first time in months she suddenly lapsed back into a few explosive and compulsive episodes of solitary drinking.

One Sunday evening during her husband's absence she went out with a married couple and a man who was a friend of theirs. Both men seemed to her dull, pompous, aggressive, domineering, bombastic. She was bored, resentful, and angry, and on returning home was restless. On such an evening as this alcoholism was particularly likely to manifest itself, but this time she restrained herself and went to bed and slept. From this sleep she wakened, shaken by a dream:

> She was a man among a large group of homosexual males, and was explaining to a woman (who turned out to be herself) that this was only a transitional phase and "nothing to worry about," but that during it she had had to submit passively to the homosexual advances of the other "men." She was perplexed by this, yet strangely reassured, and then suddenly at the end of the dream the analyst was present and gallantly picked up a glove which she had dropped, and handed it to her.

This last moment referred directly to something which had happened in the preceding analytic hour, i.e., on the afternoon before the weekend of the dream. With ritualistic regularity she had always dropped some item from among her personal belongings as she left my office (a glove, a book, a purse, a handkerchief). And quite as regularly she would dive to pick it up herself before I could move to render this courteous service, which I always tried to do as a deliberate participation in her ritual in an effort to drive home the fact that she would never allow herself to be waited on as a woman in any way. On this occasion, however, she had dropped one glove in my direction, and then stood motionless in a somewhat reflective mood. As usual I made a point of picking it up and of handing it to her in silence. Only at the last moment had she started her usual dive to retrieve it herself. Nothing had been said. We both smiled politely as she left the office. That night came the dream.

The dream had left her deeply shaken, moved, and sobered. She said, "This is the first time that I have known this from the inside. Here I was playing both roles. I was a man, yet I was in a passive homosexual relationship to other men; so I was a woman anyhow. Also you were gallantly treating me as a woman. I was telling a woman who was myself that this was a transitory phase. I cannot deny this any longer." Then, significantly enough, she went on to say that the preceding weekend, which had presented particular difficulties in her relationship to her children as well as other stressful external situations, there had been long stretches of time in which she had been relaxed and peaceful, and had enjoyed a sense of "being satisfied to be me" and "to be doing what I was doing," a feeling which she had rarely known in all her life.

This was a woman of unusual talent who in panic had fled into marriage from the promise of a great career. During her second pregnancy she had suffered a deep blow when she discovered her husband's infidelity. This had thrown her back regressively into the frame of mind which had originally driven her from her parents' home to make a career for herself. At the time of her husband's betrayal of her she still felt anchored to her marriage by their children and by the lapse of years which made it impossible for her to return to her career. At the same time her husband's behavior reactivated a rivalry with her loved, hated, and feared father, and also with her despised, weak, ineffectual, and sickly younger brother. Her contempt for the beaten, abject, enslaved figure of her mother was expressed with great intensity, as well as her fear of identifying herself solely with this mother or with the dead sister or her father, or indeed with anyone. This was the constellation of crisscrossing and rejected gender identifications out of which her problem had grown to explosive intensity.

As she worked through this phase of her treatment, her clarification and relaxation grew, and as she was able to relax, she became aware of the violence with which she had felt inwardly torn for years. She described its influence on her sexual relationships in these terms: "A moment would always come in which I had the feeling that now I had to take over, now I had to take the lead, now I had to turn the tables." The same thing was true in work, in play, in social relationships, in her relationship to her children, and in her conversational kleptomania. I have rarely known a woman more gifted as a woman who derived less happiness from even her most expert functioning, whether in domesticity or in any other way. When this particular problem began to reach its resolution, the change that occurred in her orientation toward her whole life was dramatic and moving.

One further example. A highly gifted young woman had a flair for writing, a fine dramatic gift, and great warmth in her attitudes toward children. In the course of her treatment she went through successive phases—working on the stage, writing, and teaching in nursery schools. Each one of these phases of activity brought out interesting facets of her personality and of her unconscious problems. She did each extraordinarily well; yet each also carried its multiple and conflicting meanings.

For many months secret, lifelong fantasies of going on the stage had been completely absent from her material. Then, as she approached the end of her analysis, she suddenly fulfilled a prophecy that I had made silently to myself by turning once again toward a stage career. This was buttressed by excellent rationalizations, including high praise from her dramatic coaches and her successes in certain competitions. Her battle became not "the Easter cover" versus "the circus cover" of *Lady in the Dark* (Hart, 1941), but whether to have children or to have a stage career; or, to put it another way, to be one sex or the other, or both.

Then came a dream in which she was Superman flying through the air; but to her amazement, as she flew through the air sailors down below were giving "wolf whistles" as though she were also Superwoman. (This of course is reminiscent of the famous episode in *Orlando* in which a mere glimpse of Orlando's ankle so startles a sailor as nearly to throw him from the mast.) This dream was followed by another, in which she was auditioning for the role of Blanche DuBois in *A Streetcar Named Desire* (Williams, 1947). In the dream, having auditioned successfully for the role of this unhappy, psychotic prostitute, she wandered away. Then she stooped to pick up a half dollar. But it was not a round half-dollar piece, it was one half of a round dollar, a half-moon. She picked this up, looked at it, and dissolved in tears.

In the course of time, with this warning in mind, I returned her to analysis with a woman, with whom she carried her therapy through to successful completion.

XII. Implications of the Concept for General Psychoanalytic Theory

The implication of this paper might easily be misunderstood to be an attack on psychoanalytic theories concerning the influence of anatomical differences on the relationship between the two sexes because of genital envy and castration fears. This would be a misunderstanding and misinterpretation of its implications. The concept that there is a nearly universal drive to become both sexes is not incompatible with any of these earlier, basic psychoanalytic observations. It is, rather, an extension from them into more general areas of human adjustment. Its implication is that conflicting gender identities, misidentifications, false identifications, and irreconcilable identifications give rise to unattainable and irreconcilable drives and wishes which, in turn, become fresh sources of neurotic conflict that on occasion may lead to psychotic disorganization (Kubie, 1966c, this volume, Chapter 7).

If this is true, then it becomes clear that seriously pathogenic conflicts may arise not only between basic instinctual pressures on the one hand and the conscience processes (superego) on the other, but also out of conflicting unattainable and irreconcilable identifications, false identifications, and mixed identifications, and that these in turn can give rise to irreconcilable distortions of body images and identity goals. This is an important addition to the earlier concept of intrapsychic conflicts as always arising between id processes and superego processes, but it is not irreconcilable with them. They are supplementary and in no sense mutually exclusive.

In a systematic consideration of psychoanalytic theory, what position should then be assigned to this drive to become both sexes? The question brings up more problems than I can hope to explore fully here. Indeed, throughout this paper I am limiting myself to illustrating the profusion of the interrelated manifestations and consequences of the drive. For several reasons these are complex. In the first place, not only the drive itself but also the conflicts which underlie it and those which derive from it can all be experienced and expressed concurrently on conscious, preconscious, and unconscious levels. Second, the derivative conflicts are manifested not only in different forms but also on different levels. In addition, they shift during different phases of human life, depending partly upon the stage of instinctual development through which the patient is passing (Kubie, 1956), partly on the changing nature of external circumstances and on the evolving phenomena of growth and aging.

In any systemic survey of psychodynamic sequences we must ask which conflicts are primary and which resolutions of these conflicts are primary. In this framework it is important that the drive to become both sexes has pregenital, phallic, genital, pre-Oedipal, and Oedipal ingredients, that it is repeatedly reactivated in the latency period, in puberty, in adolescence, in adult life, and again in various stages of the aging process. Furthermore, in each of these phases of life it retains manifestations which are derived from earlier phases, adding fresh accretions. Thus superimposed layers represent symptomatic derivatives of successive epochs in the life history of the drive. Consequently, merely to describe the drive, its setting, origins, evolutions, and consequences makes a canvas of enormous size and complexity, like *Orlando* itself.

A. AS MECHANISMS

Because of the richness of these ramifications, the drive to become both sexes sometimes appears to be a central axis in the development of our individual and cultural psychopathology, around which other conflicts over castration, Oedipal needs, etc., all cluster. Nevertheless, I will not claim that this drive occupies an exclusively central role in the psychodynamics of all psychopathology. I can say only that I will not be surprised if in the end its importance should prove to approximate such a central and primary position. This is of special relevance with respect to phallic envy, because the closely related phenomena of breast envy occupies a role whose importance in relation to the drive to become both sexes has never been sufficiently recognized. One man had imitated his father's career and his mother's alcoholism as though he were an automaton. Later, after his wife's mastectomy, he revealed his incorporation of her breasts by developing sweats on his breasts which were localized precisely to the area of her postoperative scars.

Yet there are important differences between breast envy and phallic envy. Thus there is the simple, elementary fact that in childhood the boy and girl are genitally unlike, but alike as to breasts. The little girl has no breasts for the little boy to envy. Consequently the small boy may covet and fear an adult's breasts but not those of an age peer. When a contemporary girl develops breasts, for the boy the breasts are likely to inherit the covetousness and the fears which had originally been directed toward both the genitals of older men and the breasts of older women. For the girl this situation has important differences. The small girl's envy and covetousness may be directed toward the male organ of the small boy as much as that of the man (Kubie, 1934a). The former, however, will be attended by less fear than is felt toward the adult phallus, where size and color play important and intimidating roles. Moreover, the adult woman possesses the breast which the little girl still lacks and which can become the object of longing, of body envy, and of fear.

Other special differences are linked to the close tie between the genitals and excretion on the one hand, and between the breasts and ingestion on the other. These are derivatives of the complex implications of apertures as avenues of intake and output. Still another difference is the fact that in most cultures there is not the same assiduous care to hide the breasts that there is to hide the genitals, either in art or in life. A fourth difference has to do with the many psychological consequences of the phenomena of erection, which are more dramatic in the genitals than in the nipples.

Despite these important differences with their special consequences, the fact that covetousness and fear may be focused on any body part remains in itself a perplexing phenomenon — perplexing, as I have pointed out above, if only because heredity has not resolved it. It has many psychological consequences which do not vary with the part envied, in addition to variables which are dependent on such special and varying features as those mentioned above.

Of all of the many problems concerning genetic influences on psychological traits there is no problem more perplexing than this. If any pattern of feelings, attitudes, and behavior should be influenced by long ages of constantly repeated racial experiences, it should be the differences, both anatomical and functional, between the sexes. Strangely, this seems not to be true either for the lower animals or for man.

These variable complexities influence the evolution of the drive to become both sexes. To have called it the drive to acquire the anatomical attributes of both sexes would have erroneously implied that anatomical parity is the sole objective of the drive, or at least that we know which comes first — whether identifications with the whole precede and determine relationships to the parts, or whether the object relationships to parts precede and determine the identifications with the whole. Unhappily, this is an unasked and therefore unanswered issue in developmental psychology.

Closely related to this problem is an issue concerning the difference between the "drive to become" and the "drive to possess" at successive stages of personality development. In other words, to *become* (depending upon identifications) and/or to *possess* (through incorporation and introjection) imply important differences in aims toward identical objects—differences whose effects can be traced on conscious, preconscious, and unconscious levels. Here again, precisely how these are interrelated has not been worked out. Yet they are essential components in the evolution of each human infant toward becoming "himself," with clearly differentiated "I" and "non-I" worlds.

B. MAGIC AND CLOTHES

The many unconscious devices by which individuals try to achieve this unattainable goal have one feature in common: they attempt to bring about a magical bodily transformation but without giving up their own sex. The result is the drive to become both, or alternatively, neither. This may be expressed through the choice of mates, hair styles, vocations and avocations, clothes, decor, intellectual and cultural interests, and sports, or, sometimes, through deliberately inviting suffering, which is often misinterpreted as a primarily masochistic perversion. It may be expressed in dreams and fantasies of death, or in behavior which invites serious accidents. Here accident proneness and even pseudosuicidal acts may have as their goal not death but to "nearly die" in order to be reborn. Thus, in the struggle to attain the desired bodily transformation, I have recently seen this particularly distressing form of the drive in a middle-aged man and in a young woman, both saying, "I want to go back to the brink of death, but not to die, as though I could thereby be reborn and start all over again as myself, but also as my brother" (in the one case), "as my sister" (in the other).

Cloaked in many disguises, this drive often leads to compulsive masturbation, in which the fantasies as well as the activity itself betray the drive to play both sexual roles. This may account in part for the extraordinary tenacity of the guilt attached to masturbation, no matter how gently and permissively a child may be reared in this respect.

The early conscious fantasies that express the relatively con-flictless phase of this drive at the dawn of the Oedipal phase include both losing something and gaining something. The boy of four or five may say, "I would be happier without a penis." The little girl will say, "I would be happier without a breast," or "I would be happier if women had penises." And ultimately, "I would be happier if I had both." Later such fantasies become increasingly disguised as the drive is sub-jected to progressive repression.

It is hardly necessary to point out how frequently the prob-lem is acted out and lived out through clothes, as a form of magic. I think of a woman whose deliberate effort was to make herself as severely masculine, somber, and even dowdy as possible. This was no small achievement in the case of this particularly attractive person. In another, the drive to be both sexes required that her clothes be neuter clothes. She dreamed of herself as a luscious nude blonde, but laid out in a casket. Nudity meant death to this woman because it would expose her state of nothingness. Because of the feeling that she had fallen between the two roles, she lived in a chronic depression with feelings of unreality and depersonalization, except when she went on drinking binges.

Comparable was the vigorous young athlete who momen-tarily simulated a woman each day as he left my office. At that special moment his every gesture was meticulously ritualized, like a woman powdering her nose. This was evident in his way of buttoning his coat, of arranging his belt, of fixing his pleats, of slicking his hair. At no other time was there any trace of effeminacy in his manner. It was interesting that this ritual-ized assumption of the female role was triggered by separation, as he left the analytic office to face the world. These mannerisms disappeared as he approached the end of his analysis.

The analysis of another patient brought to light interesting material bearing on the differences between transvestitism in-volving only the outer garments and transvestitism involving the undergarments. The undergarments closely represent the body itself and for that reason are closely related to the prob-lem of fetishism. During the course of her analysis, on a night that turned out to have been the anniversary of her mother's death, a woman dreamed that she was dressed in her stepfather's dark blue suit. This was a condensation of her grief and mourning by being "dark blue," of her envy of and identification with her stepfather, and also of replacing her mother.

C. ROLE OF CULTURAL FACTORS

I cannot leave this brief and fragmentary discussion of the multiple manifestations and evolution of the drive without referring to the role of cultural pressures in determining not the presence or absence of this conflict, but the level on which it is processed and symbolized, i.e., in shaping its forms and determining its sequences. Cultural forces influence its intensity and its distribution between the sexes. What is even more important is that cultural forces also influence the level of awareness on which it is processed, because it is this which determines whether the effort to deal with the problem will give rise to normally flexible or psychopathologically rigid adjustments and compromises. One wonders whether any culture exists in which individuals are free from this confusing, ambivalent, bisexual, and irreconcilable pair of goals.[6]

Certainly, however, our culture exacts from men and women a different price for this problem. Here girls and women are actively encouraged to be male as well as female: in dress, activities, occupations, hobbies, interests, speech, and manner. Among women the drive to become both sexes is tolerated, even encouraged, and defended on conscious and preconscious levels. Among boys and men, on the other hand, it is not encouraged. Consequently the drive is almost wholly repressed in men except for some overt homosexuals, transvestites, and "hippies." In women, on the other hand, many

[6] In *Sex and Temperament in Three Primitive Societies*, Margaret Mead (1935) makes the statement that cultures which allocate special personality traits to each sex reinforce and exaggerate the tendency of the members of each to attempt to belong to the opposite sex. This is an interesting speculation with many suggestive implications, but its basis in comparative empirical data is far from clear. My bias is to go along with it; nevertheless, it may conceivably be an example of unconscious special pleading.

conscious and preconscious manifestations of the conflict are
both tolerated and rewarded. Yet even here the core is usually
repressed. Thus cultural attitudes influence the level on which
it operates, the openness of its expression, and the accessibility
of the conflict to therapeutic influences. But they do not
create the conflict.

D. RELATION TO ORALITY AND THE PRIMACY OF AIM OR OBJECT

There is an oral component to insatiability, but contrary to
current *ad hoc* assumptions orality per se is not the only or
primary source of insatiability. More often orality merely implements other aims. This question recurs in several connections concerning the priority of aim (or "means") over object
or of object over aim (or "means"). Furthermore, it is related
to the successive phases through which drives evolve out of
their biogenetic or "instinctual" roots, how the derivative
drives come to focus on specific parts of the body as part
objects (e.g., in the face or special features of the face, genitals, hair, hips, calves, buttocks, and breasts). Someday it will
be necessary to consider how these partial components of the
drive to become both sexes can determine and limit the relationships to each sex, to neither, and to whole individuals
through early identifications and introjections, and, finally,
how all of this relates to such secondary symptomatic disturbances as exhibitionistic behavior, transvestitism, overt homosexuality, eating anomalies, the closely related buying compulsions and kleptomania, and even to that well-known social
disease which might best be called "conversational kleptomania," especially common perhaps among women but not
theirs exclusively.

Perhaps the most important consequences of the drive are
on human relations in general, because these consequences
are circular. Not only do human relationships play a role in
the development of the drive; they in turn undergo a process
of continuous deformation under a battering from these
irreconcilable and unattainable needs. Every conceivable per-
mutation and combination of these circular and irreconcilable
demands occur side by side in the same individual. And their
conscious, preconscious, and unconscious representations play

a preponderant role in marriage and occupational choices, as they do in dreams, in art and literature, and in the form and content of neuroses and psychoses.

XIII. Detour into Biography and Fiction

It would be impossible to review in full the enormous volume of fiction and biographical studies which illustrate the range of the manifestations of this problem, usually without realizing its nature. I can list here only a small sample. There are exquisite stories of childhood by James (1933) and Follett (1927), the latter tragically and appropriately called *The House without Windows* in view of the author's suicide (see McCurdy, 1966). There are records of tragic lives of sick debauchery, incest, and wasted talents, such as the life of Lord Byron (see Grebanier, 1970).

Lord Byron is such a perfect example that I will mention him first. I find that I really hate this man, pitiable certainly, but not really forgivable: at best a second-rate poet and a tenth-rate human being. His womanish beauty of face and voice made him the target for envy of many women. He must have seemed to them to have the best of both worlds. They in turn were equally targets of his hate and envy. So he ends up a compulsively overdriven sexual gourmand but never a gourmet, who knows only how to make hate in bed, never love, and with men as well as women.

His attitude toward sex and his struggle with his compulsion both to overeat and to get fat are close parallels. He had a woman's horror at the slightest tendency to overweight, and also a confused revulsion at his long simian arms and relatively short legs. It was inevitable that he should end up hating himself. Yet Grebanier never seems to realize that it was Byron's relentless but unconscious pursuit of the unattainable which led him to a merciless rapacity and hatred disguised as love. It was no accident that his alter ego was his half sister, nor that she was the only woman who even approximated being a love object for him. This was the central expression of his unconscious need not merely to exchange genders but to embody both: i.e., by taking over his sister's role in addition to his own. Fiction illustrates the theme in Thornton Wilder's (1926) *The Cabala*, and again in Norman Douglas's (1917) *South Wind*.

Turning back to biography we find it illustrated again in *The Youth of André Gide*, by Jean Delay (1963), and in *Lelia: The Life of George Sand*, by Maurois (1953). These works show in transparent ways the universality of the problem and its devastating effects on human life and human culture. In male dancers this is an important theme, and again in women of the modern dance it becomes self-evident.

We find it in the tragic depressions which infested the writings of Virginia Woolf, and particularly in her autobiographical sketches. It is found in Bell's (1972) biographical study of Virginia Woolf, in *The Moth and the Star*, by Aileen Pippett (1953), and in the book by her husband, Leonard Woolf (1963). It is transparently evident not only in the books about Virginia Woolf, but also in biographical studies of many others, both men and women.

When we turn to current "pornographic" literature we find that it too is permeated by this theme, which, although central, always remains largely unacknowledged and unrecognized. Indeed, the insatiability of human cravings constitutes the essential core of what is generally regarded as "pornography." This insatiability (the unfulfillment of the impossible) is related to the fact that human beings so often make hate in bed under the illusion that they are making love, and how often and how tragically even the full physiological gratification of sexual craving leads not to a sense of fulfillment but to sadness, terror, and anger, and most important of all to its immediate and incessant repetition. From this craving, when it is driven by unattainable and irreconcilable unconscious needs, there can be no escape, no satiation, and no rest. Immediate orgasmic fulfillment becomes a transient betrayal, an illusion, because it merely triggers a recurrence of the need. The same is true of the alcoholic who after being "on the wagon" takes one drink, only to find that it has reactivated the original craving in full force. It is true of the smoker who after months of abstinence may find that one cigarette rekindles the original craving. The same thing happens to many of us when we eat bread while waiting in a restaurant for a meal we have ordered. It happens to some with chocolate. Or consider the classical case of the child with an eating compulsion who eats until he vomits and then eats again. Why is he eating? Certainly not out of physiological need. Unwittingly the little boy may overeat to grow breasts like his mother's, while retaining his own genitalia; and the little girl may overeat to acquire a boy's genitals, while remaining a girl.

Insatiability of this kind applies to human attitudes toward money, power, clothes, shoes. I have known women whose closets bulged with clothes and shoes they could neither use nor part with. It applies to insatiability toward exercise, gambling, competitive sports, and sex. In fact, although compulsive insatiability is a striking distortion of all human cravings, it applies especially to sex.

The reason for this becomes almost self-evident in the light of my thesis. It has been said that the human animal is unique only in so far as he drinks when he is not thirsty and not dehydrated, eats when he is not hungry and has no need for calories, sleeps when he is not tired, seeks sexual gratification at any time. Certainly he is not sexually in need when he has to use artifices to whip up his sexual appetite; he is merely trying to prove something about himself, usually simply that he can have intercourse. In short, many compelling human cravings seem to serve symbolic rather than biophysical or biochemical needs, and when these symbolic needs are unconscious and are represented or misrepresented by unconscious symbols, they are insatiable. Symbolic gratification merely triggers the recurrence. Distortion occurs whenever what is sought is the gratification of unattainable, unrealizable, unconscious fantasies, and especially the gratification of pairs of opposite and irreconcilable fantasies (Kubie, 1941b, 1955, 1956).

Furthermore, these conflicting irreconcilable and unattainable desires are always so masked and disguised that the clinical student can uncover them only when he has an opportunity to study people deeply. But when we do this we find that many human beings spend much of their lives searching unwittingly and tragically for the gratification of just such unfulfillable, irreconcilable, and opposing desires.

This is why we did not have to wait for psychiatry and psychoanalysis to teach us that "success," like fame, can turn to dust and ashes. This is why even the fullest orgasm can end in tears, rage, and frustration. Devastating examples of these are shown with stark clarity in many of the relationships and episodes in current fiction and movies. Especially marked among these unconscious, irreconcilable, and unattainable needs is the frequent unconscious desire to use bodily contact in sex, this "laying on of hands," as a magical device for changing sides sexually (man into woman or woman into man) and even more frequently to end up as both sexes. This is clearly stated in *Orlando*, but even there it is not realized and faced as such. Instead, it tends to be disguised in aberrations of behavior, all marked by insatiable cravings and by mystical and pseudophilosophical formulae.

Both the insatiability and the unattainability of these fantasy goals lead to tragedy, because whenever the unconscious goal of intercourse is something unattainable (like an interchange or unification of gender roles, i.e., to become both genders), it ends in depression, terror, rage, and hatred of the sexual partner who has unwittingly cheated you. Hence the old Latin pharse, *post coitum triste*. The failure of physicians and plastic surgeons to recognize this has misled them into extensive experiments with endocrine preparations and surgery in an effort to achieve gratification of these neurotic and often psychotic needs for what is miscalled "transsexual" transformation, or better, "gender tramsmutation" (Kubie and Mackie, 1968).

Many of the sexual encounters described in current books, on the stage, and in movies are just such efforts to change sides, thinly disguised in several ways. This is usually glossed over and further disguised by translating them into more acceptable "transcendental," pseudospiritual, pseudophilosophical, and mystical terms. It plays a large role in the psychology of the so-called "encounter" groups, the Esalen groups on Big Sur, and in the Indian, Oriental, Eastern pseudophilosophical efforts to attain the unattainable and mutually irreconcilable.

Modern erotic films and stage scenes which portray sexual encounters involving several men and women in joyless bacchanalian revels give self-translating portrayals of men and women who may be grown up but not mature, caught in a febrile, hate-driven lust for the unattainable and irreconcilable, struggling to the point of exhaustion to become something they can never become. This is what the term "pornography" means, if it means anything.

To me it is one of the greatest tragedies that many so-called "cultural" movements in life are pitifully confused, ignorant, and misdirected human needs, masquerading in pseudoesthetic, pseudoreligious, pseudospiritual, pseudophilosophical language. A further consequence of this is that where there should be spiritual humility and search, we find falseness and pretentiousness. This makes me sad for the whole human race, which does not recognize its own confusion. Does it not seem strange that the human race has been divided into two sexes for so many eons, yet is still unreconciled to this simple, basic, biological fact, with its inevitable psychological consequences? Has repeated experience over the ages had no influence on genetic learning? Certainly current literary modes do not illuminate this, nor do they lessen man's confusion or heal the writers.

XIV. Epilogue: *Orlando* Again

You may recall that Orlando returned from Turkey to England as a "woman." Here she periodically resumes male garb and visits prostitutes. There is a slow gathering of threatening storm clouds. Fecundity, water, dampness, and the first intimations of a suicidal death are interwoven with fantasies of immortality. Widely spaced centuries are condensed into one. Queen Elizabeth is transmuted into Queen Victoria. Through it all persists the inability either to fuse or to remain separate. All alliances can be dissolved; none is indissoluble.

> It was strange—it was distasteful; indeed, there was something in this indissolubility of bodies which was repugnant to her sense of decency and sanitation [p. 158].

For the first time Orlando knew fear — a fear of ghosts in corridors, of robbers hiding behind trees. There was a sudden desperate need to lean on someone else. Omnipotence was gone, to be replaced by dreamlike images of falling: the falling feather, the falling sword, always of falling into depths that lead to death, falling into a magic pool. Then she breaks an ankle and a horseman comes to "save" her.

> The horse was almost on her. She sat upright. Towering dark against the yellow-sashed sky of dawn, with the plovers rising and falling about him, she saw a man on horseback. He started. The horse stopped. "Madam," the man cried, "you're hurt." "I'm dead, sir," she replied. A few minutes later, they became engaged [p. 163].

But the battle is joined again. She is sure he is a woman; he is sure she is a man.

> "You're a woman, Shel!" she cried. "You're a man, Orlando!" he cried. Never was there such a scene of protestation and demonstration as then took place since the world began [p. 164].

Their gender roles are interchanged, but the ecstasy ends again in the recurrent theme of falling: a descent into a pit. This time, however, death leads to rebirth, resurrection, transmutation. The roles of man and woman flicker and whirl like a top until finally with her marriage she becomes both. Thereupon, naturally, Shel is allowed to leave. He has served his magical purpose of transforming Orlando into both.

Here is the first brief, poignant moment of fulfillment represented in the fusion of prose and rhyme, rhyme that is both lyrical and mocking, hiding its poignancy in broken rhythms.

> Let us go, then, exploring, this summer morning, when all are adoring the plum blossom and the bee. And humming and hawing, let us ask of the starling (who is a more sociable bird than the lark) what he may think on the brink of the dust bin, whence he picks among the sticks combings of scullion's hair. What's life, we ask, leaning on the farmyard gate; Life, Life, Life! cries the bird, as if he had heard, and knew precisely, what we meant by this bothering prying habit of ours of asking questions indoors and out and peeping and picking at daisies as the way is of writers when they don't know what to say next.

Then they come here, says the bird, and ask me what life is; Life, Life, Life!

We trudge on then by the moor path, to the high brow of the wine-blue purple-dark hill, and fling ourselves down there, and dream there and see there a grasshopper, carting back to his home in the hollow, a straw. And he says (if sawing like his can be given a name so sacred and tender) Life's labour, or so we interpret the whirr of his dust-choked gullet. And the ant agrees and the bees, but if we lie here long enough to ask the moths, when they come at evening, stealing among the paler heather bells, they will breathe in our ears such wild nonsense as one hears from telegraph wires in snow storms; tee hee, haw haw, Laughter, Laughter! the moths say.

Having asked then of man and of bird and the insects, for fish, men tell us, who have lived in green caves, solitary for years to hear them speak, never, never say, and so perhaps know what life is—having asked them all and grown no wiser, but only older and colder (for did we not pray once in a way to wrap up in a book something so hard, so rare, one could swear it was life's meaning?) back we must go and straight out to the reader who waits a tiptoe to hear what life is—Alas, we don't know [pp. 176-177].

Orlando "lives" for four centuries; but the impossible cannot live. Disaster pursues her again with premonitions of death. Not even the birth of a son changes this. Instead, she becomes aware of herself not as one but as thousands of personalities, as the phase of psychotic disorganization sets in.

Choosing then, only those selves we have found room for, Orlando may now have called on the boy who cut the nigger's head down; the boy who strung it up again; the boy who sat on the hill; the boy who saw the poet; the boy who handed the Queen the bowl of rose water; or she may have called upon the young man who fell in love with Sasha; or upon the Courtier; or upon the Ambassador; or upon the Soldier; or upon the Traveller, or she may have wanted the woman to come to her; the Gypsy; the Fine Lady; the Hermit; the girl in love with life; the Patroness of Letters [p. 202].

Tragedy presses still closer.

"Haunted!" she cried, suddenly.... "Haunted! ever since I was a child." There flies the wild goose. It flies past the window out to sea.... But the goose flies too fast. I've seen it, here—there—there—England, Persia, Italy. Always it flies fast

> out to sea and always I fling after it words like nets (here she flung her hand out) which shrivel as I've seen nets shrivel drawn on deck with only sea-weed in them. And sometimes there's an inch of silver — six words — in the bottom of the net. But never the great fish who lives in the coral groves [p. 205].

Here is Orlando's sense of haunting failure, again the premonitory warning of her suicide: only an inch of silver in her net, never the great phallic fish who lives in the pink coral groves.

Then come fused images of opposite pairs; past and future, the fusion of man and woman, of birth and death, of marriage and funeral; and insistent images of water, pools, and trees where she finally goes to bury her poem, "The Oak Tree," among the roots of the great oak.

> What could have been more secret, she thought, more slow, and like the intercourse of lovers, than the stammering answer she had made all these years to the old crooning song of the woods, and the farms and brown horses standing at the gate, neck to neck, and the smithy and the kitchen and the fields, so laboriously bearing wheat, turnips, grass, and the garden blowing irises and fritillaries? [p. 212].

All moves swiftly to a close.

> All was phantom. . . . All was lit as for the coming of a dead Queen. . . . Orlando saw the dark plumes tossing. . . . A queen once more stepped from her chariot. Orlando curtsies and says, "The house is at your service, Ma'am. Nothing has been changed. The dear Lord, my father, shall lead you in" [p. 214].

The tale has moved from Elizabeth to Victoria, from the first great Queen-Father of Britain to the second.

Then like the closing bars of a symphony comes the first stroke of midnight, and out of the storm a sudden brief vision of her father-lover-husband-son. As he leaps to the ground, a wild bird springs over his head.

> "It's the goose," Orlando cried, "the wild goose.". . . And the twelfth stroke of midnight sounded; the twelfth stroke of midnight, Thursday, the eleventh of October, Nineteen Hundred Twenty-eight [p. 215].

Inexorably the fusion that can never be attained but will not be relinquished starts the slow, relentless march to Virginia Woolf's own suicide.

Was there ever a clearer or more tragic demonstration of the fact that the creative process can be used as a defense against therapeutic insight? (See Kubie, this volume, Chapter 4, 1973.)

An Acknowledgment

Over the many years during which I have been working on this paper, I have often felt indebted to Dr. Helene Deutsch. In her writings there have been intimations of insights into and concern with the various aspects of the problem with which this essay deals: to wit, *The Psychology of Women* (1944), *Selected Problems of Adolescence* (1967), and *A Psychoanalytic Study of the Myth of Dionysus and Apollo* (1969).

In her recent autobiographical volume, *Confrontations with Myself* (Deutsch, 1973), these implications become explicit (see p. 132). There the dominant focus is on a dream in which the dreamer has both masculine and feminine genital organs, and Dr. Deutsch quotes Freud as saying that it indicated a desire to be both a boy and a girl. She adds: "To wit Father's prettiest daughter and cleverest son." But the full ramifications of this drive into so many aspects of our culture and of the psychotic process are not developed or explored.

REFERENCES

Adrian, E. D. (1946), The Mental and the Physical Origins of Behaviour. *Internat. J. Psycho-Anal.,* 27:1-6.

Arlow, J. A., & Brenner, C. (1964), *Psychoanalytic Concepts and the Structural Theory.* New York: International Universities Press.

Baker, D. (1962), *Cassandra at the Wedding.* Boston: Houghton Mifflin.

Bell, Q. (1972), *Virginia Woolf: A Biography.* New York: Harcourt Brace Jovanovich.

Bernard, C. (1859), *Leçons sur les propriétés physiologiques et les altérations pathologiques des liquides de l'organisme,* 2 vols. Paris: Ballière.

Betlheim, S., & Hartmann, H. (1924), On Parapraxes in the Korsakow Psychosis. In: *Organization and Pathology of Thought,* ed. D. Rapaport. New York: Columbia University Press, 1951, pp. 288-307.

Bibring, E. (1936), The Development and Problems of the Theory of the Instincts. *Internat. J. Psycho-Anal.,* 22:102-131, 1941.

Bowlby, J., Ainsworth, W., Boston, W., & Rosenblatt, D. (1965), The Effects of Mother-Child Separation; A Follow-Up Study. *Brit. J. Med. Psychol.,* 29: 211-247.

Brickner, R. M. (1940), A Human Cortical Area Producing Repetitive Phenomena when Stimulated. *J. Neurophysiol.,* 3:125-130.

_____ & Kubie, L. S. (1936), A Miniature Psychotic Storm Produced by a Superego Conflict over a Simple Posthypnotic Suggestion. *Psychoanal. Quart.,* 5: 467-487.

Cannon, W. B. (1932), *The Wisdom of the Body.* New York: Norton.

Cobb, S. (1950), *Emotions in Clinical Medicine.* New York: Norton.

Delay, J. (1963), *The Youth of André Gide,* trans J. Guicharnaud. Chicago: University of Chicago Press.

Deutsch, H. (1944), *The Psychology of Women,* Vol. 1. New York: Grune & Stratton.

_____ (1967), *Selected Problems of Adolescence.* New York: International Universities Press.

_____ (1969), *A Psychoanalytic Study of the Myth of Dionysus and Apollo. Two Variants of the Son-Mother Relationship.* New York: International Universities Press.

_____ (1973), *Confrontations with Myself: An Epilogue.* New York: Norton.

Dobzhansky, T., & Ashley-Montagu, M. F. (1947), Natural Selection and the Mental Capacities of Mankind. *Science,* 105:587.

Douglas, N. (1917), *South Wind.* London: Secker.

Ferenczi, S., & Rank, O. (1923), *The Development of Psychoanalysis*. Washington, D.C.: Nervous and Mental Disease Monographs, No. 40, 1925.

Fisher, C. (1956), Dreams, Images, and Perceptions. *J. Amer. Psychoanal. Assn.,* 4:5-48.

Follett, B. N. (1927), *The House without Windows*. New York: Knopf.

Freud, A. (1936), *The Ego and the Mechanisms of Defence*. New York: International Universities Press, 1946.

Freud, S. (1900a), The Interpretation of Dreams. *Basic Writings*. New York: Modern Library, 1938, pp. 181-549.

————— (1900b), The Interpretation of Dreams. *Standard Edition,* 4 & 5. London: Hogarth Press, 1953.

————— (1905), *Three Contributions to the Theory of Sex,* 4th ed. Washington, D.C.: Nervous and Mental Disease Monographs, No. 7, 1930.

————— (1915a), Instincts and Their Vicissitudes. *Collected Papers,* 4:69-83. London: Hogarth Press, 1925.

————— (1915b), Repression. *Collected Papers,* 4:84-97. London: Hogarth Press, 1925.

————— (1915c), The Unconscious. *Collected Papers,* 4:98-136. London: Hogarth Press, 1925.

————— (1916-1917), *Introductory Lectures on Psycho-Analysis*. London: Allen & Unwin, 1922.

————— (1920), *Beyond the Pleasure Principle*. New York: Boni & Liveright, 1922.

————— (1925), Negation. *Collected Papers,* 5:181-185. London: Hogarth Press, 1950.

Grebanier, B. (1970), *The Uninhibited Byron*. New York: Crown.

Haldane, J. B. S. (1947), Evolution—Past and Future. *Atlantic Monthly,* 179: 45.

Hart, M. (1941), *Lady in the Dark*. New York: Random House.

Hartmann, H. (1939), *Ego Psychology and the Problem of Adaptation*. New York: International Universities Press, 1958.

————— Kris, E., & Loewenstein, R. (1946), Comments on tne Formation of Psychic Structure. *The Psychoanalytic Study of the Child,* 2:11-38. New York: International Universities Press.

Herrick, C. J. (1933), The Function of the Olfactory Parts of the Cerebral Cortex. *Proc. Nat. Acad. Sci.,* 19:7-14.

Humphrey, G. (1951), The Work of the Würzburg Group. In: *Thinking: An Introduction to Experimental Psychology*. New York: Wiley, pp. 30-65.

James, R. (1933), *Worth Remembering*. New York: Longmans, Green.

Jones, E. (1916), The Theory of Symbolism. *Papers on Psychoanalysis,* 5th ed. Baltimore: Williams & Wilkins, 1948, pp. 87-144.

Kelsen, H. (1943), *Society and Nature*. Chicago: University of Chicago Press.

Kris, E. (1952), *Psychoanalytic Explorations in Art*. New York: International Universities Press.

Kubie, L. S. (1930), A Theoretical Application to Some Neurological Problems of the Properties of Excitation Waves Which Move in Closed Circuits. *Brain,* 53:166-178.

————— (1934a), Body Symbolization and the Development of Language. *Psychoanal. Quart.,* 3:430-444.

————— (1934b), Relation of the Conditioned Reflex to Psychoanalytic Technique. *Arch. Neurol. Psychiat.,* 32:1137-1142.

———— (1937), Resolution of a Traffic Phobia in Conversations between a Father and Son. *Psychoanal. Quart.*, 6:223-226.

———— (1939), A Critical Analysis of the Concept of a Repetition Compulsion. *Internat. J. Psycho-Anal.*, 20:390-402.

———— (1941a), Preface to *Lady in the Dark*, by M. Hart. New York: Random House.

———— (1941b), The Repetitive Core of Neurosis. *Psychoanal. Quart.*, 10:23-43.

———— (1941c), The Ontogeny of Anxiety. *Psychoanal. Rev.*, 28:78-85.

———— (1941d), A Physiological Approach to the Concept of Anxiety. *Psychosomat. Med.*, 3:263-276.

———— (1943), The Use of Induced Hypnagogic Reveries in the Recovery of Repressed Amnesic Data. *Bull. Menninger Clin.*, 7:172-182.

———— (1944), A Basis for Classification of Disorders from the Psychosomatic Standpoint. *Bull. N.Y. Acad. Med.*, 20:46-65.

———— (1945a), The Therapeutic Role of Drugs in the Process of Repression, Dissociation, and Synthesis. *Psychosomat. Med.*, 7:147-151.

———— (1945b), The Value of Induced Dissociated States in the Therapeutic Process. *Proc. Royal Soc. Med.*, 38:681-683.

———— (1946), Review of *Men Under Stress*, by R. R. Grinker & J. P. Spiegel. *Psychoanal. Quart.*, 15:109-112.

———— (1948), Psychiatric Implications of the Kinsey Report. Review Essay of *Sexual Behavior in the Human Male*, by A. C. Kinsey et al. *Psychosomat. Med.*, 10:95-106.

———— (1949), The Neurotic Potential and Human Adaptation. In: *Adaptation*, ed. J. Romano. Ithaca, N.Y.: Cornell University Press, pp. 77-96.

———— (1950a), *Practical and Theoretical Aspects of Psychoanalysis*. New York: International Universities Press.

———— (1950b), The Concept of Normality and the Neurotic Process. *N.Y. Med.*, 6:19-24.

———— (1950c), The Relationship of Symbolic Function in Language Formation and in Neurosis. In: *Transactions of the Seventh Conference on Cybernetics*, ed. H. von Foerster. New York: Josiah Macy, Jr. Foundation.

———— (1951), The Neurotic Potential, the Neurotic Process, and the Neurotic State. *U.S. Armed Forces Med. J.*, 2:1-12.

———— (1952a), The Place of Emotions in the Feedback Concept. *Transactions of Ninth Conference on Cybernetics*, ed. H. von Foerster. New York: Josiah Macy, Jr. Foundation, pp. 48-72.

———— (1952b), Problems and Techniques of Psychoanalytic Validation and Progress. In: *Psychoanalysis as Science*, ed. E. Pumpian-Mindlin. Stanford: Stanford University Press, pp. 46-124.

———— (1953a), Some Implications for Pyschoanalysis of Modern Concepts of the Organization of the Brain. *Psychoanal. Quart.*, 22:21-68.

———— (1953b), The Problem of Specificity in the Psychosomatic Process. In: *The Psychosomatic Concept in Psychoanalysis*, ed. F. Deutsch. New York: International Universities Press, pp. 63-81.

———— (1954), Psychiatric and Psychoanalytic Considerations of the Problems of Consciousness. In: *Brain Mechanisms and Consciousness: A Symposium*, ed. J. F. Delafresnaye. Oxford: Blackwell, pp. 444-469.

———— (1955), Dr. Kinsey and the Medical Profession. Review of *Sexual Behavior in the Human Female*, by A. C. Kinsey et al. *Psychosomat. Med.*, 17:172-184.

_____ (1956), Influence of Symbolic Processes on the Role of Instincts in Human Behavior. *Psychosomat. Med.*, 18:189-208.

_____ (1958a), *Neurotic Distortion of the Creative Process*. Lawrence: University of Kansas Press.

_____ (1958b), The Neurotic Process as the Focus of Physiological and Psychoanalytic Research. *J. Ment. Sci.*, 104:518-536.

_____ (1959), The Relation of the Conditioned Reflex to Preconscious Functions. *Transactions of the 84th Annual Meeting of the American Neurological Association*, pp. 187-188.

_____ (1961a), Hypnotism: A Focus for Psychophysiological and Psychoanalytic Investigations. *Arch. Gen. Psychiat.*, 4:40-54.

_____ (1961b), Theoretical Aspects of Sensory Deprivation. In: *Sensory Deprivation*, ed. P. Solomon et al. Cambridge, Mass.: Harvard University Press, pp. 208-220.

_____ (1961c), Research in Protecting Preconscious Functions in Education. *Transactions of the ASDC 7th Curriculum Research Institute*, 1964, pp. 28-42.

_____ (1962), The Concept of Dream Deprivation: A Critical Analysis. *Psychosomat. Med.*, 24:62-65.

_____ (1963a), The Central Affective Potential and Its Trigger Mechanisms. In: *Counterpoint: Libidinal Object and Subject*, ed. H. S. Gaskill. New York: International Universities Press, pp. 106-120.

_____ (1963b), Neurosis and Normality. *The Encyclopedia of Mental Health*, 4:1346-1353. New York: Watts.

_____ (1964a), Editorial: A Tribute to Louis Dublin: Multiple Determinants of Suicidal Efforts. *J. Nerv. Ment. Dis.*, 138:3-8.

_____ (1964b), Review of *City of Night*, by J. Rechy. *J. Nerv. Ment. Dis.*, 139:206-207.

_____ (1966a), Review of *I Never Promised You a Rose Garden*, by H. Green. *J. Nerv. Ment. Dis.*, 142:278-280.

_____ (1966b), Psychosis—A Logical Outcome of the Neurotic "Chain Reaction." *Frontiers of Hosp. Psychiat.*, 3:6-8.

_____ (1966c), An Example of Psychotic Disorganization Arising in Early Childhood out of a Prepsychotic Neurosis. Comments on: "Say You're Sorry"—A Ten-Year Follow-Up, by R. A. Ravich & H. D. Dunton. *Amer. J. Psychother.*, 20:624-626.

_____ (1972), The Nature of Psychological Change in Individuals and Its Relation to Cultural Change. *Psychoanalysis and Contemporary Science*, 1:25-37. New York: Macmillan.

_____ (1973), Unsolved Problems concerning the Relation of Art to Psychotherapy. *Amer. J. Art Ther.*, 12:95-105.

_____ & Bartemeier, L. H., Menninger, K. A., Romano, j., & Whitehorn, J. C. (1946), Combat Exhaustion. *J. Nerv. Ment. Dis.*, 104:358-389;489-525.

_____ & Israel, H. A. (1955), "Say You're Sorry." *The Psychoanalytic Study of the Child*, 10:289-299. New York: International Universities Press.

_____ & Mackie, J. B. (1968), Critical Issues Raised by Operations for Gender Transmutation. *J. Nerv. Ment. Dis.*, 147:431-443.

_____ & Margolin, S. G. (1944), The Process of Hypnotism and the Nature of the Hypnotic State. *Amer. J. Psychiat.*, 100:611-622.

_____ _____ (1945), The Therapeutic Role of Drugs in the Process of Repression, Dissociation, and Synthesis. *Psychosomat. Med.*, 7:147-151.

Lashley, K. S. (1928), Experimental Analysis of Instinctive Behavior. *Psychol. Rev.*, 46:445.

Lewin, B. D., & Kubie, L. S. (1936), Editorial footnotes to: An Endocrine Approach to Psychodynamics, by R. G. Hoskins. *Pyschoanal. Quart.*, 5:87-107.

—— —— (1951), Mankind Discovers Man, 1801-1951. *New York Evening Post 150th Anniversary Edition,* November 12, pp. 33-34.

MacLean, P. D. (1949), Psychosomatic Disease and the Visceral Brain. *Psychosomat. Med.*, 11:338-353.

—— (1950), Developments in Electroencephalography: The Basal and Temporal Regions. *Yale J. Biol. Med.*, 22:438-451.

—— Alejandro, P., & Arellano, Z. (1950), Basal Lead Studies in Epileptic Automatisms. *J. Electroencephal. Clin. Neurophysiol.*, 2:1-16.

Mann, T. (1951), The Blood of the Wolsungs. *Stories of Three Decades.* New York: Knopf.

Margolin, S. G. (1951), The Behavior of the Stomach during Psychoanalysis. *Psychoanal. Quart.*, 20:349-373.

—— & Kubie, L. S. (1944), A Neurosis in a Merchant Seaman. *J. Abnorm. Soc. Psychol.*, 38:1-9.

—— —— Kanzer, M., & Stone, L. (1943), Acute Emotional Disturbances in Torpedoed Seamen of the Merchant Marine Who Are Continuing at Sea. *War Med.*, 3:393-408.

Marsh, J. T., & Worden, F. G. (1956), *Perceptual Approaches to Personality.* Psychiatric Research Reports, No. 6. New York: American Psychiatric Association, pp. 171-177.

Maurois, A. (1953), *Lelia: The Life of George Sand.* New York: Harper.

McCurdy, H. G. (1966), *Barbara: The Unconscious Autobiography of a Child Genius.* Chapel Hill: University of North Carolina Press.

Mead, M. (1935), *Sex and Temperament in Three Primitive Societies.* New York: New American Library, Mentor Books.

Meaker, M. J. (1964), *Sudden Endings.* Garden City, N.Y.: Doubleday.

Orr, D. W. (1942), Is There a Homeostatic Instinct? *Psychoanal. Quart.*, 11:322-335.

Pearl, R. (1933), *Constitution and Health.* London: Kegan Paul, Trench, Trubner.

Penfield, W. (1952), Memory Mechanisms. *Arch Neurol. Psychiat.*, 67:178-198.

—— & Rasmussen, T. (1950), *The Cerebral Cortex of Man.* New York: Macmillan.

Pippett, A. (1953), *The Moth and the Star: A Biography of Virginia Woolf.* Boston: Little, Brown.

Rado, S. (1922), The Course of Natural Science in the Light of Psychoanalysis. *Psychoanal. Quart.*, 1:683-700, 1932.

—— (1933), Fear of Castration in Women. *Psychoanal. Quart.*, 2:425-475.

Rapaport, D., ed. (1951), *Organization and Pathology of Thought.* New York: Columbia University Press.

Ravich, R. A. & Dunton, H. D. (1966), "Say You're Sorry"—A Ten-Year Follow-Up. *Amer. J. Psychother.*, 20:615-626.

Redlich, F. C. (1952), The Concept of Normality. *Amer. J. Psychother.*, 6:551-576.

Reiner, M. (1932), Causality and Psychoanalysis. *Psychoanal. Quart.*, 1:701-714.

Réjaunier, J. (1969), *The Beauty Trap*. New York: Trident.

_____ (1972), *The Motion and the Act*. Los Angeles: Nash.

Richter, C. P. (1927), Animal Behavior and Internal Drives. *Quart. Rev. Biol.*, 2: 307.

_____ (1941), Biology of Drives. *Psychosomat. Med.*, 3:105.

_____ (1942), Physiological Psychology. *Ann. Rev. Physiol.*, 4:561.

_____ (1943a), The Self-Selection of Diet. In: *Essays in Biology in Honor of Herbert M. Evans*. Berkeley: University of California Press, pp. 501-505.

_____ (1943b), Total Self-Regulatory Functions in Animals and Human Beings. *Harvey Lect.*, 38:63.

Schilder, P. (1942), *Mind: Perception and Thought in Their Constructive Aspects*. New York: Columbia University Press.

Scott-Maxwell, F. (1957), *Women and Sometimes Men*. New York: Knopf.

Sherrington, C. (1933), *The Brain and Its Mechanism*. Cambridge, Eng.: Cambridge University Press.

_____ (1941), *Man on His Nature*. New York: Macmillan.

Spitz, R. A. (1945), Hospitalism: An Inquiry into the Genesis of Psychiatric Conditions in Early Childhood. *The Psychoanalytic Study of the Child*, 1:53-74. New York: International Universities Press.

_____ (1946), Hospitalism: A Follow-Up Report. *The Psychoanalytic Study of the Child*, 2:113-119. New York: International Universities Press.

_____ & Wolf, K. M. (1946), Anaclitic Depression. *The Psychoanalytic Study of the Child*, 2:313-342. New York: International Universities Press.

Stein, L. (1950), *Journey into the Self*, ed. E. Fuller. New York: Crown.

Sterba, R. (1931), *Introduction to the Psychoanalytic Theory of the Libido*. New York: Nervous and Mental Disease Monographs, No. 68, 1942.

Thunberg, T. (1926), Der Barospirator. *Skandinav. Arch. Physiol.*, 49:234.

Watson, B. B. (1964), *A Shavian Guide to the Intelligent Woman*. London: Chatto & Windus.

Wheeler, W. M. (1939), *Essays in Philosophical Biology*. Cambridge: Harvard University Press.

Wilder, T. (1926), *The Cabala*. New York: Boni.

Williams, T. (1947), *A Streetcar Named Desire*. New York: New Directions.

Woolf, L., ed. (1953), *A Writer's Diary; Being Extracts from the Diary of Virginia Woolf*. New York: Harcourt, Brace.

_____ ed. (1963), *Beginning Again: An Autobiography of the Years 1911 to 1918*. New York: Harcourt, Brace & World.

Woolf, V. (1926), *The Moment and Other Essays*. New York: Harcourt, Brace, 1948.

_____ (1928), *Orlando: A Biography*. New York: Harcourt, Brace.

_____ (1929), *A Room of One's Own*. New York: Harcourt, Brace.

INDEX

Adler, A., 49
Adrian, E. D., 57, 58
Affect, 15, 33, 46, 171, 181
  central affective position, 12-13, 20, 33, 170, 184, 190
  see also Emotion(s)
Alejandro, P., 115, 125
Alexander, F., 75
Arellano, Z., 115, 125
Arlow, J. A., 163
Ashley-Montagu, M. F., 56
Awareness, levels of, 5-6, 11, 19-21, 27-32, 35, 36, 95-96, 98-105, 115, 144-145, 153, 156, 159, 160, 170, 207-208; *see also* Conscious processes; Preconscious processes; Psychoanalysis, topographic principles in; Unconscious processes

Baker, D., 196
Barach, A. L., 70
Bartemeier, L. H., 134
Beach, F., 74, 127
Behavior
  bodily needs and, 57-61, 119-122
  determinants of, 36, 52, 128, 146, 160
  information processing and, 34-35
  neurophysiology of; *see* Neurophysiology of instincts
  quantitative evaluation of; *see* Psychoanalysis, quantitative variables in
  see also Drive(s); Instinct(s); Sexual behavior
Bell, Q., 200, 256
Benjamin, J., 127

Bergson, H., 31
Bernard, C., 58
Betlheim, S., 96
Bibring, E., 56
Bichat, M. F. X., 121
Body
  drive to become both sexes and, 226, 249-251, 254
  image, 100, 119-126
  needs, 57-61, 119-122, 166; *see also* Instinct(s), vital
  see also Neurophysiology; Symbolic process, bipolarity of
Bordley, J., 166
Boston, W., 190
Bowlby, J., 190
Brain; *see* Neurophysiology
Bremer, F., 78
Brenman, M., 127, 150-152, 154
Brenner, C., 163
Brentano, F., 23
Breuer, J., 30
Brickner, R. M., 137, 142
Brody, E. B., 1-2
Byron, Lord, 255-256

Camus, A., 6
Cannon, W. B., 58
Child development, 3, 185, 186, 188, 190
  drive to become both sexes and, 211-215, 217, 223-225, 249-250
  psychopathology and, 12-13, 92-95
  symbolic process and, 8-9, 101
  see also Instinct(s), elaboration of
Clinical cases
  drive to become both sexes, 202-203,

271

212-213, 231, 249; clothes and, 252, 253; disappearance of a parent and, 233; drinking and, 235-236; influence on work, 238-241; influence on psychotherapy, 242-247; marriage and, 228-229; unconscious, 205

neurosis and psychosis, 173-180

Cobb, S., 88, 104

Conflict
between drives, 5, 17-19, 26, 42, 48, 177, 184
psychology of, 16-19, 160
psychopathology and, 24, 48, 106, 138, 144, 149-150, 155, 158, 171-172, 184
symbolic process and, 112, 121-122, 171-172, 184
between symptoms, 20, 26, 172, 184
unconscious, 14, 15, 47, 48, 70-71, 106, 149, 155, 158, 160, 171-172, 184

Conscious processes (Cs), 15, 27-31, 33, 35, 36, 90, 93, 95-105, 115, 136-140, 143, 145-148, 151, 153, 156-159

Creativity and creative thinking, 3, 17, 18, 32, 96, 139-141, 150, 160, 185-188

Defense(s), 10, 28, 47, 83, 98
language as, 9
unconscious, 92, 98, 149, 155-158
see also Neurosis; Repression

Deikman, A. J., 35

Delay, J., 194, 256

de No, L., 103

Determinism; see Psychoanalysis, freedom and determinism in

Deutsch, F., 157

Deutsch, H., 157, 263

Development, child; see Child development

Dobzhansky, T., 56

Douglas, N., 256

Dunton, H. D., 179

Dreams and dreaming, 17, 32, 96-98, 123, 144, 162-169, 189
drive to become both sexes and, 217, 238, 242-245, 247

neurophysiology of, 111-112, 166-168
perception in, 109-110, 166-167, 186
preconscious processes and, 32, 162-168
structural approach to, 163-164
theoretical fallacies and, 162-164
topographical aspects of, 162-163
unconscious processes and, 163-164

Drive(s)
to become adult and child, 223-225
compulsive, 14, 17, 48, 54, 73, 131, 135, 203
conflict between, 5, 17-19, 26, 42, 177
emotions in, 45-46, 80; see also Affect; Emotion(s)
idea of, 17-19, 44, 203-208
instincts and, 48, 54-55, 68, 75, 83-84
preconscious, 204-208
quantification of, 42-44, see also Psychoanalysis, quantitative variables in
symbolic process and, 17-20, 22-23, 118-119, 204
unconscious, 17, 22, 26, 149, 150-151, 171, 172, 204-208
see also Conflict; Drive to become both sexes; Instinct(s); Psychic energy; Sexual behavior

Drive to become both sexes, 19, 181, 191-263
aging process and, 198, 234-235
in biography and fiction, 255-259
body change and, 226, 249-251, 254
child development and, 211-215, 217, 223-225, 249-250
clinical cases, 202-203, 205, 208-213, 228-229, 231, 233, 235-236, 238-247, 249, 252, 253
clothes and, 251-253
courtship and, 225-227, 255
creativity and, 200, 204, 205, 255-259, 263
cultural factors in and consequences of, 197, 223-225, 253-255
disappearance of a parent and, 233-234
drinking and, 235-237
heredity and, 196-197, 201-203, 250

"hippie" culture and, 198, 222, 253
homosexuality and, 232-233, 253
influence on psychotherapy, 241-247
influence on work and play, 237-241
manifestations, 196, 197, 215-218, 254, 255
marriage choice and, 227-229, 255
masturbation and, 232-233
neurosis and, 218-223
perception and, 214-215
pornography and, 217-218, 256-257, 259
psychoanalytic theory and, 201, 247-255
psychodynamic implications, 197, 204-208, 248-249, 254-255
psychosis and, 199-200, 218-223
sexual behavior and, 199-200, 229-231, 256-257
transvestitism and, 196, 253, 254
see also Instinct(s), sexual; Sexual behavior
Dunton, H. D., 179

Education; see Child development
Elizabeth, Queen, 259, 262
Emotion(s)
  instincts and, 45-46, 79, 80, 82
  psychopathology and, 12, 94, 107, 113, 121
  see also Affect
Erickson, M., 5
Existentialism, 23-25
Experience, 17, 28
  neurophysiology of, 7-8
  see also Awareness; Behavior; Drive(s); Instinct(s)
External environment (Non-I); see Perception; Symbolic process, bipolarity of

Feedback, 7-8, 13, 14, 26, 163, 182
Ferenczi, S., 49
Fingarette, H., 23
Fisher, C., 165, 167
Follett, B. N., 196, 197, 255
Freedom, 6, 21-27, 38
  to change, 11, 142, 185-190
Freud, A., 157
Freud, S., 4, 8, 10, 13, 16-18, 20-28, 30-36, 41-43, 48, 49, 51, 52, 55-56, 58, 77, 83, 85, 95, 96, 98, 105, 108, 146, 147, 154, 156, 157, 159, 162-165, 168, 171, 181, 194, 195, 263
Fulton, J., 1

Gill, M. M., 31, 127
Glover, E., 4-5
Grebanier, B., 199, 255
Grinker, R. R., 50

Habermas, J., 30
Haldane, J. B. S., 56
Hallucinations, 11, 107-114, 153, 166
Harrower, M. R., 127, 153-154
Hart, M., 194, 247
Hartmann, H., 50, 96, 127, 152, 154-157
Health vs. illness, 143-144, 150-151
  biochemical factors and, 128
  genetic factors and, 154
  holistic approach to, 129
  ontogenetic approach to, 129-130, 135-136
  phenomenological distinction between, 130-133
  see also Neurosis vs. psychosis; Psychopathology
Henderson, L. J., 141, 208
Herrick, C. J., 125
Holt, R. R., 2
Homeostasis; see Instinct(s); Neurophysiology
Hoskins, R. G., 43
Humphrey, G., 164
Hutchinson, G. E., 74-75

I; see Body; Symbolic process, bipolarity of
Information processing, 32-36
Instinct(s)
  biochemistry of, 53-55, 58, 67, 71, 73-76, 78, 83-86, 118
  child development and, 18, 81-82
  drives and, 48, 54-55, 68, 75, 83-85
  elaboration of, 61, 79-86; see also Child development
  emotional components of, 45-46, 79, 80, 82; see also Affect

executive (tertiary), 61, 76-79, 82
Freud's theory of, 48, 54-56, 85-86
neurophysiology of, 53-54, 57-60, 62-63, 75-79, 83-86, 118, 120
perception and, 80-81
physiology of, 58-73, 76-83, 85-86, 120
psychological influences on, 68, 71-73, 76, 82-86, 118
sexual (secondary), 61, 73-76, 78, 82, 137; *see also* Drive to become both sexes; Sexual behavior
vital (primary), 61-73, 76, 81-83, 117-119; respiration, 62, 65, 66, 68, 70, 72, 79-81, 84; tissue maintenance, 65, 66, 69, 70, 72, 80; warning mechanisms of, 67-73, 76, 83, 85, 86; water balance, 65-68, 70, 72, 80
see also Drive(s)
Internal world (I); *see* Body; Symbolic process, bipolarity of
Israel, H. A., 179

James, R., 194, 226, 255
James, W., 31, 32, 35, 100
Jones, E., 96, 97, 102

Kanzer, M., 134
Kelsen, H., 53
Kierkegaard, S., 25
Klein, G. S., 8, 14, 26-28, 34
Klein, M., 93
Knight, R. P., 127
Knowledge and knowing; *see* Awareness, levels of; Experience
Kris, E., 28, 50, 127, 146, 150, 160
Kubie, L. S., 1-39, 43-44, 50, 58, 63, 64, 70, 77, 78, 88, 99-100, 110, 115, 116, 119-121, 123, 134, 135-140, 142, 149, 165, 166, 170, 171, 179, 181, 188-190, 194, 195, 197, 199, 200, 202, 204, 205, 208, 214, 219, 225, 248, 249, 257, 258, 263

Langer, S., 16, 32
Lashley, K. S., 55, 62, 67-68, 73
Lewin, B. D., 43-44, 121, 127, 158-159, 165

Libido, 44, 48-50, 72, 85; *see also* Drive(s); Drive to become both sexes; Instinct(s), sexual; Psychic energy
Loewenstein, R., 50, 127

Mackie, J. B., 195, 202, 258
MacLean, P. D., 5, 9, 10, 103, 104, 115, 124-125
Mann, T., 197
Margolin, S. G., 5, 7, 11, 30, 70, 110, 120, 127, 134, 166, 214, 219
Marsh, J. T., 167
Matte Blanco, I., 28, 36-37
Maurois, A., 199, 256
McCulloch, W., 8
McCurdy, H. G., 197, 255
Mead, M. 197, 253
Meaker, M. J., 192
Miller, H., 218
Murdock, H., 2

Neurophysiology
of dreams, 111-112, 166-168
of experience and behavior, 4, 5, 7-8, 58
of instincts, 53-54, 57-60, 62-63, 75-79, 83-86, 118, 120
psychoanalysis and, 5, 115
of symbolic process, 8-11, 102-106, 111-112, 115, 123-126
Neurosis, 11-12, 14, 48-49, 83, 154, 166, 190
clinical cases, 13, 173-180
drive to become both sexes and, 218-223
drive conflict and, 137, 149, 155, 177, 184
masked, 134
vs. normality, 127, 128, 130, 132-135, 137-138, 140-146, 155, 159, 161
ontogenetic approach to, 135-136
phenomenology of, 130-133
preconscious processes in, 37, 139, 144, 170-171, 185-190
vs. psychosis, 11, 87, 89-91, 105-106, 170-173, 184, 187-188
repetition in, 11, 14, 136-137, 143, 154, 190

sociological factors in and consequences of, 133-135
symbolic process in, 11, 14-16, 19, 27, 92-95, 101, 102, 105-106, 122, 137, 139, 140, 171, 184
symptoms of, 11, 137, 143, 146, 170-173, 184, 187-188
unconscious processes in, 153-156, 158-161, 181
see also Health vs. illness; Psychopathology; Psychosis; Symbolic process, distortion in
Non-I; *see* Symbolic process, bipolarity of
Normality, 149-151, 153
vs. neurosis, 127, 128, 130, 132-135, 137-138, 140-146, 155, 159, 161
vs. psychopathology, 150-152, 155-156, 158
see also Health vs. illness; Neurosis; Psychopathology; Psychosis
Nunberg, H., 4

Orlando, fusion of sexes in, 191-194 259-263
Orr, D. W.. 55

Papez, J. W., 125
Pearl, R., 64, 115, 117
Penfield, W., 5, 9, 123, 124, 142
Perception, 31-32, 153-154
as ego function, 92, 106, 107
in dreams, 34, 109-111, 166-168, 186
drive to become both sexes and, 214-215
see also Awareness; Experience; Instinct(s)
Pippett, A., 192, 200, 256
Preconscious processes (Pcs), 11, 18, 20-21, 27-31, 33-35, 95-97, 141, 143, 146, 152-153, 156, 159, 163, 164, 170
control, 17
in creative thinking, 150, 185; *see also* Creativity
dreaming and, 32, 162-168
drives and, 204-208
in neurosis, 37, 139, 144, 170-171, 185-190

symbolic process and, 98-105, 115, 139, 185-190
see also Awareness, levels of; Conscious processes; Psychoanalysis, topographic principles in; Unconscious processes
Psychic energy, 4, 28, 42-44, 47, 57
see also Drive(s); Instinct(s); Libido; Psychoanalysis, dynamic principles in
Psychoanalysis
dynamic principles in, 41-51, 104, 108, 138-139, 145-146, 149, 159-160, 163-164, 171, 203-208
economic principles in, 42, 48-51
freedom and determinism in, 21-27, 38
meaning in, 26-27
need for change in, 3-4, 7, 168-169
neurophysiology and, 5, 115
quantitative variables in, 41-51, 148-149, 159
as science, 3-6
structural principles, 4, 41-42, 50, 163-164, 171
theoretical fallacies in, 87-91, 130-131, 135-136, 147-150, 157, 162-164
topographic principles in, 20-23, 27-31, 35-37, 51, 156-157, 162-164
see also Awareness, levels of; Conscious processes; Preconscious processes; Unconscious processes
Psychopathology
affective and emotional components of, 12, 94, 107, 113, 121
child development and, 12-13, 92-95
classical view of, 87-88, 90
conflict and, 17, 24, 48, 106, 138-144, 149-150, 155, 158, 171-172, 184
interpersonal approach to, 88-89
Kraepelinian view of, 89, 135
metapsychological view of, 156-157
Meyerian view of, 89-90, 135-136
vs. normality, 87-114, 127, 136
ontogenetic approach to, 89-91, 99, 129-130, 135-136
preconscious processes in, 37, 139, 144, 170-171, 185-190

repression and, 19, 26-27, 48, 49, 104-105, 158; *see also* Defense(s); Repression
role of personality in, 89-91, 105, 136, 151, 152, 159
symbolic process in, 9-12, 14-17, 19, 27, 37, 92-95, 101, 102, 105-106, 108-112, 122, 137-140, 171, 183, 184, 204
theories of, 87-91, 105, 130-131, 135-136, 147-150, 157, 182
unconscious processes in, 136-139, 149-151, 153, 155-156, 159-161, 181
vulnerability to, 37, 91-92
see also Clinical cases; Health vs. illness; Neurosis; Normality; Psychosis; Schizophrenia; Symbolic process, distortion in
Psychosis
clinical cases, 173-180
drive to become both sexes and, 199-200, 218-223
hallucinations in, 107-100, 113-114, 153, 166
vs. neurosis, 11, 87, 89-91, 105, 107, 170-173, 184, 187-188
perception and, 108-109
regression in, 20, 181-182
symbolic process in, 11, 19, 92-95, 101, 105-112, 140, 172, 183-184
see also Health vs. illness; Normality; Psychopathology; Symbolic process, distortion in
Psychosomatic disorders
body image and, 119-122, 125
categories of body organs and, 116-119
symbolic process in, 115-116, 120, 121, 123-126
Psychotherapy, 10, 22, 25, 135, 144, 152-153
drive to become both sexes and, 241-247

Rado, S., 228
Rank, O., 49, 96
Rapaport, D., 28, 96, 97, 127, 153
Rasmussen, T., 124
Ravich, R. A., 179

Redlich, F. C., 127, 135, 148-150
Réjaunier, J., 199, 218
Repression, 19, 26-27, 48, 49, 104-105, 107, 158, 253; *see also* Defense(s)
Richter, C. P., 58-60
Ricoeur, P., 23

Sachs, H., 96
Sackville-West, V., 193
Sartre, J.-P., 23, 25
Schafer, R., 23-25, 35
Schilder, P., 152
Schizophrenia, 152-153
Schutz, A., 31, 32, 34
Science, 18, 41, 133, 146, 148-149, 160
psychoanalysis and, 3-6
Scott-Maxwell, F., 199
Sensation; *see* Perception
Sexual behavior, 8, 199-200, 229, 231, 256-257
biochemical substrates of, 74-76
physiology of, 74-76
see also Drive to become both sexes; Instinct(s), sexual
Sexual identity; *see* Drive to become both sexes
Sherrington, C., 53, 57, 61, 64, 77-78
Smith, E., 125
Somers, M. R., 65
Spiegel, J. P., 50
Spillane, M., 218
Spitz, R. A., 3, 12, 93-95, 127, 179, 190
Stein, L., 202
Sterba, R., 56
Strauss, R., 181
Sutherland, A., 228
Symbolic process and symbolization
bipolarity of, 5, 9-11, 15, 19, 32, 98-105, 107-108, 112-113, 119, 122-123, 140-141
body as referent, 8-9, 14, 19, 121-122; *see also* Body image
distortion in, 11, 14-16, 18-20, 27, 37, 94, 106-110, 139, 170-172, 183-186, 188-190, 220; *see also* Neurosis; Normality; Psychopathology; Psychosis
drives and, 17-20, 22-23, 118-119, 204

freedom to change and, 185-190
neurophysiology of, 8-11, 102-105, 111-112, 115, 123-126
in neurosis, 11, 14-16, 19, 27, 92-95, 101-102, 105-106, 122, 137, 139, 140, 171, 184
preconscious processes and, 98-105, 115, 139, 185-190
in psychosis, 11, 19, 92-95, 101, 105-112, 140, 172, 183-184
in psychosomatic disorders, 115-116, 120, 121, 123-126
somatic and neural base of, 8-11, 116-122
unconscious processes and, 98-105, 117, 119, 139, 143, 186-187; *see also* Conflict; Drive(s); Instinct(s)

Thunberg, T., 70

Unconscious processes (Ucs), 5, 6, 11, 12, 20-22, 24, 27-31, 35-37, 46, 90, 95-97, 115, 140, 141, 143, 146, 147, 149, 155-157, 160-161, 170, 189, 205

in dreaming, 163
in drives, 17, 22, 26, 149-151, 171, 172, 204-208
in psychopathology, 136-139, 152, 153, 155-156, 159-161, 171, 181
see also Awareness, levels of; Conscious processes; Preconscious processes; Psychoanalysis, topographic principles in

Victoria, Queen, 259, 262
Virchow, R., 121

Watson, B. B., 202
Webster, N., 162-163
Wheeler, W. M., 58, 60-61
Wilder, T., 256
Williams, T., 247
Wolf, K. M., 93, 179
Wolfe, T., 6
Woolf, L., 192, 200, 256
Woolf, V., 191-194, 256
Worden, F. G., 167
Wurmser, L., 16, 32
Wurzberg School, 164, 185, 188

ABOUT THE AUTHORS

EUGENE B. BRODY is Professor of Psychiatry and Human Behavior and Director, Program of Humanistic Studies in Medicine, at the University of Maryland School of Medicine, where between 1959 and 1975 he was Chairman of the Department of Psychiatry and Director of the Institute of Psychiatry and Human Behavior. He received an M.A. in experimental psychology at the University of Missouri, took his M.D. at Harvard Medical School, is a graduate of the New York Psychoanalytic Institute, and was trained in psychiatry at Yale where he remained on the faculty until moving to Maryland. He has been a visiting professor at the Federal University of Brazil in Rio de Janeiro and at the University of the West Indies in Jamaica, and in 1975-76 was a Fellow of the Center for Advanced Study in the Behavioral Sciences at Stanford. He is coeditor of *Psychotherapy with Schizophrenics* (1952), *Psychiatric Epidemiology* (1967), and *Adult Clinical Psychiatry* (1974), Vol. 3 of the *American Handbook of Psychiatry;* editor of *Minority Group Adolescents in the United States* (1968) and *Behavior in New Environments: The Adaptation of Migrant Populations* (1970); and author of *The Lost Ones: Social Forces and Mental Illness in Rio de Janeiro* (1973) and *To Have a Baby for Him: A Psychosocial Study of Sex and Contraception in Urban Jamaica* (forthcoming). Since 1968 he has been Editor-in-Chief of the *Journal of Nervous and Mental Disease.*

LAWRENCE S. KUBIE received his M.D. from Johns Hopkins University in 1921, and his psychoanalytic training at the London Institute of Psycho-Analysis, 1928-1930. In addition to engaging in the private practice of psychoanalysis, he became a member of the faculty of the New York Psychoanalytic Institute in 1932, and was Clinical Professor of Psychiatry at Yale University (1947-1960), Lecturer in Psychiatry at Columbia University College of Physicians and Surgeons (1955-1960) and Johns Hopkins University (1960-1973), Senior Associate in Training and Research at Sheppard and Enoch Pratt Hospital (1959-1964), and Clinical Professor of Psychiatry at the University of Maryland (1959-1973). From 1960 to 1968 he was Editor-in-Chief of the *Journal of Nervous and Mental Disease*. He was the author of over 300 articles, reviews, and books, including *Neurotic Distortion of the Creative Process* and *Practical and Theoretical Aspects of Psychoanalysis*. Kubie died in 1973.

PSYCHOLOGICAL ISSUES

No.   1 — ERIK H. ERIKSON: *Identity and the Life Cycle; Selected Papers.* Historical Introduction by David Rapaport

No.   2 — I. H. PAUL: *Studies in Remembering; The Reproduction of Connected and Extended Verbal Material*

No.   3 — FRITZ HEIDER: *On Perception, Event Structure, and the Psychological Environment.* Preface by George S. Klein.

No.   4 — RILEY W. GARDNER, PHILIP S. HOLZMAN, GEORGE S. KLEIN, HARRIET LINTON, and DONALD P. SPENCE: *Cognitive Control; A Study of Individual Consistencies in Cognitive Behavior*

No.   5 — PETER H. WOLFF: *The Developmental Psychologies of Jean Piaget and Psychoanalysis*

No.   6 — DAVID RAPAPORT: *The Structure of Psychoanalytic Theory; A Systematizing Attempt*

No.   7 — OTTO POTZL, RUDOLF ALLERS, and JAKOB TELER: *Preconscious Stimulation in Dreams, Associations, and Images; Classical Studies.* Introduction by Charles Fisher

No.   8 — RILEY W. GARDNER, DOUGLAS N. JACKSON, and SAMUEL J. MESSICK: *Personality Organization in Cognitive Controls and Intellectual Abilities*

No.   9 — FRED SCHWARTZ and RICHARD O. ROUSE: *The Activation and Recovery of Associations*

No. 10 — MERTON M. GILL: *Topography and Systems in Psychoanalytic Theory*

No. 11 — ROBERT W. WHITE: *Ego and Reality in Psychoanalytic Theory: A Proposal regarding the Independent Ego Energies*

No. 12 — IVO KOHLER: *The Formation and Transformation of the Perceptual World.* Introduction by James J. Gibson

No. 13 — DAVID SHAKOW and DAVID RAPAPORT: *The Influence of Freud on American Psychology*

No. 14 — HEINZ HARTMANN, ERNST KRIS, and RUDOLPH M. LOEWENSTEIN: *Papers on Psychoanalytic Psychology*

No. 15 — WOLFGANG LEDERER: *Dragons, Delinquents, and Destiny; An Essay on Positive Superego Functions.* Introduction by Roy Schafer

No. 16 — PETER AMACHER: *Freud's Neurological Education and Its Influence on Psychoanalytic Theory*

No. 17 — PETER H. WOLFF: *The Causes, Controls, and Organization of Behavior in the Neonate*

No. 18/19 — ROBERT R. HOLT, Ed.: *Motives and Thought; Psychoanalytic Essays in Honor of David Rapaport*

No. 20 — JOHN CHYNOWETH BURNHAM: *Psychoanalysis and American Medicine, 1894-1918; Medicine, Science, and Culture*

No. 21 — HELEN D. SARGENT, LEONARD HORWITZ, ROBERT S. WALLERSTEIN, and ANN APPELBAUM: *Prediction in Psychotherapy Research: A Method for the Transformation of Clinical Judgments into Testable Hypotheses*

No. 22 — MARJORIE GRENE, Ed.: *Toward a Unity of Knowledge*

No. 23 — FRED SCHWARTZ and PETER H. SCHILLER: *A Psychoanalytic Model of Attention and Learning*

No. 24 — BERNARD LANDIS: *Ego Boundaries*

No. 25/26 — EMANUEL PETERFREUND in collaboration with JACOB T. SCHWARTZ: *Information, Systems, and Psychoanalysis; An evolutionary Biological Approach to Psychoanalytic Theory*

No. 27 — LOUIS BREGER, IAN HUNTER, and RON W. LANE: *The Effect of Stress on Dreams*

No. 28 — EDITH LEVITOV GARDUK and ERNEST A. HAGGARD: *Immediate Effects on Patients of Psychoanalytic Interpretations*

No. 29 — ERICH GOLDMEIER: *Similarity in Visually Perceived Forms*. Foreword by Irvin Rock

No. 30 — MARTIN MAYMAN, Ed.: *Psychoanalytic Research: Three Approaches to the Experimental Study of Subliminal Processes*

No. 31 — NANETTE HEIMAN and JOAN GRANT, Eds.: *Else Frenkel-Brunswik: Selected Papers*

No. 32 — FRED SCHWARTZ, Ed.: *Scientific Thought and Social Reality: Essays by Michael Polanyi*

No. 33 — STANLEY I. GREENSPAN: *A Consideration of Some Learning Variables in the Context of Psychoanalytic Theory*

No. 34/35 — JOHN E. GEDO and GEORGE H. POLLOCK, Eds.: *Freud: The Fusion of Science and Humanism; The Intellectual History of Psychoanalysis*

No. 36 — MERTON M. GILL and PHILIP S. HOLZMAN, Eds.: *Psychology versus Metapsychology; Psychoanalytic Essays in Memory of George S. Klein*

No. 37 — ROBERT N. EMDE, THEODORE J. GAENSBAUER, and ROBERT J. HARMON: *Emotional Expression in Infancy: A Biobehavioral Study*

No. 38 — DAVID SHAKOW: *Schizophrenia: Selected Papers*

No. 39 — PAUL E. STEPANSKY: *A History of Aggression in Freud*

No. 40 — JOSEPH DE RIVERA: *A Structural Theory of the Emotions*. Introductory Essay by Hartvig Dahl

No. 41 — HANNAH S. DECKER: *Freud in Germany: Revolution and Reaction in Science, 1893-1907*

No. 42/43 — ALLAN D. ROSENBLATT and JAMES T. THICKSTUN: *Modern Psychoanalytic Concepts in a General Psychology* — Parts 1 & 2